First World War
and Army of Occupation
War Diary
France, Belgium and Germany

5 CAVALRY DIVISION
Secunderabad Cavalry Brigade
Headquarters,
'N' Battery Royal Horse Artillery,
7th Dragoon Guards (Princess Royal),
20 Deccan Horse, 34 Poona Horse,
Brigade Signal Troop,
13 Cavalry Machine Gun Squadron and Royal Army
Veterinary Corps
Mobile Veterinary Section
1 January 1917 - 31 May 1917

WO95/1165

The Naval & Military Press Ltd
www.nmarchive.com
Published in association with The National Archives

Published by

The Naval & Military Press Ltd

Unit 10 Ridgewood Industrial Park,

Uckfield, East Sussex,

TN22 5QE England

Tel: +44 (0) 1825 749494

www.naval-military-press.com

www.nmarchive.com

This diary has been reprinted in facsimile from the original. Any imperfections are inevitably reproduced and the quality may fall short of modern type and cartographic standards.

© **Crown Copyright**
Images reproduced by permission of The National Archives, London, England, 2015.

Contents

Document type	Place/Title	Date From	Date To
Heading	Bde Headquarters. Jan 1917-Apl 1918		
Heading	War Diary of Headquarters, Secunderabad Cavalry Brigade. From 1st January 1917 To 31st January 1917		
War Diary	Feuquieres Carroy Aigneville Frettenevle Harcelaines Buighy	01/01/1917	31/01/1917
Heading	Secunderabad Cavalry Brigade. From 1st to 28th February 1917.		
War Diary	Feuquieres Carroy Aigneville Frettenevle Harcelaines Buighy	01/02/1917	31/03/1917
Heading	War Diary For March 1917 Sec'bad Cavalry Bde. Vol IX		
War Diary	Feuquieres Carroy Aigneville Frettenevle Harcelaines Buighy	01/03/1917	20/03/1917
War Diary	Inval Boiron	21/03/1917	21/03/1917
War Diary	Prevzel	22/03/1917	23/03/1917
War Diary	Prisnun Camp Hamel	24/03/1917	25/03/1917
War Diary	Bois de Mereaucourt	27/03/1917	27/03/1917
War Diary	Halle	28/03/1917	30/03/1917
War Diary	Clery	31/03/1917	31/03/1917
Heading	Headquarters, Secunderabad Cavalry Brigade. From 1st to 30th April 1917.		
War Diary	Bayonvillers	01/04/1917	30/04/1917
Heading	War Diary For month of may 1917 From 1st May to 30th June 1917 Secunderabad Cavalry Brigade Vol XI		
War Diary	Trefcon	01/05/1917	31/05/1917
Operation(al) Order(s)	Secunderabad Cavalry Brigade Operation Order No. 37.	14/05/1917	14/05/1917
Operation(al) Order(s)	Secunderabad Cavalry Brigade Operation Order No. 38.	30/05/1917	30/05/1917
War Diary	Secunderabad Cavalry Brigade Operation Order No. 39	25/05/1917	25/05/1917
Operation(al) Order(s)	Secunderabad Cavalry Brigade Operation Order No: 40.	27/05/1917	27/05/1917
Map	Appx. A.		
Miscellaneous	Trench Stores To Be Handed Over To 4th Cavalry Division.		
Miscellaneous	S.A.A. Grenades Etc. To Be Handed Over To 4th Cavalry Division.		
Miscellaneous	S.A.A., Grenades, Etc. To Be Handed Over To Canadian Cavalry Brigade.		
Operation(al) Order(s)	Secunderabad Cavalry Brigade. Subsidiary Order To O.O. No. of 27-5-17	28/05/1917	28/05/1917
Operation(al) Order(s)	Secunderabad Cavalry Brigade Operation Order No: 41.	27/05/1917	27/05/1917
Miscellaneous	Reclassification of S.A.A., Grenades and Trench Stores Consequent On Relief Of Ambala Cavalry Brigade		
Miscellaneous	Normal O. O. distribution,	28/05/1917	28/05/1917
Miscellaneous			
Diagram etc	Diagram of Visual Circuits		
Diagram etc	Circuit Diagram.		
Heading	War Diary Sec'bad Cavalry Brigade From 1st June to 30th June 1917. Vol. I		
War Diary	Montigny Farm	01/06/1917	14/06/1917
War Diary	Trefcon	15/06/1917	23/06/1917
War Diary	Vadencourt Ch.	23/06/1917	30/06/1917

Operation(al) Order(s)	Secunderabad Cavalry Brigade Operation Order No. 42. Appx "A"	03/06/1917	03/06/1917
Operation(al) Order(s)	Secunderabad Cavalry Brigade Operation Order No: 43.	12/06/1917	12/06/1917
Operation(al) Order(s)	Machine Gun Barrages. Issued with Sec'bad Cavalry Brigade O.O. No.43.		
Miscellaneous	Barrage Table Issued with Sec'bad Cavalry Brigade Operation Order No.43.		
Miscellaneous	Normal O.O. Distribution No. 23 Ambala Cav Bde. No. 24 Canadian Bde No. 25 Mhow Cav Bde.	12/06/1917	12/06/1917
Miscellaneous	The 5th Cavalry Division G.	13/06/1917	13/06/1917
Miscellaneous	Field 13-6-17		
Operation(al) Order(s)	Secunderabad Cavalry Brigade Operation Order No: 44. Apx "C"	11/06/1917	11/06/1917
Operation(al) Order(s)	Administrative Instruction Issued with Secunderabad Cavalry Brigade Operation Order No.44		
Miscellaneous	Relief Table issued with Sec'bad Cav. Bde O.O. 44 d/11-6-17		
Operation(al) Order(s)	Secunderabad Cavalry Brigade Operation Order No: 45. Apx "D"	22/06/1917	22/06/1917
Miscellaneous	March Table issued with Secunderabad Cav. Brigade O.O. 45.		
Operation(al) Order(s)	Administrative Instructions Issued With O.O.45.		
Heading	War Diary of Secunderabad Cavalry Brigade from 1st July 1917 to 31 July 1917 Vol l		
War Diary	Vadencourt Chateau Map Ref 1/20,000 62.C. N.E. 62.C. S.E. 62.b. N.E. 62.b. S.W.	01/07/1917	13/07/1917
War Diary	Trefcon.	13/07/1917	14/07/1917
War Diary	Map. Ref. 1/100,000 St. Quentin, Amiens, Lens.	14/07/1917	15/07/1917
War Diary	Lens.	16/07/1917	31/07/1917
Miscellaneous	App A Report On The Operations On The Night 4th/5th July.		
Miscellaneous	The 5th Cavalry Division. app k	08/07/1917	08/07/1917
Operation(al) Order(s)	Secunderabad Cavalry Brigade Operation Order No: 47.	07/07/1917	07/07/1917
Miscellaneous	Relief Table Issued With Sec'bad Cavalry Brigade Operation Order No: 47.		
Heading	Secunderabad Cavy Bde War Diary From 1st August 1917 To 31st August 1917		
War Diary	Monchy Cayeux-Anvin-Eps-Herbeval Hestrus	01/08/1917	31/08/1917
War Diary	Monchy Cayeux-Anvin-Eps-Herbeval	01/08/1917	31/08/1917
Heading	War Diary Sec'bad Cavalry Brigade From 1st September 1917 To 30th September 1917		
Heading	War Diary Secunderabad Cavalry Brigade From 1st October 1917 To 31st October 1917 Vol I		
War Diary	Monchy Cayeux-Anvin-Eps-Herbeval Hestrus.	01/10/1917	06/10/1917
War Diary	Boeseghem	07/10/1917	07/10/1917
War Diary	Watou	08/10/1917	15/10/1917
War Diary	Renescure area	16/10/1917	16/10/1917
War Diary	Hervare	17/10/1917	17/10/1917
War Diary	Fruges.	18/10/1917	31/10/1917
Operation(al) Order(s)	Secunderabad Cavalry Brigade Operation Order No 53 Apx "A"	05/10/1917	05/10/1917
Operation(al) Order(s)	Secunderabad Cavalry Brigade Operation Orders No. 54. Apx "A"	06/10/1917	06/10/1917
Miscellaneous	Administrative Instructions Issued with O.O. 7th October 1917.	07/10/1917	07/10/1917

Operation(al) Order(s)	Secunderabad Cavalry Brigade Operation Order No: 54. Apx "C"	14/10/1917	14/10/1917
Operation(al) Order(s)	Secunderabad Cavalry Brigade Operation Order No: 56. Apx "D"	15/10/1917	15/10/1917
Miscellaneous	Administrative Instructions Issued With O.O. No. 56.		
Operation(al) Order(s)	Secunderabad Cavalry Brigade Operation Order No; 57. Apx "E"	16/10/1917	16/10/1917
Miscellaneous	March table issued with Sec'bad Cav. Bde. O.O. No. 57.		
War Diary	Fruges Coupielle Vielle-Crecquy-Royon-Coupielle Neuve	01/11/1917	09/11/1917
War Diary	Le Meillard	10/11/1917	10/11/1917
War Diary	Querrieu	11/11/1917	11/11/1917
War Diary	Mericourt	12/11/1917	12/11/1917
War Diary	Vraignes	19/11/1917	19/11/1917
War Diary	Fins	20/11/1917	23/11/1917
War Diary	Mericourt	27/11/1917	27/11/1917
War Diary	Trefcon	29/11/1917	30/11/1917
Operation(al) Order(s)	Secunderabad Cavalry Brigade Operation Order No: 58. Apx "A"	08/11/1917	08/11/1917
Operation(al) Order(s)	Administrative Instructions Issued With O.O. No. 58.	08/11/1917	08/11/1917
Miscellaneous	Distribution of Billets.	09/11/1917	09/11/1917
Operation(al) Order(s)	Secunderabad Cavalry Brigade Operation Order No: 59. Apx "B"	09/11/1917	09/11/1917
Operation(al) Order(s)	Administrative Instructions Issued With O.O. No 59.	09/11/1917	09/11/1917
Operation(al) Order(s)	Secunderabad Cavalry Brigade Operation Orders No: 60. Apx "C"	11/11/1917	11/11/1917
Miscellaneous	Secunderabad Cavalry Brigade.March tables issued with O.O. No:-60.	11/11/1917	11/11/1917
Operation(al) Order(s)	Administrative Instructions issued with O.O. No. 60.	11/11/1917	11/11/1917
Operation(al) Order(s)	Continuation Operation Order No 61. Apx "D"	19/11/1917	19/11/1917
Operation(al) Order(s)	Secunderabad Cavalry Brigade. Operation Order No 61	16/11/1918	16/11/1918
Miscellaneous	Administrative Instructions issued with O.O. No-of date.	18/11/1917	18/11/1917
Operation(al) Order(s)	Secunderabad Cavalry Brigade Operation Order No. 63. Apx "E"	19/11/1917	19/11/1917
Miscellaneous	Secunderabad Cavalry Brigade. Apx "F"	20/22/1917	20/22/1917
Miscellaneous	Secunderabad Cavalry Brigade	21/11/1917	21/11/1917
Operation(al) Order(s)	Secunderabad Cavalry Bde Operation Order No. 63. Apx "G"	26/11/1917	26/11/1917
Miscellaneous	Secunderabad Cavalry Brigade. Apx "H"	04/12/1917	04/12/1917
War Diary	In Valley S. of Heudicourt.	01/12/1917	02/12/1917
War Diary	Saulcourt.	03/12/1917	08/12/1917
War Diary	SE. of Devise	09/12/1917	10/12/1917
War Diary	Trefcon.	17/11/1917	31/01/1918
Heading	War Diary Sec'bad Cavalry Brigade 1st to 28th Feby 1918		
War Diary	Trefcon	01/02/1918	02/02/1918
War Diary	Belloy Sur Somme.	03/02/1918	28/02/1918
War Diary	Creuse.	01/03/1918	30/03/1918
War Diary	At Sea.	01/04/1918	11/04/1918
War Diary	Tel El Kebir.	11/04/1918	16/04/1918
War Diary	Egypt.	20/04/1918	30/04/1918
Heading	N Battery R.H.A. Jan 1917-Feb 1918.		
War Diary	Beauchamps	01/01/1917	19/03/1917
War Diary	Villeroy	20/03/1917	20/03/1917
War Diary	St Aubin	21/03/1917	21/03/1917

War Diary	Taisnil	22/03/1917	22/03/1917
War Diary	Le Hanel	23/03/1917	24/03/1917
War Diary	Bwouac (near Frise)	25/03/1917	26/03/1917
War Diary	Halle	27/03/1917	28/03/1917
War Diary	Clery	29/03/1917	31/03/1917
Heading	War Diary "N" Battery R.H.A From 1st April 1917 To 30th April 1917		
War Diary	Bayonvillers	01/04/1917	16/04/1917
War Diary	Near Trefcon	14/04/1917	08/05/1917
War Diary	Near Hamelet	09/05/1917	10/05/1917
War Diary	Trefcon	11/05/1917	27/05/1917
War Diary	Near Verguies	01/06/1917	18/06/1917
War Diary	Le Verguier	01/07/1917	11/07/1917
War Diary	Festny	12/07/1917	18/07/1917
War Diary	St. Pol.	19/07/1917	20/07/1917
War Diary	Sautrecourt	21/07/1917	28/07/1917
War Diary	Lievin	29/07/1917	13/09/1917
War Diary	Hestrus	13/09/1917	08/10/1917
War Diary	Watou.	08/10/1917	16/10/1917
War Diary	Bout-De-La Ville	14/10/1917	29/10/1917
War Diary	Fruges	01/11/1917	12/11/1917
War Diary	Brusle	12/11/1917	20/11/1917
War Diary	Near Marcoing	20/11/1917	22/11/1917
War Diary	La-Neuville	23/11/1917	23/11/1917
War Diary	Trefcon	24/11/1917	30/11/1917
War Diary	Near Heudecourt	01/12/1917	03/12/1917
War Diary	Saulcourt.	04/12/1917	16/12/1917
War Diary	R.9.c.i.s	01/01/1918	20/02/1918
War Diary	Trefcon	21/02/1918	28/02/1918
Heading	7th Dragoon Guards Jan 1917-Feb 1918.		
Heading	War Diary of 7th Dragoon Guards. From 1st January 1917 To 31st January 1917		
War Diary	Feuquieres.	01/01/1917	31/01/1917
Heading	7th Dragoon Guards. From 1st to 28th February 1917.		
War Diary	Feuquieres	01/02/1917	28/02/1917
Heading	War Diary For March 1917 7th D Guards Slad Cav: Bde		
War Diary	Feuquieres	01/03/1917	20/03/1917
War Diary	Le Quesne.	20/03/1917	21/03/1917
War Diary	Namps Au Mont.	21/03/1917	22/03/1917
War Diary	Near Hamel.	23/03/1917	24/03/1917
War Diary	Bois de Mereaucourt	24/03/1917	27/03/1917
War Diary	Halle	27/03/1917	27/03/1917
War Diary	Clery.	28/03/1917	30/03/1917
War Diary	Bayonvillers	30/03/1917	31/03/1917
Heading	War Diary 7th D Guards From 1st April 1917 to 30th April.		
War Diary	Bayonvillers.	01/04/1917	14/04/1917
War Diary	Trefcon.	15/04/1917	30/04/1917
Heading	War Diary For month of May 1917 From 1st-31st May 1917 1st Dragoon Guards. Vol XI		
War Diary	Trefcon	01/05/1917	15/05/1917
War Diary	1 1/2 m S.E. of Le Verguier.	15/05/1917	31/05/1917
Heading	War Diary 7th Dragoon Guards June 1st to June 30 1917		
War Diary	1 1/2 miles S.E. of Le Verguier.	01/06/1917	14/06/1917

War Diary	Trefcon	15/06/1917	23/06/1917
War Diary	Vadricourt.	23/06/1917	30/06/1917
Heading	War Diary 7th Dragoon Guards From 1st July 1917 to 31st July 1917. (Vol I)		
War Diary	Vadencourt. 1/2 N of Hassemy.	01/07/1917	07/07/1917
War Diary	Vadencourt	07/07/1917	09/07/1917
War Diary	Trefcon.	10/07/1917	10/07/1917
War Diary	Buire.	14/07/1917	14/07/1917
War Diary	Suzanne	15/07/1917	15/07/1917
War Diary	Ville sur Corbie.	16/07/1917	16/07/1917
War Diary	Sarton.	17/07/1917	17/07/1917
War Diary	Bryas.	18/07/1917	19/07/1917
War Diary	Anvin Le Petit.	20/07/1917	31/07/1917
Heading	War Diary 7th Dragoon Guards From 1st August 1917 To 31st August 1917		
War Diary	Anvin.	01/08/1917	30/08/1917
Heading	War Diary Sec'bad Cavalry Brigade 7th Dragoon Guards From 1st to 30 Sept 1917		
War Diary	Anvin	01/09/1917	30/09/1917
Heading	War Diary 7th Dragoon Guards. From 1st October 1917 To 31st October 1917		
War Diary	Anvin	01/10/1917	06/10/1917
War Diary	Boesinghem	07/10/1917	07/10/1917
War Diary	Watou.	08/10/1917	15/10/1917
War Diary	Campagne	16/10/1917	16/10/1917
War Diary	Thiembrone	17/10/1917	17/10/1917
War Diary	Coopelle-Veille.	20/10/1917	31/10/1917
War Diary	Anvin	01/10/1917	06/10/1917
War Diary	Boesinghem	07/10/1917	07/10/1917
War Diary	Watou	08/10/1917	15/10/1917
War Diary	Campagne	16/10/1917	16/10/1917
War Diary	Thiembrone	17/10/1917	17/10/1917
War Diary	Coopelle-Veille	20/10/1917	09/11/1917
War Diary	Autheux.	10/11/1917	10/11/1917
War Diary	Querrieu	11/11/1917	11/11/1917
War Diary	Cappy	12/11/1917	12/11/1917
War Diary	Bouvaincourt	15/11/1917	19/11/1917
War Diary	Bois de Dessart	20/11/1917	21/11/1917
War Diary	Marcoing	21/11/1917	21/11/1917
War Diary	1 Mile W 9-Villars-Pluich	21/11/1917	22/11/1917
War Diary	Froissy	23/11/1917	27/11/1917
War Diary	Coopelle Veille	01/11/1917	09/11/1917
War Diary	Autheux.	10/11/1917	10/11/1917
War Diary	Querrieu	11/11/1917	11/11/1917
War Diary	Cappy	12/11/1917	12/11/1917
War Diary	Bouvaincourt	15/11/1917	20/11/1917
War Diary	Bois de Dessart.	21/11/1917	21/11/1917
War Diary	Marcoing	21/11/1917	21/11/1917
War Diary	1 Mile W 9-Villars-pluich	21/11/1917	22/11/1917
War Diary	Sy.	23/11/1917	30/11/1917
War Diary	Trefcon.	30/11/1917	30/11/1917
War Diary	Heudecourt	01/12/1917	03/12/1917
War Diary	Saulcourt	03/12/1917	08/12/1917
War Diary	Buire	09/12/1917	17/12/1917
War Diary	Trefcon.	18/12/1917	25/01/1918
War Diary	Leverguier	26/01/1918	31/01/1918

War Diary	Trefcon.	01/02/1918	01/02/1918
War Diary	Bayonvillers	02/02/1918	02/02/1918
War Diary	St Sauveur. (Vernand)	03/02/1918	03/02/1918
War Diary	St Sauveur	15/02/1918	15/02/1918
War Diary	Picquigny	20/02/1918	28/02/1918
War Diary	Longpre.	28/02/1918	28/02/1918
Heading	20th Deccan Horse Jan 1917-Feb 1918		
Heading	War Diary of 20th Deccan Horse. From 1st January 1917 To 31st January 1917		
War Diary	Harcelaines	01/01/1917	26/01/1917
Heading	20th Deccan Horse. From 1st to 28th February 1917.		
Miscellaneous	Daily List of ? in Adjutant?		
War Diary		06/02/1917	28/02/1917
Heading	War Diary For March 1917 XXth Deccan Horse Sbad Cav Bde Vol IX		
War Diary	Harcelaines	01/03/1917	19/03/1917
War Diary	Andaineville.	20/03/1917	20/03/1917
War Diary	Neuville-Sous-Loeuilly.	21/03/1917	21/03/1917
War Diary	Hamel.	22/03/1917	22/03/1917
War Diary	Feuilleres.	24/03/1917	26/03/1917
War Diary	Halle	27/03/1917	27/03/1917
War Diary	Clery.	28/03/1917	28/03/1917
War Diary	Curlu	29/03/1917	29/03/1917
War Diary	Framerville	30/03/1917	30/03/1917
Heading	20th Deccan Horse From 1st April to 30th April		
War Diary	Framerville	02/04/1917	06/04/1917
War Diary	Trefcon	14/04/1917	30/04/1917
Heading	War Diary For month of may 1917 From 1st-31st May 1917 20th Deccan Horse Vol XI		
War Diary	62c/L.28.a.	15/05/1917	26/05/1917
War Diary	Field	28/05/1917	31/05/1917
Heading	War Diary 20th Deccan Horse 1st June to 30th June 1917.		
War Diary	Field	01/06/1917	26/06/1917
Miscellaneous	App. C.		
Miscellaneous	Report by Listening Patrol.		
Miscellaneous			
Miscellaneous	App D		
Miscellaneous	App. E	13/06/1917	13/06/1917
Miscellaneous	App. E.		
Miscellaneous	App E		
Miscellaneous	App F		
Heading	War Diary of XXth Deccan Horse. From 1st July 1917 to 31st July 1917. (Vol I)		
War Diary	Field	03/07/1917	29/07/1917
Heading	War Diary 20th Deccan Horse From 1st August 1917 To 31st August 1917		
War Diary	The Field	01/08/1917	31/08/1917
Heading	War Diary 20th Deccan Horse S'bad Cavalry Bde. From 1st to 30th Sept. 1917		
War Diary	The Field	08/09/1917	30/09/1917
Heading	War Diary of 20th Deccan Horse From 1st October 1917 To 31st October 1917		
War Diary	The Field	03/10/1917	24/12/1917
War Diary	Field	23/12/1917	27/01/1918
War Diary	Field	25/01/1918	31/01/1918

Heading	War Diary 20th Deccan Horse 1st to 28th Feby 1918.		
War Diary	Field	01/02/1918	28/02/1918
War Diary	Field	01/02/1918	15/02/1918
Heading	34th Poona Horse Jan 1917-Mar 1918		
Heading	War Diary of 34th Poona Horse. From 1st January 1917 To 31st January 1917		
Heading	34th Poona-Horse War Diary From 1st January 1917 To 31st January 1917.		
War Diary	Aigneville	01/01/1917	28/01/1917
Heading	War Diary of 34th Poona-Horse From 1st Feb 1917 to 28th Feb 1917 (Vol VIII)		
War Diary	Aigneville	01/02/1917	22/02/1917
Heading	War Diary of 34th Poona-Horse From 1st March 1917 to 31st March 1917 (Vol IX)		
War Diary	Aigneville	01/03/1917	20/03/1917
War Diary	Fresneville	21/03/1917	21/03/1917
War Diary	Plachy Buyon	22/03/1917	24/03/1917
War Diary	Bois de Mereaucourt	25/03/1917	27/03/1917
War Diary	Halle	27/03/1917	30/03/1917
War Diary	Buyonvillers	30/03/1917	30/03/1917
Heading	War Diary 34th Poona-Horse From 1st April 1917 to 30th April 1917. (Vol I)		
War Diary	Bayonvillers.	01/04/1917	29/04/1917
Heading	War Diary of 34th Poona-Horse From 15th May 1917 to 30th May 1917 Vol XI		
War Diary	Caulaincourt	15/05/1917	31/05/1917
Heading	War Diary of 34th Poona-Horse From 1st June to 30 June 1917 (Vol I)		
Miscellaneous			
War Diary		01/06/1917	30/06/1917
Heading	War Diary of 34th Poona-Horse From 1st July 1917 to 31st July 1917 (Vol I)		
War Diary			
War Diary		01/07/1917	09/07/1917
War Diary	Caulaincourt	10/07/1917	13/07/1917
War Diary	Cartigny	14/07/1917	14/07/1917
War Diary	Suzanne	15/07/1917	15/07/1917
War Diary	Morlanecourt	16/07/1917	16/07/1917
War Diary	Authie	17/07/1917	17/07/1917
War Diary	Belval	18/07/1917	19/07/1917
War Diary	Eps	20/07/1917	31/07/1917
Heading	War Diary of 34th Poona Horse From 1st August 1917 to 31st August 1917		
War Diary	Eps.	01/08/1917	31/08/1917
Heading	War Diary of 34th Poona Horse From 1st September to 30th September 1917		
War Diary	Eps.	01/09/1917	30/09/1917
Heading	War Diary of 34th Poona Horse From 1st October to 31st October 1917.		
War Diary	Eps.	01/10/1917	06/10/1917
War Diary	Les. Ciseaux	07/10/1917	07/10/1917
War Diary	Watou	08/10/1917	15/10/1917
War Diary	Heuringhen	16/10/1917	16/10/1917
War Diary	Merck St. Lievin	17/10/1917	17/10/1917
War Diary	Crequy	18/10/1917	31/10/1917

Heading	War Diary of 34 Poona Horse From 1st November 1917 To 30 November 1917		
War Diary	Crequy	01/11/1917	05/11/1917
War Diary	Heuzecourt St Acheul	10/11/1917	10/11/1917
War Diary	Beaucourt	11/11/1917	11/11/1917
War Diary	Merricourt Sur Somme.	12/11/1917	12/11/1917
War Diary	Hancourt	13/11/1917	20/11/1917
War Diary	Near X Roods Ki miles N of C of La. Vacquerie Which J W of Villers Plouich	21/11/1917	21/11/1917
War Diary	Bivouack NE of Villers Plouich	22/11/1917	22/11/1917
War Diary	Fins	23/11/1917	23/11/1917
War Diary	Chuignolles	24/11/1917	27/11/1917
War Diary	Trefcon	28/11/1917	30/11/1917
Heading	War Diary of 34th Poona Horse From 1st December 1917 To 31st December 1917.		
War Diary	Valley 1/4 Mile. S. Of Sugar Factory Heudicourt.	01/12/1917	01/12/1917
War Diary	Bois Gauche	02/12/1917	02/12/1917
War Diary	1/2 Sugar Factory Heudicourt	03/12/1917	03/12/1917
War Diary	1/2 Mile. S.W. of Saulcourt in Shnkem Road.	04/12/1917	07/12/1917
War Diary	Devise	08/12/1917	17/12/1917
War Diary	Trefcon	18/12/1917	26/01/1918
War Diary	Vadencourt	26/01/1918	28/01/1918
War Diary	Trefcon	29/01/1918	29/01/1918
War Diary	Vadencourt	29/01/1918	29/01/1918
War Diary	Trefcon	30/01/1918	30/01/1918
War Diary	Vadencourt	30/01/1918	31/01/1918
Heading	War Diary of 34th Poona Horse For the month of February 1918. (From 1st to 28th February 18)		
War Diary	Trefcon	01/02/1918	01/02/1918
War Diary	Vadencourt	01/02/1918	01/02/1918
War Diary	La Motte	02/02/1918	02/02/1918
War Diary	Vadencourt	02/02/1918	02/02/1918
War Diary	Havernas	03/02/1918	03/02/1918
War Diary	3/4 Mile E of Vadencourt	03/02/1918	03/02/1918
War Diary	Havernas	04/02/1918	04/02/1918
War Diary	3/4 Mile E of Vadencourt	04/02/1918	04/02/1918
War Diary	Havernas	05/02/1918	05/02/1918
War Diary	Trenches 3/4 Mile E of Vadencourt	05/02/1918	05/02/1918
War Diary	Havernas	06/02/1918	06/02/1918
War Diary	Trenches 3/4 mile E of Vadencourt	06/02/1918	06/02/1918
War Diary	Havernas	07/02/1918	07/02/1918
War Diary	Trenches 3/4 mile E of Vadencourt	07/02/1918	07/02/1918
War Diary	Havernas	08/02/1918	08/02/1918
War Diary	Trenches 3/4 mile E of Vadencourt	08/02/1918	08/02/1918
War Diary	Havernas	09/02/1918	09/02/1918
War Diary	Trenches 3/4 mile E of Vadencourt	09/02/1918	09/02/1918
War Diary	Havernas	10/02/1918	10/02/1918
War Diary	Trenches 3/4 mile E of Vadencourt	10/02/1918	10/02/1918
War Diary	Havernas	11/02/1918	11/02/1918
War Diary	Trenches 3/4 mile E of Vadencourt	11/02/1918	11/02/1918
War Diary	Havernas	12/02/1918	12/02/1918
War Diary	Trenches 3/4 mile E of Vadencourt	12/02/1918	12/02/1918
War Diary	Havernas	13/02/1918	13/02/1918
War Diary	Trenches 3/4 mile E of Vadencourt	13/02/1918	13/02/1918
War Diary	Havernas	14/02/1918	14/02/1918
War Diary	Trenches 3/4 mile E of Vadencourt	14/02/1918	14/02/1918

Type	Location	Start	End
War Diary	Havernas	15/02/1918	15/02/1918
War Diary	Trenches 3/4 mile E of Vadencourt	15/02/1918	15/02/1918
War Diary	Havernas	16/02/1918	28/02/1918
Heading	War Diary of 34 Poona Horse From 1st March 1918 to 31st March 1918		
War Diary	Pissy	01/03/1918	21/03/1918
War Diary	Marseilles	22/03/1918	31/03/1918
Heading	Signal Troop. Jan 1917-Apl 1918		
Heading	War Diary of Signal Troop, Secunderabad Cavalry Brigade. From 1st January 1917 To 31st January 1917		
War Diary	Feuquieres	01/01/1917	31/01/1917
Heading	Signal Troop, Secunderabad Cavalry Brigade. From 1st to 28th February 1917.		
Miscellaneous	Issued to Section		
War Diary	Feuquieres	01/02/1917	28/02/1917
Heading	War Diary For March 1917 Signal Troop Sbad Cavy Bde V & IX		
War Diary	Feuquieres	01/03/1917	31/03/1917
Heading	Signal Troop Sec'bad Cavalry Bde From 1st April to 30th April		
War Diary	Bayonvillers	01/04/1917	30/04/1917
Heading	War Diary For month of may 1917 From 1st-31st May 1917 Signal Troop Vol XI		
War Diary	Trefcon	01/05/1917	19/05/1917
War Diary	Mintigny Farm.	19/05/1917	31/05/1917
Diagram etc	Circuit Diagram P.I.I		
Miscellaneous	Key To Diagram. A		
Diagram etc	Circuit Diagram. P.11.		
Diagram etc	Diagram of Visual Circuits		
Heading	War Diary Signal Troop Sec'bad Cavalry Bde 1st June to 30th June 1917		
War Diary	Montigny Farm	01/06/1917	30/06/1917
Diagram etc	Circuit Diagram "S"		
Heading	War Diary Signal Troop, Secunderabad Cav Bde. From 1st July 1917 to 31st July 1917 (Vol I)		
War Diary	Vadencourt	01/07/1917	10/07/1917
War Diary	Bivouac Trefcon	10/07/1917	20/07/1917
War Diary	Chateau Monchy-Cayeux.	20/07/1917	31/07/1917
Heading	War Diary Signal Troop S'bad Cavy Bde From 1st August 1917 To 31st August 1917		
War Diary	Monchy-Cayeux	01/08/1917	31/08/1917
Heading	War Diary Sec'bad Cavalry Brigade Signal Troop From 1st to 30th Sept. 1917		
War Diary	Monchy-Cayeux	01/09/1917	30/09/1917
Heading	War Diary Sbad Bde Signal Troop From 1st October 1917 To 31st October 1917		
War Diary	Monchy-Cayeux	01/10/1917	31/10/1917
War Diary	Trefcon	01/01/1918	24/01/1918
War Diary	Vadencourt	25/01/1918	31/01/1918
War Diary	At Sea.	01/04/1918	11/04/1918
War Diary	Tel El Kebir Egypt.	11/04/1918	30/04/1918
Heading	Machine Gun Squadron Jan 1917-Feb 1918.		
Heading	War Diary of Machine Gun Squadron, Secunderabad Cavalry Brigade. From 1st January 1917 To 31st January 1917		
War Diary	Buigny	01/01/1917	31/01/1917

Heading	13th Squadron, Machine Gun Corps, (Cavalry) (Secunderabad Cavalry Brigade). From 1st to 28th February 1917.		
Miscellaneous	Issued to Section		
War Diary	Buigny	01/02/1917	28/02/1917
Heading	War Diary For March 1917 13th M G Sqdn-Cavalry Vol IX Sbad Cav: Bde		
War Diary	Buigny	01/03/1917	19/03/1917
War Diary	Le Mazis.	20/03/1917	20/03/1917
War Diary	Rumaisnil	21/03/1917	21/03/1917
War Diary	Hamel	22/03/1917	24/03/1917
War Diary	Bois de Moreaucourt	25/03/1917	26/03/1917
War Diary	Halle	27/03/1917	27/03/1917
War Diary	Clery	28/03/1917	28/03/1917
War Diary	Hem	29/03/1917	29/03/1917
War Diary	Bayonvillers	30/03/1917	31/03/1917
Heading	War Diary 13th Sqdn: M.G. Corps (Cavalry) From 1st April to 30th April		
War Diary	Bayonvillers	01/04/1917	02/04/1917
War Diary	Raincourt	03/04/1917	13/04/1917
War Diary	Trefcon	14/04/1917	15/04/1917
War Diary	St Martin des Pres	16/04/1917	30/04/1917
Heading	War Diary For month of may 1917. From 1st-31st May 1917 13th Sqdn M Gun Sqdn (Cavalry) Vol XI		
War Diary	St. Martin-des-Pres.	01/05/1917	01/05/1917
War Diary	Near Trefcon	02/05/1917	14/05/1917
War Diary	Jeancourt	15/05/1917	31/05/1917
Heading	War Diary 13th Sqdn. M. Gun Corps (Cavy) 1st June to 30th June 1917.		
War Diary	Jeancourt	01/06/1917	13/06/1917
War Diary	St Martin Les Pres	14/06/1917	23/06/1917
Heading	War Diary 13th Squadron (M.G.C.) Cavalry From 1st July 1917 to 31st July 1917 (Vol. I).		
War Diary	St. Martin des Pres.	01/07/1917	13/07/1917
War Diary	Buire 2 miles E of Suzanne.	14/07/1917	15/07/1917
War Diary	Morlancourt	16/07/1917	16/07/1917
War Diary	Sarton	17/07/1917	17/07/1917
War Diary	Crossart	18/07/1917	19/07/1917
War Diary	Monchy Cayeux	20/07/1917	31/07/1917
Heading	Sec'bad Cavalry Bde. 13th Sqn M.G. Corps. War Diary From 1st August 1917. To 31st August 1917. Vol I		
War Diary	Monchy-Cayeux	01/07/1917	05/07/1917
War Diary	Fleury	06/07/1917	31/07/1917
Heading	War Diary S'bad cavalry Brigade 13th Sqn M.G Corps From 1st to 30th Sept 1917		
War Diary	Fleury	01/09/1917	30/09/1917
Heading	War Diary 13th M G Squadron From 1st October 1917 To 31st October 1917		
War Diary		01/10/1917	31/10/1917
War Diary	Coupelle-Neuve	01/11/1917	08/11/1917
War Diary	Mt Renault Farm.	09/11/1917	09/11/1917
War Diary	St Gratien	10/11/1917	10/11/1917
War Diary	Chuignolles.	11/10/1917	11/10/1917
War Diary	Vraignes	12/10/1917	19/11/1917
War Diary	Cambrai Area	20/11/1917	20/11/1917
War Diary	Near Marcoing	21/11/1917	21/11/1917

Type	Location	Start	End
War Diary	Fins.	22/11/1917	22/11/1917
War Diary	Marley Camp	23/11/1917	26/11/1917
War Diary	St Martin des Pris.	27/11/1917	30/11/1917
War Diary	Sq. W 23.	01/12/1917	07/12/1917
War Diary	Brusle	08/12/1917	12/12/1917
War Diary	Gomiecourt	13/12/1917	19/12/1917
War Diary	Trefcon	20/12/1917	25/01/1918
War Diary	Leverguier	26/01/1918	31/01/1918
Heading	War Diary 13th M G Sqdn 1st to 28th February 1918.		
War Diary	Leverguier	01/02/1918	15/02/1918
War Diary	Flesseles	16/02/1918	27/02/1918
War Diary	Cocquerel	28/02/1918	28/02/1918
Heading	Mobile Veterinary Section Jan-May 1917		
Heading	War Diary of Mobile Veterinary Section, Secunderabad Cavalry Brigade. From 1st January 1917. To 31st January 1917		
War Diary	Feuquieres.	01/01/1917	31/01/1917
Heading	Mobile Veterinary Section, Secunderabad Cavalry Section From 1st to 28th February 1917.		
Miscellaneous	?Correspondence received		
War Diary	Fequieres.	01/02/1917	13/02/1917
Heading	Mobile Veterinary Section, Secunderabad Cavalry Brigade. From 1st to 31st March 1917.		
War Diary		14/02/1917	28/02/1917
War Diary	Feuquieres.	01/03/1917	20/03/1917
War Diary	Provzel	21/03/1917	21/03/1917
War Diary	Hamel	22/03/1917	23/03/1917
War Diary	Bois de Mereaucourt.	24/03/1917	24/03/1917
War Diary	Biaches	25/03/1917	28/03/1917
War Diary	Cappy	29/03/1917	31/03/1917
Heading	Mobile Veterinary Section, Secunderabad Cavalry Brigade. From 1st to 30th April 1917.		
Miscellaneous	Issued to Section		
War Diary	Bayonvillers	01/04/1917	14/04/1917
War Diary	Trefcon	15/04/1917	30/04/1917
Heading	Mobile Veterinary Section, Secunderabad Cavalry Brigade. From 1st May to 31st May 1917.		
Miscellaneous	Issued to Section		
War Diary	Trefcon	01/05/1917	31/05/1917

1917-18
5TH CAVALRY DIVISION
SECUNDERABAD CAV. BDE.

BDE HEADQUARTERS.

JAN 1917 - APL 1918

1917-18
5TH CAVALRY DIVISION
SECUNDERABAD CAV. BDE.

SERIAL NO. 119

Confidential

War Diary

of

HEADQUARTERS, SECUNDERABAD CAVALRY BRIGADE.

FROM 1st January 1917 **TO** 31st January 1917

Staff Carol Bde Vol VII

Army Form C. 2118.

WAR DIARY
INTELLIGENCE SUMMARY

(Erase heading not required.)

Page 1

Instructions regarding War Diaries and Intelligence Summaries are contained in F.S. Regs., Part II. and the Staff Manual respectively. Title Pages will be prepared in manuscript.

Place	Date	Hour	Summary of Events and Information	Remarks and references to Appendices
FEVRIERES CARROY RUMMEDILLE METTENEUVE HARCEIANES BUIGNY	1/1/17 3.4.17 1st to 3rd		The Brigade remained in Billets as per margin. Pioneer Battalion reported from XIVth Bgde. Training, in Mounted and Dismounted Work, Bombing, Musketry, Sniping and Lewis Gun Practices Carried out during the month. WR 1.2.17	

Serial No: **119**

Headquarters,

Secunderabad Cavalry Brigade.

From 1st to 28th February 1917.

Army Form C. 2118.

3rd Cavalry Bde

Vol VIII Page 1

WAR DIARY
or
INTELLIGENCE SUMMARY
(Erase heading not required.)

Instructions regarding War Diaries and Intelligence Summaries are contained in F. S. Regs., Part II. and the Staff Manual respectively. Title Pages will be prepared in manuscript.

Place	Date	Hour	Summary of Events and Information	Remarks and references to Appendices
FEUQUIERES	1-2.17		The Brigade remained in Billets as per margin.	
CARROY				
AIGNEVILLE				
FRETTEMEULE				
HARDELAINES				
BUIGNY				
	8.2.17		Headquarters of Sector Forces XIII and X Reserve Horse Company proceeded to join XIIIth Corps - Strength - O.R.B. 29. O.R.1 - 261	
	9.2.17		Bona Horse Company proceeded to join XIIIth Corps - Strength as follows: - B.Os- 7, 1.Os - 3, O.R.B. 3, O.R.1. 246	
	10.2.17		7th Guards Company proceeded to join XIII th Corps - Strength as under - B.Os. 5. O.R.B. 2. O.R. 154.	
	1st to 31st		Training in mounted and dismounted work, Bombing, Musketry, Sniping and Hotchkiss Gun practice carried out during the month.	

RCP

2449 Wt. W14957/M90 750,000 1/16 J.B.C. & A. Forms/C.2118/12.

Serial No: 119.

Confidential.

War Diary

for March 1917

Sec'd a Cavalry Bde.

Vol. IX

Army Form C. 2118.

Staff & O/C Pioneer Bn

WAR DIARY
or
INTELLIGENCE SUMMARY
(Erase heading not required.)

Page I

Instructions regarding War Diaries and Intelligence Summaries are contained in F. S. Regs., Part II. and the Staff Manual respectively. Title Pages will be prepared in manuscript.

Place	Date	Hour	Summary of Events and Information	Remarks and references to Appendices
FOUQUIERES CARROY- DIGNEVILLE FRETTEMEULE	1.3.17		The Brigade remained in Billets, as per margin	
HARELAINES BUIGNY	12.3.17		Bde. marches to & shown notes.	
	14.3.17		Pioneer Bn. reported from XIIIth Corps - Strength - B.O. - 11 - O.R.B. - 283. O.R.1 = 507.	
	20.3.17	10.30am	Bde. moved to Ste Colen LE QUESNE - ARGUEL - CAMPSPORT - FRESNEVILLE - ANDAINVILLE - INVAL BOIRON - ST. AUBIN RIVIERE via MARTAINNEVILLE Sn. - OISEMONT - QUATRE. Arrilles at INVAL BOIRON.	
INVAL BOIRON	21.3.17	10.30am	Bde. marched to CONA - NAMPTY - HEBE COURT - BUJON - NAMPS-au-MONT - NAMPS-au-VAL - NEUVILLE via HORNOY - THIEULLOY - FRICAMPS. Arrived at PREUZEL.	
PREUZEL	22nd to 23rd	11am	Bde. marched to Americans Pioneers Camps, HAMEL near BOVES - VILLERS BRETONNEUX - Reput Centre (Americans Camp)	
Pioneer Camp HAMEL	24th 25th	6.45am	Bde. marched to Bivouacs in Bois du MEREAUCOURT via CAPPY. South of FRISE - le Bois du MEREAUCOURT. Reput Centre 1 of Brig. at MEREAUCOURT.	
Bois de MEREAUCOURT	27th	1 pm	Bde. marched to Bivouacs near HALLE via HERBECOURT - Reput Centre - HALLE. HERBECOURT - BIACHES.	

Army Form C. 2118.

WAR DIARY
INTELLIGENCE SUMMARY
(Erase heading not required.)

Page 11

Instructions regarding War Diaries and Intelligence Summaries are contained in F. S. Regs., Part II. and the Staff Manual respectively. Title Pages will be prepared in manuscript.

Place	Date	Hour	Summary of Events and Information	Remarks and references to Appendices
HALLE	28th 29.3.17	3pm	Bn. moved to a bivouac between CLERY and FRISE via CLERY.	
CLERY	30.3.17 31.3.17	11.30a	Bn. marched to BAYONVILLERS via SUZETTE - via - FRISE - CAPPY - PROYART. Bon-Cours opposite school - BAYONVILLERS. 1st to 19th training in Mounted & Dismounted Bombing, Musketry, Sniping & Hotchkiss Gun Practice carried out. Weather during month very cold and wet. A.R.	

Serial No. 119.

Headquarters, Secunderabad Cavalry Brigade.

From 1st to 30th April 1917.

Sec'ted Cavalry Brigade Vol 10

Army Form C. 2118.

Pg. I

WAR DIARY

INTELLIGENCE SUMMARY.

(Erase heading not required.)

Instructions regarding War Diaries and Intelligence Summaries are contained in F. S. Regs., Part II, and the Staff Manual respectively. Title pages will be prepared in manuscript.

Hour, Date, Place.	Summary of Events and Information	Remarks and references to Appendices.
BAYONVILLERS 1-4-1917	The Brigade in Billets in and around BAYONVILLERS.	Ref. Map 1/100000 AMIENS.
14.4.17 9. am.	Bde marched to a bivouac in the vicinity of TREFCON via HARBONNIERES – LIHONS – CHAULNES – ST CHRIST – ENNEMAIN – FOURQUES – MONCHY LAGACHE. Bde Hd Qrs. – TREFCON.	Ref. map 1/100000 ST. QUENTIN
15.4.17 to 30.4.17	Training in mounted & dismount. Work, Bombing, musketry, Sniping & Hotchkiss Gun Practice carried out.	

Serial No. 119.

Confidential

From 1st May to 30th June 1917

War Diary for month
of May 1917

From 1st May 3rd to 30th June 1917.

Secunderabad Cavalry Brigade

Vol. XI

Army Form C. 2118.

WAR DIARY

Secld Cavalry Brigade.

INTELLIGENCE SUMMARY.

(Erase heading not required.)

Page 1

Instructions regarding War Diaries and Intelligence Summaries are contained in F. S. Regs., Part II, and the Staff Manual respectively. Title pages will be prepared in manuscript.

Hour, Date, Place.	Summary of Events and Information	Remarks and references to Appendices.
TREFCON. 1-5-17 to 8.5.17	The Brigade remained in bivouacs at TREFCON. Weather fine.	Ref Map:- 1/100000 St QUENTIN.
11.5.17	Fourth Army Commander inspected Brigade & met N.E. of BEAUVOIS.	
12.5.17	Orders received to organise Dismounted Bde. Strength as follows:- B.O:- 51. 1.O:- 18. O.R.B 453. O.R 1 = 582.	
14-5-17/15.5-17	Dismt Regts from 9th Hodson's Horse, 18th Lancers and Dismt Sqdn from 14th K Edwards (Cavaly) attached to Brigade. Midnight 14th/15th May. Dismounted Brigade relieved 174th Infantry Bde.	O.O. 34 attached.
15.5.17/16.5.17		
16.5.17	Command passed Genl. Bde Hd Qrs. MONTIGNY FERM. Bde Front. GRAND PRIEL WOOD - L.18.b. DEAN COPSE - RED WOOD. G.31.D - roughly 4000 yd. Advanced Regt.- 7th Hussars + Poona Horse Support Regt.- 9th Hodson's Horse + 26th Horse Bde in Reserve - 18th Lancers	Map:- 1/20000 62 c. N.E + 62 c. S.E. 62 B.N.W + 62 B. S.W.

Army Form C. 2118.

WAR DIARY
Sected Cavalry Bde.
INTELLIGENCE SUMMARY.
(Erase heading not required.)

Page II

Hour, Date, Place.	Summary of Events and Information	Remarks and references to Appendices.
16-5-17 contd.	Situation normal. Weather wet muddy. Hostile artillery on enemy's part. A few shells dropped around ASCENSION FARM.	
17.5.17	Situation normal. Weather slightly improved. No 9 Post shelled with Shrapnel - 1 am. Casualties - 1 Indian Officer. 6.I.O.R's. Unebolts por.	
18.5.17	Enemy Artillery more active. G.R. 3.15 am. No. 10 Post attacked by an enemy Patrol of 30 men. These were driven off & no casualties were suffered. Touch obtained with enemy Patrols by both Advanced Posts.	
19.5.17	In the early hours a German Patrol 20-30 strong attempted to turn No 15 Post. These were driven off without casualties. Quiet day & shelling light. Light Support Regt. (9th Hrse) relieved 12 Advanced Regt. (7th 19 Guards). 18th Lancers still in Bde Reserve	G.O.O. 38 attached
night 19/20		
20.5.17.	Situation normal. Intermittent shelling during day. Left Support Regt. (30th Horse) relieved the Advanced left (Poona Horse)	

Army Form C. 2118.

Sialkot Cav. Bde.

WAR DIARY

or

INTELLIGENCE SUMMARY. Page 111

(Erase heading not required.)

Instructions regarding War Diaries and Intelligence Summaries are contained in F. S. Regs., Part II, and the Staff Manual respectively. Title pages will be prepared in manuscript.

Hour, Date, Place.	Summary of Events and Information.	Remarks and references to Appendices.
21.5.17.	Situation unchanged. No 9 Post again shelled. Casualties - 4.O.R.1. Fine day. Aeroplanes good.	
22.5.17	Situation normal - 2.O.R.1. wounded by Shell fire.	
23.5.17	Situation normal - Night of 23rd/24th A patrol of Horse raided an enemy post in G.19.L.9.5. under Lieut. A.S. GODFREE. 20th Deccan Horse held by an N.C.O. and 12 men - 3 prisoners were captured - 2 enemy killed, the remainder fled to their own line. Our patrol returned without casualties. Prisoners were of 73rd Fusiliers 111th Division. normal.	
24.5.17	Situation normal weather fine.	Enemy Artillery activity
25.5.17	" " "	normal.
26.5.17	" " "	
27.5.17	Situation normal. weather fine. Intermittent shelling. about 1 - 100 Shells dropped around ASCENSION FARM. Left Support line shelled with 5.9. H.E. Casualties 3 Killed 4 wounded. Following relief took place night 27/28th. Right Support Regt (7th Hussars) relieved Rt. Advanced Regt (9th Horse) Left Support Regt (Poona Horse) relieved Left Advanced Regt (2nd Horse) S.W. Lancers Still in Bde Reserve.	

Army Form C. 2118.

Jeelalaew Bde

Page IV

WAR DIARY
—OF—
INTELLIGENCE SUMMARY.

(Erase heading not required.)

Hour, Date, Place.	Summary of Events and Information.	Remarks and references to Appendices.
28.5.17.	No request on 4" Cavalry Divn coming into the line the Bde front was shortened as follows:— Northern Boundary. PIEUMEL WOOD - GRAND PRIEL FM - 6.20. Central. Southern Boundary. R.5.b.7.9. - RED.HOOD - 6.27 Central. 4" Cavalry Divn on the NORTH taking over 4 posts, 2 Supports, & Left Wing Regt Headquarters. Canadian Bde on the SOUTH taking over 2 posts, 1 support & Wing Hd Qrs. Ambala Cav. Bde. troops withdrawn (less 3 sect. 14" Sqdn. m.gns.(army)). Bde front now consists of 9 Advanced Posts & 8 counter-attack troop pts situated amounts 2 Subsectors held as follows:— Right Regt. 7 Kriegan Eurrs. Left Regt. 24 Poona Horse. Bde Reserve. 20" Deccan Horse.	
29.5.17.	Situation normal, weather true but cooler. Situation normal - shelling light, weather hot inclut.[?] good. An Officers Patrol was attacked from the rear on their way back from a point 500 yds E. of ASCENSION FARM. Casualties 1 - B.O. 1 - N.C.O. wounded.	

Army Form C. 2118.

Shed Law Bn

WAR DIARY
or
INTELLIGENCE SUMMARY   V

(Erase heading not required.)

Place	Date	Hour	Summary of Events and Information	Remarks and references to Appendices
29.5.17 continued			Enemy patrol in ASCENSION FARM chased by one of our patrols were fired on by 2 enemy patrols with bombs. One casualty I.O.R. killed. 3 O.R. wounded.	
	30/5/17		Situation unchanged. Shelling light. Patrols ascertained that ASCENSION WOOD, LITTLE BILL & Rifle pits in G.26.c. are held by enemy during night.	
	31/5/17		100 shells 5.9 H.E. dropped into the area between LE VERGIER and PIEUMAL WOOD. Two Battery ceased shelling when our Counter-batteries were turned on to them. Patrols again ascertained that ASCENSION WOOD & LITTLE BILL are held by the enemy at night, also that enemy enter dug outs in G.32.b.o.8. Weather fine. Visibility good.	
			General.— All posts. Supports. Numbers of resistance by additional wire. Existing M.G. emplacements improved & strengthened & 2 new Support Posts Commenced. No. 5 post. ASCENSION Avenue & Battle H.Q. at JEANCOURT completed. Advanced Troops. Amtals Cavalry Brigade under 2 Lieut. R.E. Supervision new dug outs completed.	

2449   Wt. W14957/M90 750,000 1/16 J.B.C. & A.   Forms/C.2118/12.

Copy No.....

S E C R E T

SECUNDERABAD CAVALRY BRIGADE OPERATION ORDER NO.37.

Ref: Maps Sheets 62.C.N.E.& 62.C.S.E.-1/20,000   14th May 1917.

1. The Secunderabad Cav.Bde, 9th Hodson's Horse, 18th Lancers, 14th Sqdn: M.G.C.(Cav) and 1 Field Troop attached, will take over the line from the 177th Infantry Bde. on May 15th & night 15th/16th in accordance with attached table.

2. The Brigade frontage will be L.22.a. to R.5.d.3.5.divided into 2 sub-sections: the dividing line between sub-sections being S. end of PIEUMEL WOOD (L.28.c.9.7) - L.30.b.8.8.- road junction G.20.d.6.5.

3. The Brigade will be disposed as follows:-

   Right Sub-section. Advanced Troops - 7th D.Guards. H.Q.R.5.a.6.0
                                        relieving 2 Coys 4/Lincolns

                      Support.- 9th Hodson's Horse.H.Q.L.33.d.3.3.
                                relieving 2 Coys 4/Lincolns.

   Left Sub-section. Advanced Troops - Poona Horse H.Q.L.28.a.5.9
                                       relieving 4/Leicesters.

                     Support.Deccan Horse.H.Q.L.28.a.5.9.
                             relieving 5/Leicesters

   Brigade Reserve.   18th Lancers - L.28.c.1.9.

   Brigade H.Q.   MONTIGNY FARM.

   Advanced H.Q.& Relay Post.- JEANCOURT.

4. Os. C. 13th & 14th M.G. Sqdns will arrange direct with O.C.,177th M.G.Coy: the relief of guns by day 15th May and night 15th/16th May.

5. All details of reliefs will be arranged direct between Os.C. Regiments and Os.C Battalions, including the number of Officers and O.R. to spend the night 14th/15th and 15th May in the line.

6. All Maps, Air Photographs, and Trench Stores will be taken over and receipts given.

7. Transport and Administrative Orders issued under S.C.O.857 d/14-5-17.

8. No troops will proceed mounted by day N. of the line VENDELLES-ETRIES - JEANCOURT or E. of the line VENDELLES - BOIECOURT.

9. Completion of reliefs will be reported by the code word 'TREFCON'

10. An advanced Report Centre will open at JEANCOURT from 9.30.am onwards.

    Report Centre closes at TREFCON at 7.pm.15th May.

                    (Sgd) A. CAMPBELL ROBB.   Major
                    Brigade Major, Secunderabad Cavalry Brigade.

Issued by D.R. at 4.30.pm.

         Normal   O.O.Distribution.

S E C R E T   Copy No........

SECUNDERABAD CAVALRY BRIGADE OPERATION ORDER NO.38.

30th May 1917.

1. The following Reliefs will be carried out on night 30th/31st May:-

    Right A.3.   Supports 9th Hodson's Horse will relieve Advanced Troops 7th Dragoon Guards.

    Left A.3.   Supports XXth Deccan Horse will relieve Advanced Troops 34th Poona Horse.

    Brigade Reserve.-   18th Lancers will remain in Brigade Reserve.

2. All details of the relief will be arranged between Os.C. concerned.

3. Os.C. Supports will arrange with Os.C. Advanced Troops that a proportion of Officers and other ranks spend 24 hours in the front line trenches, before the relief takes place.

4. The relief will not commence before 9.30.p.m.

5. All Trench Stores will be handed over to incoming Units who will give receipts for same.

6. The strictest silence will be observed during the relief, which will be carried out under cover of a covering party to be arranged for by Os.C concerned.

7. Relieved Troops will not leave a Post until the Commander Relieving is satisfied that all is correct.

8. The Brigade Reserve (except that portion used for working and carrying Parties) will stand to during the hours of the relief.

9. The completion of the Relief will be reported by the code word 'TERTRY'

10. Acknowledge.

                                                Major,

                      Brigade Major, SECUNDERABAD CAVALRY BDE.

Issued by D.R.

            Ordinary O.O. distribution.

SECRET   Copy No........

SECUNDERABAD CAVALRY BRIGADE OPERATION ORDER NO. 30

25th May 1917.

1. The following Reliefs will be carried out on night 27th/28th May:-

    Right A.S.   Supports 7th Dragoon Guards will relieve Advanced Troops 9th Hodson's Horse,

    Left A.S.   Supports 34th Poona Horse will relieve Advanced Troops, XXth Deccan Horse.

    Brigade Reserve.-   18th Lancers will remain in Brigade Reserve.

2. All details of the relief will be arranged between Os.C concerned.

3. The relief will not commence before 9.30.pm.

4. All Trench Stores will be handed over to incoming Units who will give receipts for same.

5. The strictest silence will be observed during the relief which will be carried out under cover of a covering party to be arranged for by Os.C. concerned.

6. Relieved troops will not leave a post until the Commander Relieving is satisfied that all is correct.

7. The Brigade Reserve (except that portion used for working and carrying parties) will stand to during the hours of the relief.

8. Detail of working parties during relief will be issued later.

9. The completion of the relief will be reported by the code word 'FLEZ'

10. Acknowledge.

                (Sgd) A.CAMPBELL ROSS,   Major

          Brigade Major, Secunderabad Cav.Bde.

Issued by D.R.

    Ordinary O.O.Distribution.

        Copy No.23 - Canadian Cav.Bde.
           " 24 - M'how
           " 25 - R.E.Liaison Officer

SECRET   Copy No. An. E

SECUNDERABAD CAVALRY BRIGADE OPERATION ORDER NO: 40.

                                                27th May 1917.
                  ----

1.   The 4TH CAVALRY DIVISION and CANADIAN CAVALRY BRIGADE are taking over part of Sub-sector A.2. on the night 28th/29th May, 1917.

2.   The following reliefs will take place on the night of May 28th/29th, 1917.

   (a) CANADIAN CAVALRY BRIGADE will take over from the 7th Dragoon Guards as far NORTH as the line: Valley which runs through G.36.Central – RED WOOD (Canadian) – RED HOUSE (Secunderabad).–R.5.c.0.7.

   (b) The N'HOW CAVALRY BRIGADE will take over from the 34th Poona Horse as far SOUTH as the line: G.36 Central – GRAND PRIEL FARM – N.side of PIEUMEL WOOD – L.27.b.8.5. (all inclusive to Secunderabad)

3. (a) The 7th Dragoon Guards will hand over No.1.Post, RED WOOD, the Southern portion of No.2.Post. (The small Communication Trench which runs into the Post at the bend will be the line of demarcation between Brigades) No.1.Support Post and Right Wing Headquarters will also be handed over.

        Code word for completion of Relief – 'AULT'

   (b) The 34th Poona Horse will hand over:–

        Posts, 11, 12, 13, & 14,
        Support Posts, 7 & 8,
        Observation Posts, old 7 & 9,
        Left Wing Headquarters,
        Regimental Headquarters.

        Code word for completion of Relief – 'TREFCON'.

4.   Command Pass/on completion of Relief.

5.   All Ammunition, Grenades and Trench Stores, in all Posts and Headquarters handed over, will also be handed over and receipts obtained. returned

6.   All details of the relief will be arranged between Officers Commanding concerned.

7.   The relief will not commence before 9.30.p.m.

8.   The strictest silence will be observed during the relief, which will be carried out under cover of a covering party to be arranged for by Os.C.concerned.

9.   Relieved Troops will not leave a Post until the Commander Relieving is satisfied that all is correct.

10.   Detail of all Ammunition and Trench Stores to be handed over attached.

                                                11..........

II

11. The AMBALA CAVALRY BRIGADE TROOPS (less H.Q. and 2 Sections, 14th Machine Gun Squadron) will return to the Back Area on 28th/29th May, as follows:-

    (a) The 14th Machine Gun Squadron (less 1 Section), will remain in its present location.

    (b) 18th Lancers and Transport which came with Regt: will march to the head of the VENDELLES Valley, where led horses will meet them at Q.12 Central at 3.30.p.m.

        Transports will march by the MONTIGNY FARM - BERNES - FLECHIN Road.

    (c) 9th Hodson's Horse and Transport which came with Regiment.

        Led Horses will be brought to L.25.d.central at 10.p.m. will march via MONTIGNY FARM - BERNES - FLECHIN Road.

        Transport will move along the VENDELLES - SOYECOURT Road.

    (d) 1 Section 14th M.G.Squadron will move independently after 9.30.p.m.

12. East of the Line SOYECOURT - VENDELLES, *BERNES* the following intervals will be maintained:-

	By day.	By night.
Between troops,	400 yards	200 yards
wagons,	400 "	150 "

13. Relief by Secunderabad Troops will be reported by the code word 'PARIS'.

14. All Ammunition, Grenades, and Trench Stores will be handed over as in Appendix attached.

15. Acknowledge.

                                                  Major
Brigade Major, SECUNDERABAD CAVALRY BDE.

Issued by D.R.

    Ordinary O.O.distribution.
    No.23 - M'how Cavalry Brigade,
    " 24 - Canadian Cavalry Brigade,
    " 25 - Ambala Cavalry Brigade,
    " 26 - R.E.Liaison Officer.
       27 - 4 Cavalry Bn.

TRENCH STORES TO BE HANDED OVER TO 4TH CAVALRY DIVISION.

	Gas Rockets	Strombos Horns	Gas Gongs	Gas Fans	Gas Alert Boards	Gas Testing Tubes	Bludgeons	Shovels	Picks	Trench Covers	Prowlers	Mallets	Scrapers	Scoops
Regtl: H.Q.) L.28.a.6.8.)	7	3	18	18	1	1	14	140	5	60	1	1	14	
Reserve Regt:) L.22.c.7.3.)	-	-	1	-	-	-	-	4	-	12	-	-	-	1

S.A.A. GRENADES ETC. TO BE HANDED OVER TO 4TH CAVALRY DIVISION.

	S.A.A.	Webley.	Grenades			Very Lights		S.O.S.	Ground Flares.
			No.5.	No.23.	No.20 or 3.	1"	1½"		
A.2.Left. Forward Regt: Left Sqdn:H.Q L.23.d.5.5.	20	-	21	4	3	1	-	2	-
Regtl: H.Q. L.28.a.6.8.	73	-	68	20	18	5	4	3	75
Reserve Regiment L.23.c.7.3.	17	-	90	-	-	-	-	2	-

The Locations given are those at which relieved Unit will hand over to relieving Unit.

Forward Regiment is 34th Poona Horse,

Reserve Regiment is 18th Lancers.

O.C., 9th Hodson's Horse will hand over to O.C., XXth Deccan Horse. *all SAA Grenades & Trench Stores*.

---oOo---

S.A.A., GRENADES, ETC. TO BE HANDED OVER TO
CANADIAN CAVALRY BRIGADE.

	S.A.A. Boxes.	GRENADES			Very Lights.		S.O.S. Tins.
		No.5. (Boxes)	No.23.	No.3. or 30.	1" Boxes	1½" Boxes	
Right Sqdn H.Q.) 7th D.Gds)	28	12	-	2	1	1	1

TRENCH STORES.

All Trench Stores in Posts and Headquarters as ordered in
O.O.No.40., para: 3.

SECRET

SECUNDERABAD CAVALRY BRIGADE.

SUBSIDIARY ORDER TO O.O.No.40 of 27-5-17

28th May 1917

The Officer Commanding 13th Machine Gun Squadron will keep his Guns in the positions they occupy now until relieved by the 4th CAVALRY DIVISION, or until further orders.

2. Acknowledge.

[signed] Campbell Ross
Major
Brigade Major, SECUNDERABAD CAVALRY BDE.

Issued by D.R.

Normal O.O. distribution.

Copy No. 23 — 4th Cavalry Division
" 24 — M'how Cavalry Brigade
" 25 — Canadian " "
" 26 — Ambala " "
" 27 — R.E. Liaison Officer.

A.P.E.

Copy No.........

SECUNDERABAD CAVALRY BRIGADE OPERATION ORDER NO:41.

27th May 1917.

1. Consequent on the withdrawal of the Regiments of the AMBALA CAVALRY BRIGADE, and the taking over of a portion of Sub-sector A.2. by 4th CAVALRY DIVISION and CANADIAN CAVALRY BRIGADE, the front of A.2.sub-sector held by SECUNDERABAD CAVALRY BRIGADE will be:-

   Northern Boundary.-

   G.20.Central - Gd.PRIEL Fm - N.side of PIEUMEL WOOD - L.27.b.9.5.

   Southern Boundary.-

   G.27 central - RED WOOD (Canadian) - RED HOUSE (Secunderabad) - R.5.c.9.7.

   Dividing Line between Regiments.-

   G.26.central - ASCENSION FARM - HILL SPINNEY (All inclusive to A.2.L)

2. In consequence A.2.sub-sector will be held as follows:-

   A.2.R.   7th Dragoon Guards.

             3 Squadrons Outpost Line and Counter attack Troops,

             1 Squadron Support in Intermediate Line, at R.5.a & c.

             Headquarters.- R.5.b.3.2.

   A.2.L.   34th Poona Horse.-

             3 Squadrons Outpost line and counter attack Troops,

             1 Squadron Support in Intermediate Line, at R.28.a.

             Headquarters.- L.28.a.4.3.

   Reserve.- The XXth Deccan Horse will be in Brigade Reserve.

             2 Squadrons in old German Trench at L.28.c

             2 Squadrons in Intermediate Line.-L.34.d. and R.4.b.

             Headquarters.- L.33.d.3.3.

3. All arrangements for taking over will be made direct by Os.C. concerned, and Relieved Troops will not leave until the Commander Relieving is satisfied that all is correct.

4................

II.

4. Detail of Ammunition, Grenades, and Trench Stores to be handed over is attached.

5. Completion of Relief in New A.2. will be reported by the code word 'PARIS'.

6. Defence Standing orders in case of attack hold good.

7. <u>Acknowledge</u>.

Campbell Ross
Major
Brigade Major, SECUNDERABAD CAVALRY BDE.

Issued by D.R.   Normal O.O. distribution 1-22

```
Copy No. 23  -  M'how Cavalry Brigade
     "   24  -  Canadian Cavalry Brigade
     "   25  -  Ambala Cavalry Brigade
     "   26  -  4th Cavalry Division,
     "   27  -  R.E. Liaison Officer.
```

RECLASSIFICATION OF S.A.A., GRENADES and TRENCH STORES CONSEQUENT ON RELIEF OF AMBALA CAVALRY BRIGADE

----

1. IN A.2.L.-

  O.C., XXth Deccan Horse will hand over to O.C., 34th Poona Horse.-

  (a) All S.A.A., Grenades, etc.

  (b) All Trench Stores,

which are now on charge of Support Regiment, A.2.L

These Stores will then form Regimental Reserve of A.2.L Forward Regiment.

2. IN SUPPORT.-

  O.C., 9th Hodson's Horse will hand over to O.C., XXth Deccan Horse,

  (a) All S.A.A., Grenades, etc,

  (b) All Trench Stores,

which are now on charge of Support Regiment, A.2.R

These Stores will then form reserve of Reserve Regiment.

3. Receipts will be obtained in each case, and copies will be forwarded to Brigade Headquarters by 6.p.m. tomorrow, 28th May.

4. Issues will be made to complete Units to scale of S.A.A. as given in Appendix "F" Defence Scheme.

B.M.O.565.

28th May 1917.

To/
Normal O.O.distribution,
5th Cavalry Division,
4th   "   "
M'how Cavalry Brigade,
Canadian   "   "
Ambala   "   "
R.E.Liaison Officer.

MEMORANDUM.-

Reference O.O.41,d/27-5-17.,-

The following additions will be made:-

para.1.line 3 after 'BRIGADE' insert 'on 28th/29th May 1917'

para.5.after 'New A.2' insert 'at times laid down in O.O.40 of 27th May'

[signature]
Major
Brigade Major, Secunderabad Cavalry Bde

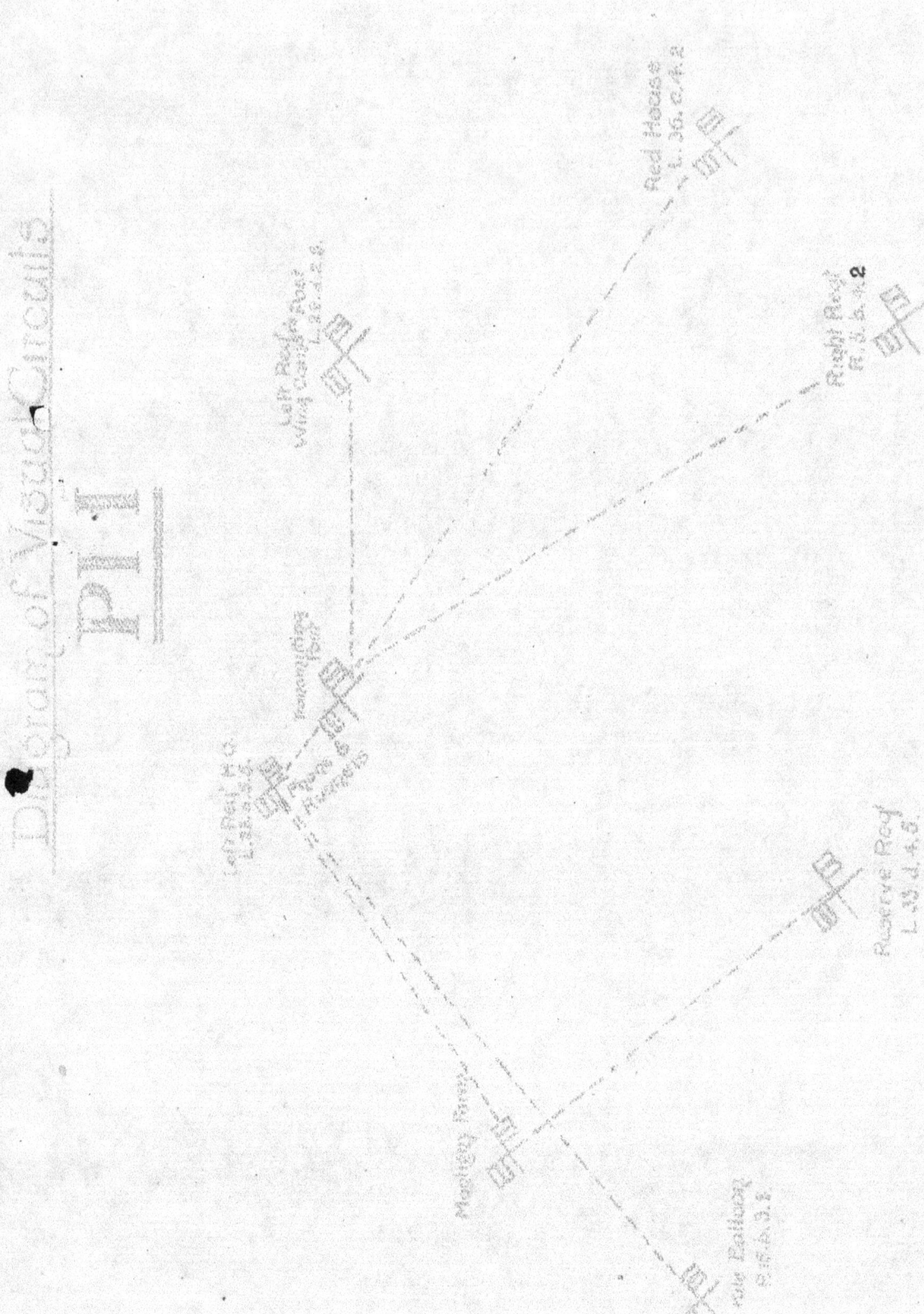

'F'

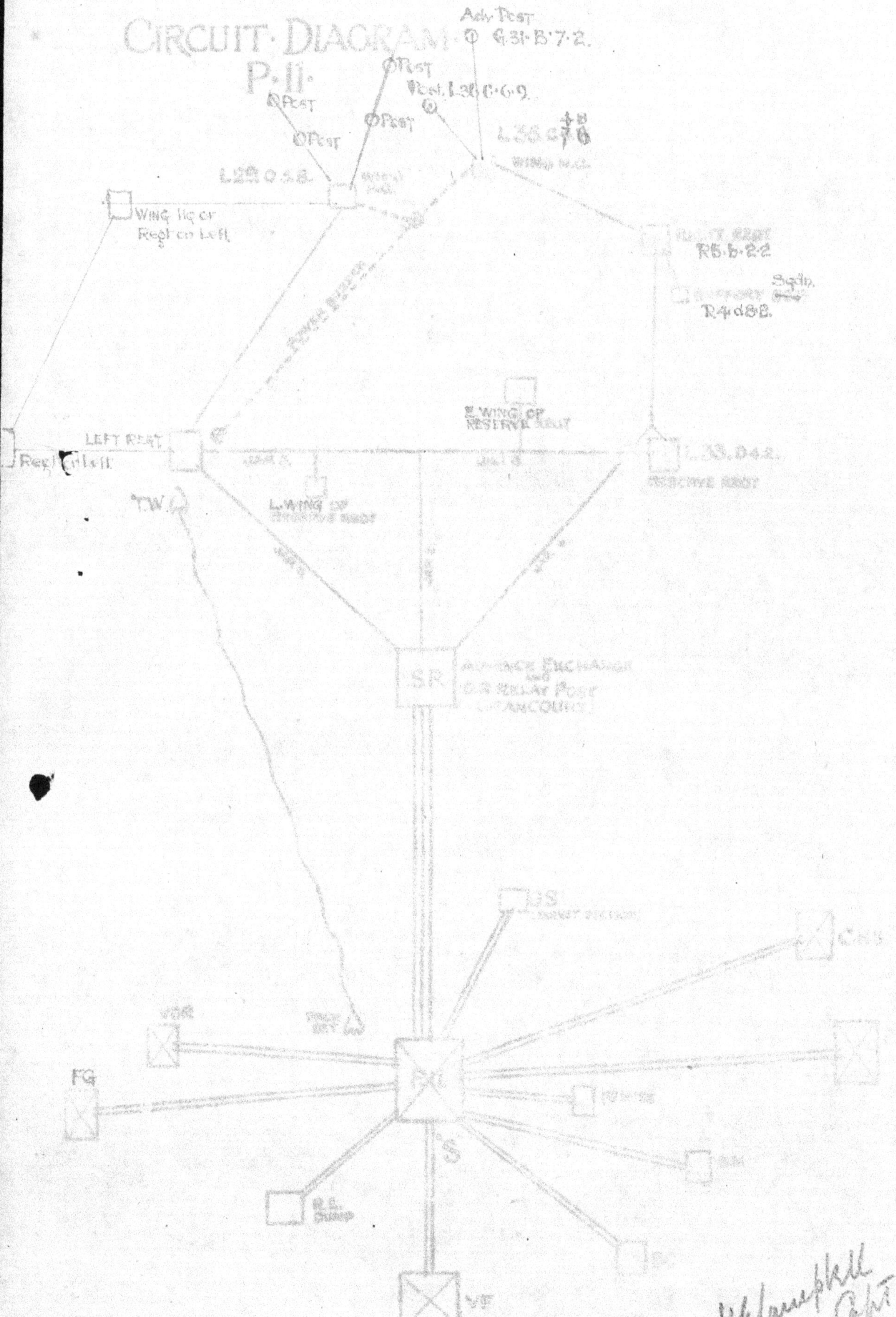

A.W. Campbell Capt
Sigs P11

War Diary
-
Sec'ted Cavalry Brigade.

From 1st June to 30th June 1917.

Vol. I

Army Form C. 2118

WAR DIARY of Scotstoun Cavalry Bde.
INTELLIGENCE SUMMARY. Page I

June 1917.

(Erase heading not required.)

Place	Date	Hour	Summary of Events and Information	Remarks and references to Appendices
MONTIGNY FARM	1/6/17		Bde.dere'manean in A.2 Sub sect.- Nn. Boundary- PIEUMEL WOOD - - GRAND PRIEL FM - G30 central. Southern Boundary.- R.S. & 7.9.- RED HOO. B27 Central. Rt. Regt. 7th (Queen). Lt. Regt. - 34th Horse. Bde Reserve- Patrol of 7th Guards found enemy in strength about B.32.a. Patrol withdrew	Map referenced 1/20000 B20.NE B27.SE B23.NW B2.S.N.
	2/6/17		Situation quiet.	
	3/6/17		Our Artillery concentrated on enemy trenches in front. uform night. Patrol of 34th Poona Horse went out to ASCENSION WOOD & LITTLE BILL to clear up situation. A party of 40 Germans were seen to enter B.18.3.1.d.	
	4/6/17		Following relief took place night 4th/5th (O.O.42 attached) Reserve Regt. 20th Deccan Horse relieved left advanced regt 34th Poona Horse "7" 34th Poona Horse now being in Bde Reserve Situation unchanged. Weather fine	9.9 O.O. "7"
	5/6/17		Situation quiet. No Patrol encounter. Casualties 34th Poona Horse killed - 3. O.R.1. wounded - one O.R.1. 20th Deccan Horse.- Killed no O.R.1. Situation quiet. No patrol encounter.	
	6/6/17		" " " " " "	
	7/6/17		" " " " " " Casualties 20th Horse. killed one O.R.	
	9/6/17		" " " " " "	
	10/6/17		Increased artillery activity. ASCENSION FARM shelled. Patrol from 7th Guards visited Nankin G.32.a. Enemy ex barrage behind them	

Army Form C. 2118

Scotch Sicily 1Bn.

WAR DIARY
INTELLIGENCE SUMMARY
(Erase heading not required.)

Instructions regarding War Diaries and Intelligence Summaries are contained in F. S. Regs., Part II. and the Staff Manual respectively. Title pages will be prepared in manuscript.

Place	Date	Hour	Summary of Events and Information	Remarks and references to Appendices
MONTIGNY FARM	10/6/17		S.O.S. was put up left of 17.1 Subsector. Four guns opened on their S.O.S. lines. Patrol withdrew w/o casualties. Heavy storm of rain.	
	11/6/17		Situation normal. Visual reconnaissance of ASCENSION WOOD. Patrol of 7 Guards found small party of enemy G.26.c, but could not engage them. Heavy thunderstorm.	
	12/6/17		Enemy artillery activity above normal. Preparations for raid on ASCENSION WOOD completed.	
	13/6/17		Raid carried out on ASCENSION WOOD. (O.O. raid & report on raid attached.) Casualties:- Major A. CAMPBELL ROSS, D.S.O. Brigade Major, wounded by grenade fire 20". Meecin Horze - Killed 4. O.R.1. Wounded - Lieut. L. A. GLASSPOOLE. 17 O.R.1. + 6 O.R.1 slightly at duty. Missing - Lieut. E. E. LAWFORD and 4 O.R.1.	Apx "B"
			Situation quiet. Outpost line shelled. Heavy Artillery retaliated at 5.30 pm and enemy fire checked. It re-opened at 11 pm. A direct hit on No.6 Post at 3.30 am killed 4 and wounded 3 O.R.1 of 20". Meecin Horze. At 9pm a H.E. Shrapnel killed 1 and wounded 3 O.R.1 in same post. Relief by Cameron Bn. commenced 10pm completed 2 am without incident. Reinforcements attached.	Apx "C"
	14.6.17			

Army Form C. 2118

Sirhind Coy. WAR DIARY
INTELLIGENCE SUMMARY.
(Erase heading not required.)

Instructions regarding War Diaries and Intelligence Summaries are contained in F. S. Regs., Part II. and the Staff Manual respectively. Title pages will be prepared in manuscript.

Place	Date	Hour	Summary of Events and Information	Remarks and references to Appendices
TREFCON	15/6/17		Coy returned to bivouacs in vicinity of TREFCON.	
	16/6/17		Inspection of Horses of Coy by the Corps Commander.	
	17/6/17 to 22/6/17		Training carried out in mounted & dismounted work. Bombing, musketry & M. Gun practice.	
	23/6/17		Coy relieved Ambala Cav. Bde in outposts 17.1 (C.O. attached)	App "D"
WADENCOURT			Southern Boundary - R. OMIGNON	
Cav.			Northern Boundary - CAUBRIERES Wood No.2 (excl) - Trench junction R.5.c.9.7.	
			- RED HOUSE (excl) - G.31.b.72 - Bottom of valley wheeling thro' S.25 Central.	
			7 7/O Evans on night - 34th Poona Horse on left - 20th Deccan Horse in reserve	
	24/6/17		Situation quiet. Patrol of 34th Poona Horse met enemy and drove back patrol at G.33.a.4.9. Patrol lost 1 killed & 2 slightly wounded.	
	25/6/17		Situation quiet. No patrol encounters	
	26/6/17		Situation quiet. Mutual patrols out. No encounters took place.	
	27/6/17		Strong patrol of 34th Poona Horse would ELEVEN TREES to clear up activities. About 20 of enemy were dislodged & casualties inflicted on	

Army Form C. 2118

1st Bedad Bn: 15ac
WAR DIARY or INTELLIGENCE SUMMARY.   IV

(Erase heading not required.)

Instructions regarding War Diaries and Intelligence Summaries are contained in F. S. Regs., Part II. and the Staff Manual respectively. Title pages will be prepared in manuscript.

Place	Date	Hour	Summary of Events and Information	Remarks and references to Appendices
VADENCOURT Co.	27/6/17 Contd		on there with bombs and Hotchkin rifle. One man killed in our Patrol.	
	28/6/17		Unable to go owing to heavy rain. No patrols out. 5 Officers and 80 O.R.'s 7/8 Guards selected to prepare for raid.	
	29/6/17		A patrol of enemy was seen at M.3.a.2.2. but no encounter took place. A patrol of 2nd Bn Home Force encountered about 50 of enemy about Q.33.a.3.9. and inflicted casualties on him by rifle fire.	
	30/6/17		Situation normal. Usual patrols out but no encounter took place.	

G.N. Knoll Cpt.
15th Major Comm 8 &
15th Bn
Second Bedad Comm 8 &

A.5834. Wt. W.4973/M687 750,000 8/16 D, D, D, & L. Ltd. Forms/C.2118/13.

SECRET   Apx "A"   Copy No..........

SECUNDERABAD CAVALRY BRIGADE OPERATION ORDER NO. 42

3rd June 1917

1. The following Relief will be carried out on night 4th/5th June :-

A.2.L - Reserve Regiment XXth Deccan Horse will relieve Advanced Regt. 34th Poona Horse.

Brigade Reserve - 34th Poona Horse will be in Brigade Reserve.

2. All details of the relief will be arranged between Os.C. concerned.

3. The relief will not commence before 9.45 p.m.

4. All Trench Stores will be handed over to incoming Units who will give receipts for same.

5. The strictest silence will be observed during the relief, which will be carried out under cover of a covering party to be arranged for by Os.C. concerned.

6. Relieved Troops will not leave a post until the Commander Relieving is satisfied that all is correct.

7. Detail of working Parties during relief will be issued later.

8. The completion of the relief will be reported by the code word 'DUMPED'.

9. ACKNOWLEDGE.

(signed)

Major,
Brigade Major, SECUNDERABAD CAVALRY BRIGADE.

Issued by D.R.

Ordinary O.O. distribution.

Copy No. 23 - 4th Cavalry Division,
" 24 - Canadian Cavalry Brigade,
" 25 - M'how " "
" 26 - R.E. Liaison Officer.

Apx. 'B'

S E C R E T

Copy No .

SECUNDERABAD CAVALRY BRIGADE OPERATION ORDER NO: 43.

Reference Map BELLENGLISE 1/20,000.   12th June, 1917.

1. A Raid on ASCENSION WOOD will be carried out on the night 12th/13th June, 1917, at Zero hour, with the intention of killing and capturing Germans who are holding the Wood, and destroying his Posts.

2. Zero hour will be notified later.

3. At half-an-hour before Zero hour one Squadron XXth Deccan Horse will be disposed as follows:-

    <u>1 Troop</u> from G.25.b.8.9. to G.26.a.0.8. Objective /From N.W. corner of Wood to centre road (both inclusive) - S.W. face of Wood up to and including centre road.

    <u>1 Troop.</u> From G.26.a.0.8. - G.26.a.2.7. Objective,- Northern face of Wood from centre road (exclusive) to Eastern corner of Wood (inclusive) - Southern face of Wood from centre road (exclusive) to S.E. corner (inclusive).

    <u>2 Troops</u> in support in rear (to the North of) of the above.

In addition, 1 British Officer and 1 Troop will proceed with the raiding party to point where Supporting Troops are disposed, to act as a covering Party, and to take over prisoners.

4. At Zero hour both parties will move forward to their objectives, under cover of Artillery and Machine Gun fire.

25% of the party will carry two No.5.Grenades to deal with any dug-outs.

5. The Party will withdraw clear of the objective by Zero plus 30 minutes, when the Artillery fire will cease.

6. A Red & Green Rocket will be fired from No.2.O.P. at Zero plus 28 minutes, to indicate the time for withdrawal.

The Staff Captain will issue the necessary Rockets.

7. The O.C., 13th Squadron M.G.C.(C) will arrange for the attached M.G.Barrages.

All other Machine Guns will remain in their normal positions and will not fire.

The O.C., XXth Deccan Horse will arrange for an escort to advanced machine guns.

8. Watches will be synchronised by sending a representative at 7.pm. to Brigade Headquarters on June 12th.

    17th Brigade R.H.A.
    XXth Deccan Horse,
    13th Squadron M.G.C.(C)   (only)

O. O. C., Poona Horse

9. The O.C., 34th Poona Horse will have one Squadron at L.29. central from Zero minus 30 minutes to Zero plus 1 hour.
This Squadron will come under the orders of the O.C., XXth Deccan Horse, if required.

10. Artillery and Machine Gun Barrages attached.

11. ACKNOWLEDGE.

A. Campbell

Major,
Brigade Major, SECUNDERABAD CAVALRY BRIGADE.

Issued by D.R.

Copy No. 23	-	AMBALA CAVALRY BRIGADE.	
" 24	-	CANADIAN " "	
" 25	-	M'HOW " "	
" 26	-	O.C. 17th R.H.A. Bde.	
" 27	-	R.E. Liaison Officer.	

MACHINE GUN BARRAGES.

Issued with Sec'bad Cavalry Brigade O.O.No.43.

----

3 Guns at G.25.d.0.0.

    Objectives. - LITTLE BILL.
    Range.-   750 yards.
    Bearings.-   63 deg. to 75 deg. (true)

2 Guns at G.25.d.5.3. just North of the I in ASCENSION FARM.

    Objective.- BIG BILL.
    Range.-   From 850 yards to 1,150 yards.
    Bearings.-   35 deg. to 45 deg. (true)

1. Gun at Post MOLLY.

    Objectives.- From G.20.a.9.6. to G.20.d.10.6.
    Bearings.-   49 deg. to 70 deg (true).-

1. Gun at Post DONG.

    Objectives.- From G.20.d.9.5. to G.27.a.9.3.
    Bearings.-   30 deg. to 80 deg. (true)

BARRAGE TABLE

Issued with Sec'bad Cavalry Brigade Operation Order No. 43.

Battery.	1st Objective.	Time.	Rate of fire.
B/295.	G.19.d.5.5.-LITTLE BILL (inclusive)	Zero to zero plus 30 minutes.	2 rds. per gun per min. A. AX.
Q, RHA.	LITTLE BILL (exclusive) - G.26.a.60.75.	-do-	2 rds. per gun per min. N. NX.
A/295.	G.26.a.60.75 - G.26.a.6.0.	-do-	2 rds. per gun per min A. AX.
X. RHA.	G.26.a.6.0.- G.26.c.0.5.	-do-	2 rds. per gun per min. N. X.
N. RHA.	G.25.d.9.1.- G.26.c.3.6.	-do-	-do-
D/298.	ASCENSION WOOD	Zero to zero plus 2 minutes.	2 rds. per gun per min. BX.
D/298	Second Objective LITTLE BILL & BIG BILL.	Zero plus 8 min. to zero plus 30 min.	1 rd. per gun per min. BX.

SECRET
10

Normal O.O. distribution
No 23. Ambala Cav Bde   26. 17 Bde RHA
  " 24. Canadian Bde   27. R.E. Recon
  " 25. Mhow Cav Bde   Officer

Memo

Ref. O.O. 43 of date.

Zero time .. " 2 am 13th June '17 "

13/6/17

A Campbell Ross
        Major
Brigade Major
      5th Cav Bde

CONFIDENTIAL.   B.M.O.631.   13th June, 1917.

To/

The 5th Cavalry Division G.

I forward herewith the report of the O.C., XXth Deccan Horse on the raid carried out by a squadron of that Regiment on the night 12th/13th June.

2. I have but little to add to the report.

3. The artillery barrage was promptly put down and lifted, but that on G.25.d.5.4. was a little too close in and necessitated the shifting of a machine gun which was posted in this position to cover the valley between ASCENSION WOOD and BIG BILL.

4. I think it was a little unfortunate that almost at the precise moment the raid was timed to start, the Germans should have seen fit to commence an enterprise on the posts to the North.

5. I much regret the loss of Lieut: LAWFORD (reported missing) who was a very promising young officer.

6. I wish to bring to the notice of the G.O.C., Division, the conduct of Major A. CAMPBELL ROSS, D.S.O., Brigade Staff. On seeing that the Germans were occupying the sunken road, he gathered together a few men and rushed down on the flank and rear of the party holding the road. Unfortunately before he had proceeded far enough to get into position to cut off the withdrawal of the enemy he was rather severely wounded by grenade fire in both legs. Most of the few men with him were wounded at the same time.

7. I would like to endorse the remarks of the O.C., Deccan Horse as to the leadership of Captain MULLOY.

8. It is most gratifying to know that a good deal of the damage done to the enemy was with the 'cold steel' and this reflects credit on the dash and spirit of the regiment.

9. The power buzzer which was installed in ASCENSION WOOD by the advanced party proved of value in maintaining communication with Squadron Headquarters in 'GRAHAM's POST', but I have to suggest for future operations that the Amplifier be not installed in the same dugout as telephones, as the latter if working are liable to jam the former.

10. The M.G. barrage seemed effective and the guns must have been in good order and well tuned up as no jams occurred.

(Sgd) C. GREGORY, Brig:General,
Commanding SECUNDERABAD CAVALRY BRIGADE.

Field 13-6-17

In accordance with Sec'bad Bde O.O.43, a raid was carried out in ASCENSION WOOD, with the object of killing and capturing Germans who were holding the wood, and of destroying the posts.

I ordered a Squadron under Captain MULLOY to carry out the actual raid, sending a troop under Lieut: BARROW to act as covering party, and afterwards to take over prisoners.

Covering troops were put out well to the front (i.e.East) of posts Nos. 8 & 9 down the hill towards ASCENSION WOOD.

The raiding Squadron left GRAHAM's POST at 12.30.am. and passed through our wire Near No. .post about 20 mins. later - just after they had passed through our wire a Post on our left was apparently attacked by an enemy bombing party, which necessitated the Regiment on our left opening Hotchkiss Rifle fire and using Very Lights. This somewhat delayed the arrival of the two rear troops at the position of readiness, which was some 150 yards to the N. of the Wood.

At zero hour (2.am) the artillery opened fire and Captain MULLOY advanced on the wood, which he entered two or three minutes later, without opposition. There appear to have been some Germans in the wood who left it on hearing our approach.

The raiding party destroyed some dugouts, cut wire where it existed, and having thoroughly searched the wood, left it in accordance with orders, at 2.30.am.

Troops having been ordered to return to our line as follows:-
1 Troop to No.9.Post, 1 to No.8.Post, 1 to the N. of the Sunken road and 1 to the S. of the same.

On emerging from the wood the squadron came under very heavy rifle and M.G.fire from the sunken road, which they attacked, but owing to the intensity of the fire and the free use of hand grenades, it was found impossible to surround the enemy. In this conflict several Germans were killed, but under the conditions existing at the moment, it was impracticable to carry out a systematic examination of the bodies. One of these was carried back for purposes of identification; from his shoulder straps and identity disc, he belonged to the 73.Fus.R. A shoulder strap bearing No.453 was taken from another body.

The Squadron carried out its task without casualty, but during the action on the return to our lines, I regret to report Lieut: LAWFORD to be missing. It is said that he was seen to be wounded, but this has yet to be confirmed. Lieut: GLASSPOOLE was wounded slightly, as was Ressaidar DALIP SINGH, four other ranks were killed, four other ranks are missing, and reported by individual sowars as being killed: this latter statement requires further confirmation. Twenty two other ranks are wounded, of whom 5 are slightly, and at duty.

The Squadron carried out its mission, and having completed its task returned to our lines about 3.15 am.

I consider the leading of the Squadron reflects considerable credit on Captain MULLOY, who was undoubtedly assisted by the fire of the artillery and M.G.Squadrons.

(Sgd) F.ADAMS Lt-Col.
Commandant S.O.

SECRET.   Apx. "C"   Copy No......

SECUNDERABAD CAVALRY BRIGADE OPERATION ORDER NO: 44

Reference Map 1/40,000.   11th June, 1917.

1. The SECUNDERABAD CAVALRY BRIGADE will be relieved by the CANADIAN CAVALRY BRIGADE in Sunsector A.2. on June 14th and night June 14th/15th, in accordance with the attached Table.

2. Relief of Forward Regiments will not commence before 10.pm. No post will be withdrawn till the Commander relieving is satisfied that all is correct.
Command will pass on completion of relief.

3. All details of relief will be mutually settled between C.O's concerned. All Headquarters (Stores, amm: &c may) be relieved by day.

4. The 13th M.G. Squadron (less 1 Section) will remain in the line, and will come under orders of the G.O.C., CANADIAN CAV.BDE.

5.(a) The Dismounted Reinforcements of the SECUNDERABAD CAVALRY BDE. will, on relief, march to VENDELLES, where they will take over the Billets now occupied by the Dismounted Reinforcements of the CANADIAN CAVALRY BRIGADE.

   (i) In Command. - Major O.M. DYKE - XXth Deccan Horse.

   (ii) 2 British Officers, 4 I.O's, & 100 O.R. will be detailed by each Regiment.

(b) The Secunderabad Field Ambulance will detail a water cart to report to Major O.M. DYKE at VENDELLES at 6.pm. 14th June.

(c) Advanced Parties from each Regiment will be sent to VENDELLES where the O.C. will allot billets at 6.pm. on 14th June.

6. On relief, the SECUNDERABAD CAV.BDE will come into Divisional Reserve, and Brigade Report Centre will open at TREFCON at 2.am.

7. Relief will be reported by the code expression 'Sandbags urgently required.'

8. ACKNOWLEDGE.

                                           A. Campbell Ross
                                                    Major
                               Brigade Major, SECUNDERABAD CAVALRY BDE.

Issued by D.R.-

              Normal O.O. distribution.
       Copy No. 23   - CANADIAN CAVALRY BRIGADE.
            "   24   - ALIBALA
       Copies Nos: 25, 26, & 27, - O.C., Dismounted Details,
       Copy No. 28   - O.C., Dismounted Reinforcements.
         "   " 29   - C.R.H.A.
         "   " 30   - R.E. Liaison Officer.

ADMINISTRATIVE INSTRUCTIONS

issued with Secunderabad Cavalry Brigade Operation Order No.44

----

1. RATIONS.
    (a) On 14th June Rations for consumption on 15th will be delivered in the Back Area, except those for the Dismounted Reinforcements, which will be delivered in VENDELLES after 6.p.m. on 14th June.

    (b) All Reserve Rations and Water Tins held on charge in Advanced and Support Posts will be handed over to relieving Units, and also the reserve at Brigade H.Q.

2. AMMUNITION.
    All S.A.A., Grenades etc., except S.A.A. held on Regimental charge will be handed over on relief and receipts obtained.

3. TRENCH STORES.
    All Trench Stores, Trench covers, petrol tins, etc., will be handed over on relief. Receipts will be obtained in each case, and copies forwarded to Brigade H.Q.
    Rifles specially issued for firing Rifle Grenades will be retained by Regiments, and not handed over.

4. GUARDS.
    Guards and Fatigues furnished by the Reserve Regiment will be relieved by Lord Strathcona's Horse.

5. TRANSPORT.
    Os.C.Units, Back Area, will send up Transport with the led horses as under:-

    For each Regiment - 2.G.S.Wagons.
                          2.L.G.S. "

    Of the above, 1 G.S.Wagon is allotted to each Regiment for the carriage of Kits of Dismounted Reinforcements and will remain at VENDELLES.

    Squadron entrenching Tools will be withdrawn on pack.

G. Simson.

Lieut:
for Staff Captain, Sec'bad Cav. Bde.

Relief Table used with Cav. Bde. O.O.44 of 11-6-17

Horses of

Date	Unit relieved	Relieving Unit	Area taken over	Grecides meet relieving unit at	Incoming Units arrive at	Outgoing Units arrive at	Remarks
Day 14th June.	2 Sqdns Pomn Horse.	1 Sqdn L.S.Hse.	Reserve line A.2.L.	Q.12.Central	L.27.c. 2-3.p.m.	Q.12.Central 5.30.p.m.	No of led horses to be 20 by day for outgoing units. 115 Led horses & 1 pack
	-do-	2 Sqdns L.S.Hse.	Reserve line A.2.R.	L.33.a.Central	L.33.a.Central 10.30.p.m.	L.33.a.Central 12.p.m.	105 Led horses & 1 pack
night	Mt.D. Guards	R.C.D.	A-2-R.	-do-	L.33.a.Central 11.p.m.	L.33.a.Central 1.a.m.	205 Led horses 16 pack
14th/15th June.	XX R Regt. Ryecan Horse.	F.G.H.	A-2-L.	L.27.c.	L.27.c. 11.30.p.m.	L.27.c. 1.30.A.m.	205 Led horses 7 Pack
	1 Section 13th M.G. Sqdn Signal Troops Brigade Hdqrs	} To be arranged by O's.C. concerned.					

Note:-
(a) Guides will be in proportion of 1 per troop for front line units, 1 per post for supports.
(b) East of VENDELLES-BERNES line troops move at 400 yds distance by day and 200 yds by night.
(c) By day incoming units will not proceed mounted beyond the VENDELLES-BERNES line.
(d) Led horses of outgoing units will move up along the unmounted route via the POEUILLY - BOYECOURT - VENDELLES Valley.
(e) All traffic except that of forward Regiment A-2-R. will move on a left-handed circle returning to Bivets via JEANCOURT-MONTIGNY Fm - BERNES to Bivets.
(f) Canadian Cavalry Bde will proceed mounted to VENDELLES, thence dismounted to locations as given in Relief Table.
(g) Transport of Canadian Cav Bde will come in by day to MONTIGNY Fm, that of Dismounted Cav Bde will go out in by day to MONTIGNY Fm, that of Dismounted Bde will go out in rear of Regiments.

Apx "D"

Copy No. ....

SECUNDERABAD CAVALRY BRIGADE OPERATION ORDER NO: 45

Ref: Map 1/40,000.   22nd June, 1917.

1. The SECUNDERABAD CAVALRY BRIGADE will relieve the AMBALA CAVALRY BRIGADE in Subsector A.1. on the 23rd June and night 23rd/24th June, in accordance with the attached Table.
Command passes on completion of relief.

2. (a) 7th Dragoon Guards and Poona Horse will relieve the 8th Hussars and 9th Hodson's Horse respectively.

(b) XXth Deccan Horse will relieve the 18th Lancers at 3.pm. in Brigade Reserve at VADENCOURT Ch.

(c) 1 Section No.13. Squadron (M.G.C)(C) - now in Back Area, will relieve 1 Section No.14. Squadron M.G.C.(C) on the evening of 22nd June, under arrangements to be made between Os.C.13th & 14th Squadrons M.G.C.(C).

(d) 14th Squadron M.G.C.(C) (less 1 Section) and No.9.L.A.C. Battery will remain in the line.

3. All details of relief and guides will be arranged between C.Os concerned.
No post will be withdrawn until the Commander relieving is satisfied that all is correct.

4. Horses will not be taken beyond VERMAND before 9.30.p.m., nor beyond VADENCOURT by night.

5. Dismounted Reinforcements of the Brigade will come under orders of Os.C.Regiments after work on the night of 22nd/23rd June. Os.C. will issue orders to Os.C. their respective parties direct, as to their disposal.

6. The Transport under Lieut: H.PEMBERTON as laid down for Dismounted Establishment will rendezvous at the cross-roads CAULAINCOURT - BEAUVOIS and TREFCON - ETREILLERS at 8.pm. and proceed to Bivouac in VERMAND.

7. All Maps, air photos, trench stores, ammunition, shelters, etc will be taken over and receipts given.

8. (a) Reliefs will be completed by 2.am. on 24th June.

(b) Completion of relief will be reported by the code expression 'WAIT AND SEE'.

9. Brigade Report Centre will close at TREFCON at 9.pm., and open at Chateau VADENCOURT at the same hour.

10. Administrative Instructions attached.

11. ACKNOWLEDGE.

M.C.Raymond
Captain,
for Brigade Major, SECUNDERABAD CAV.BDE

Issued by D.R.

Normal O.O.distribution.
Copy No.23. - CANADIAN CAV.BDE.
" 24 - AMBALA
" 26 - 120th French D.I.Bde, HARTEVILLE.
" 27 - No.9.L.A.C.Battery
" 28 - C.R.H.A., 5th Cav.Dn.
" 29 - O.C., Back Area Details.
" 30 - O.C., Dismounted Reinforcements
" 31 - R.E.Liaison Officer.

March Table issued with Secunderabad Cav. Brigade O.O. 45.

Date	Relieving Unit	Unit to be relieved	To move mounted to	Route	Remarks
22nd	1. Section 13th M.G.Sqn.	1. Section 14th M.G.Sqn.	VERMAND	CAULAINCOURT thence across country	To be relieved under orders of O.C. 14th M.G. Squadron.
23rd	S.S. Queens Own	18th Lancers Bde. Reserve.	— do —	— do —	1. Relief to commence by 3. p.m. 23rd. 2. Will maintain 10 min. interval between Squadrons.
23rd	34th Poona Horse	9th R. H. Horse in A.I.L.	R.21.a.	CAULAINCOURT thence across country to BIHECOURT Sta.	1. Not to be to E. of VERMAND before 9.30 p.m. 2. Relief to start at 10.30 p.m. 3. Will maintain 5 min. interval between Squadrons.
23rd	7th Dragoon Guards	8th Hussars in A.I.R.	R.21.b. (BIHECOURT)	— do —	1. Not to be to E. of VERMAND before 10.30 p.m. 2. Relief to start at 11.30 p.m. 3. Will maintain 5 min. interval between Squadrons.
23rd	Brigade H.Q. Signal Troop	} Relief to be arranged by O.C. concerned			Brigade H.Q. will arrive at VADENCOURT at 10.30. p.m.

NOTE
1. NO HORSES TO MOVE EAST OF VERMAND BY DAY.
2. Led horses will return on Northern side of VADENCOURT–VERMAND Road.

ADMINISTRATIVE INSTRUCTIONS ISSUED WITH O.O.45.

SUPPLIES.

1. (a) All troops will take with them their rations for the 24th June.

   (b) All ranks must be in possession of one Iron Ration and a filled water-bottle.

   (c) On the night 23rd/24th June and subsequent nights, Rations will be brought up by the limbered train under Lieut: KEEFE.
   From the Refilling Point at MONTECOURT to the cross-roads at BIHECOURT where Units will have guides waiting at 8.45.pm.nightly.

   (d) Regiments and 13th M.G. Squadron will each detail one N.C.O. to check and load up rations at the refilling point and march with the limbered train under Lieut: KEEFE. These details will report to Captain SHORT at 10.am. on 23rd June and will remain at the refilling point. Brigade H.Q. will detail 1 trench cover for British Ranks and Poona Horse 1 trench cover for Indian Ranks.

   (e) Units in the Forward Area must submit their own A.B.55 to include transport details, and extra trench rations This indent will be given to Units' representatives at Forward Regimental H.Q. each night and will be for supplies four days in advance.

   (f) <u>Reserve Rations & Water.</u>
   Two days British and two days British and Indian special scale Reserve Rations are maintained in all forward posts in the Right and Left portions of Sub-sector A.1. respectively. In addition, a reserve of Rations is kept at Advanced Brigade H.Q. VADENCOURT. On taking over, Units will forward to Brigade H.Q. a list showing the number and location of all reserve rations and water tins received from outgoing Units.

TRANSPORT

2. (a) The Brigade Transport for the Forward Area will be parked at VERMAND under the orders of Lieut: PEMBERTON B.T.O.
   Detail as under.-

   Brigade H.Q............ 3.L.G.S.Wagons,
   Per Regiment.......... 3   "   "
   Per M.G.Sqdn......... 2   "   "
   For Medical Equipment, 2 half limbers.
   Per Regiment......... 1 G.S.Wagon.

   (b) 7th D.Guards, Poona Horse, and IXth Leccan Horse will each detail 2 Pack horses (with dismounted leaders) to march and park with the Brigade Transport. They will take empty tool packs and two pairs pack ropes per animal, and will be used for carrying water and rations to Advanced Posts.

   (c) All Handcarts will be taken.

   (d) Each Unit will detail 1.N.C.O. to be in charge of the Transport.

   Poona Horse will detail 1 Farrier,
   Deccan Horse "   "   " 1 Mochi.

II

WATER. 3. (a) The following water carts will be taken.-

    7th D.Guards........ 1.
    Poona Horse,........ 1.
    M'how I.C.F.A...... 1.

The water carts of the two regiments will remain and fill at VERMAND and will proceed each night to Units with the ration limbers.

M'how I.C.F.A. water cart will remain at the Advanced Dressing Station and will supply Brigade H.Q.Units and the Reserve Regiment.

(b) There is a spring at VADENCOURT giving good drinking water.

(c) The reserve of water held in advanced posts must be changed every three days.

AMMUNITION. 4.

(a) All S.A.A. grenades etc will be taken over by Units from the Units of the AMBALA CAV.BDE they relieve.

(b) The XXth Deccan Horse will detail 1 Dafadar to remain in permanent charge of the Brigade S.A.A. Dump at VADENCOURT.

R.E.STORES. 5. The Advanced Divisional Dump is at VERMAND. The Brigade Dump is at VADENCOURT.

Units' Indents for R.E.Stores will reach Advanced Brigade H.Q. by 2.p.m.daily, and the stores will be sent up by night.

RETURNS. 6. The following Returns must be sent in punctually by 9.pm.-

(i) Daily Casualty Return (12 noon to 12 noon)
(ii)   " Expenditure of S.A.A.
(iii)   " Fighting Strength.

These Returns will be submitted by D.R.

On taking over, the following Returns will be submitted by midday on the 25th June to the Staff Captain.-

(i) S.A.A., Grenades, Very Lights, etc. taken over by Units;
(ii) Trench Stores, R.E.Stores, Tents, Trench Covers, Petrol tins (other than those for reserve water ration) taken over.
(iii) Strombos Horns and anti-gas appliances taken over: locations of strombos horns will be given.
(iv) Reserve of Rations and water taken over: locations must be given.

Forward Units will also submit the following Returns.-

    Fridays 2.pm. Weekly Fighting Strength,
    1st July, 2.pm. War Diary
    "   "   "   Return of self-inflicted wounds.

POSTAL. 7. Back Area details will send letters and newspapers for Forward Units by mounted orderlies to Advanced Bde H.Q.

Parcels will be sent up from Back Area on Ration Limbers.

Forward Units will send their outgoing mails to Advanced Brigade H.Q. by 1.pm. daily.

III

MEDICAL ARRANGEMENTS 8. (a) Personnel are detailed as follows:-

Captain R.C.P. BERRYMAN, I.M.S.
Senior Medical Officer will be in medical charge of Left Sector and Reserve Regiment.

Captain J.H. CRUICKSHANK, R.A.M.C.
will be in charge of Right Sector, Brigade H.Q. and Transport.

Sub-Asst-Surgeon from Poona Horse.

Ward Orderlies (1 from Poona Horse,
(1 " Deccan Horse.

Orderlies for (1 " 7th D. Guards,
M.Os. (1 " Deccan Horse.

Stretcher Bearers, 24. - 8 per Regiment.

R.A.M.C. for water duties. - 1 from 7th D. Guards.

For Sanitary (2.O.R.B. - 7th D. Guards.
duties. (2.O.R.I. from Divnl Sanitary
(section for each Indian Regt:

Batmen for M.Os. - 3.

(b) Transport.
1 half L.G.S. Wagon for Medical Equipment to be detailed by 7th D. Guards,
1 half L.G.S. Wagon for Medical Equipment to be detailed by XXth Deccan Horse.

(c) Equipment.

2 Pairs Medical Panniers. - 1 pr. with M.O. 7th D. Guards
1 " " " Deccan Hse.

2 Field Surgical Haversacks -----------do-----------

2 Field Medical Companions, -----------do-----------

2 Haversacks Shell Dressings -----------do-----------

100 spare First Field Dressings) Will be supplied
12 Field Stretchers   ) from A.D.S. M'how
50 Ammonia Capsules,   ) I.C.F.A. to be
) handed over by M.Os
) of outgoing Units
) to those of incoming
                                 (units on relief.

The lance pattern Regimental Stretcher will not be taken into the line.

3. DRESSING STATIONS.

Advanced Dressing Station. VADENCOURT-R.16.a.9.4
(M'how I.C.F.A)
Regtl: Aid Posts.

A.1. Right.   (FLEMING's CRATER-R.11.b.8.6.
               (not completed.

A.1. Left   (COCKER's QUARRY-R.11.c.7.9.

IV.

Advanced Regtl: Aid Posts. For use as occasion requires.-

    A.1.Right.-   M.7.b.3.0.

    A.1.Left   TWIN CRATERS-R.6.c.6.1.

The evacuation of all wounded unable to walk is by hand under Regimental arrangements from the line to Regimental Aid Posts, thence by Bearer Party with wheeled carriers or by horse ambulances. After dark to the advanced Dressing Station.

ROAD CONTROL. 9. (a) By day a M.M.P. patrol will be posted at cross-roads VADENCOURT to prevent any loitering. By night a M.M.P. patrol will be posted on the BIHECOURT - VADENCOURT road and will ensure that there is an interval of 100 yards between all vehicles going to and coming from Forward H.Q.

    (b) The road running N.E. beyond the road junction at R.11.c.0.6. will not be used in daylight by any but single men, who must keep close to the hedge on the Southern side.

    (c) The reserve regiment will detail a sentry for duty to prevent motor cars and horses passing the barricade at VADENCOURT.

CEMETERIES. 10.   British - R.16.b.3.4.
            Indian - R.16.b.4.3.
Burial Returns will be submitted by the Staff Captain.

ORDNANCE. 11. Forward Units will arrange with their details in the Back Area for Ordnance Stores to be sent up on ration limbers from the refilling point.

BATHS. 12. Brigade Baths are at VERMAND.

LAUNDRY. 13. Underclothing will be sent to Sec'bad Cav.Bde Field Ambulance for disinfection by 10.am on the 27th June. Arrangements for transport will be notified later.

GUARDS & SENTRIES. 14. The Reserve Regiment will detail the following.-

    (a) 1.N.C.O.& 3 men   -   Brigade H.Q.Guards.
    (b) -------do--------   -   Bde Ammn: Dump Guard.
    (c) 1 sentry   -   Aeroplane look-out.

                                     Captain,
for Staff Captain, SECUNDERABAD CAVALRY BRIGADE.

Normal O.O.distribution.

     Copy No. 23   -   AMBALA CAV.BDE.
       "   24   -   R.E.Liaison Officer.
       "   25   -   S.M.O.
       "   26   -   B.B.O.

Serial No. 119

War Diary
of
Secunderabad Cavalry Brigade

From 1st July 1917 to 31st July 1917

(Vol I).

Army Form C. 2118.

Secunderabad Cavalry Brigade

WAR DIARY
—or—
INTELLIGENCE SUMMARY.   Page 1.
(Erase heading not required.)

Instructions regarding War Diaries and Intelligence Summaries are contained in F. S. Regs., Part II. and the Staff Manual respectively. Title pages will be prepared in manuscript.

Place	Date	Hour	Summary of Events and Information	Remarks and references to Appendices
VADENCOURT Chateau. Map Ref. 1/20 000 - G.31.b.7.2. 62.c.N.E. 62.c.S.E. 62.b.N.W. 62.b.S.W.	1/7/17		Brigade remained in Divisional A.I. Southern Boundary River OMIGNON. Northern Boundary BAVRIERES WOOD No 2(incl.) - Trench Junction R.S.c.9.7. - RED HOUSE (excl.) - G.31.b.7.2. - Bottom of Valley which runs through G.28 Central. 7th Dragoon Guards on Right. 34th Poona Horse on Left. 20th Deccan Horse in Reserve. Situation Normal. Vicinity of FILLER Redoubt patrolled - no encounter.	
	2/7/17		Situation Normal. Usual Patrols, Vicinity of FILLER Redoubt patrolled. No encounter. Enemy wiring party was seen.	
	3/7/17		Enemy Artillery activity above normal. The TUMULUS, incoming line and PONTRU-VADENCOURT Valley being intermittently shelled throughout the day and night. Situation normal. Usual Patrols out. No encounter. A party of 15 Germans approached a Listening Post in SOMERVILLE WOOD and on being challenged answered "KAMERAD." Bursts were thrown at them and they retired.	
	4/7/17		Situation normal. Usual patrols out. Preparations for Raid on FILLER Redoubt and SQUARE Copse and the adjoining Trenches completed. Raid was attempted but could not be carried out.	of Report attached 2/7/17. A.
	5/7/17.		Situation Normal. A strong Patrol endeavoured to search for bodies or any means of identification that might have been left from Patrol of enemy killed on night 4th/5th. One R.H.A. Battery co-operated by shooting enemy wire in front of FILLER Redoubt. Patrol reached N. of ELEVEN TREES without incident. Two small parties of the enemy were seen working about in front of SQUARE COPSE and FILLER Redoubt. Owing to the bright moonlight it was found impracticable to go over the ground where recently had been killed. The Patrol made a circuit of No Mans Land but no more enemy were seen.	

Canadian Cavalry Brigade

Army Form C. 2118.

WAR DIARY
INTELLIGENCE SUMMARY.   Page 11.
(Erase heading not required.)

Place	Date	Hour	Summary of Events and Information	Remarks and references to Appendices
	6/9/17		Situation Normal. Novel Patrols out. No encounter.	
	7/9/17		Situation Normal. Usual cover of an Artillery and Machine Gun barrage on enemy positions about THE ELEVEN TREES by Hostile Troops & the 7th Dragoon Guards.	Copy of Report attached Appx B.
	8/9/17		Situation Normal. Usual patrols out. Reported rumoured out watching ASCENSION Valley owing raid by Canadian Cavalry Brigade. No encounter.	
	9/9/17		The Brigade relieved in the line by part of 101st Infantry Brigade. Situation normal. Brigade returned to Bivouacs about TREFCON. Relief completed without incident by 2.30. a.m. 10th mo Count	Copy orders attached Appx C.
TREFCON.	10/9/17 - 13/9/17		Brigade remained in Bivouacs in vicinity of TREFCON.	
Map Ref 1/100,000 ST QUENTIN, AMIENS, LENS.	14/9/17		Orders received for Division to move Northwards. Brigade (less "N" Battery, R.H.A) with 5th Field Squadron. R.E. Commenced S.C.F.A. attached, marched Northwards, billeting on night 14th/15th: CARTIGNY - BUIRE - COURCELLES. Brigade Report Centre BUIRE.	
	15/9/17		March continued. S.C.F.A. attached, billeting night 15th/16th in area. VAUX - SUZANNE. Brigade Report Centre SUZANNE.	
LENS.	16/9/17		March continued Northwards. Brigade billeting night 16th/17th in area. MORLANCOURT - VILLE - SOUS - CORBIE - TREUX. Brigade Report Centre TREUX.	

Army Form C. 2118.

Secunderabad Cavalry Brigade

WAR DIARY
or
INTELLIGENCE SUMMARY.
(Erase heading not required.)

Page III

Instructions regarding War Diaries and Intelligence Summaries are contained in F. S. Regs., Part II. and the Staff Manual respectively. Title pages will be prepared in manuscript.

Place	Date	Hour	Summary of Events and Information	Remarks and references to Appendices
	17/7/17		March continued to MARIEUX Area. Brigade Report Centre AUTHIE.	
	18/7/17		March continued to the ST. POL Area. Brigade Report Centre RAMECOURT.	
	20/7/17		Brigade moved to new Billets, and were billeted as follows:—	
			Brigade H.Q. ⎫ Signal Troop. ⎪ M.V. Section. ⎬ MONCHY – CAYEUX. 20th Dorsey Yeo. ⎪ 13th M.G. Squadron. ⎪ Ind. Fd. A. ⎭	
			'N' Battery R.H.A. – SAUTRECOURT. 4th Dragoon Gds. – ANVIN. 34th Poona Horse – EPS & HERBEVAL.	
	27/7/17 – 31.7.17		Brigade Report Centre Chateau MONCHY–CAYEUX. 'N' Battery R.H.A. left Ste. under OC. 19th DHQ. bde. to come under orders of 1st Army. Brigade remained in present Area. Training carried out in Mounted and Dismounted Work. Casualties during month:— 5-7-17 1.B.O. 3.O.R.8. 3.O.R.1. Wounded. 8-7-17 2.O.R.B. Killed Wounded. 1.B.O., 8.O.R.B., 1.I.O. 9-7-17 1.I.O. Wounded.	

R.K.K.

App. A

REPORT ON THE OPERATIONS ON THE NIGHT 4TH/5TH JULY.

------------oOo------------

The raiding party under Lieut: HASTINGS left our lines at 10.pm. and reached the point of assembly without incident at 11.pm.

2. On reaching this point some talking was heard about XI TREES and towards SQUARE COPSE. Nothing however occurred except that a few Very Lights were shown.

3. A little after 11.30.pm. the Torpedo Party (Lieut: MACBEAN) advanced, covered by scouts.
After crawling about 100 yards, odd parties of the enemy in twos and threes were seen moving across the front; the scouts reported a Patrol or covering party in the direction of SQUARE COPSE.

4. The torpedo party advanced another 50 yards or so, and three of the enemy passed close to them without discovering them.
The torpedo party moved on a little distance, from which point the German Patrol (referred to above,- para:3), of 15 to 20 men could be clearly seen against the skyline.

5. The party was now some 50 yards from the wire, when two Germans passed across their front, one of them shouting an order to some others who were about 30 yards behind. Of these, two advanced straight on to the party, and when they got to about 5 yards away, and it was evident that they had discovered our party, Lieut: MACBEAN fired his revolver and another man of the party his rifle, knocking over both the enemy.

6. The German patrol came down upon the left flank of the torpedo party, and it withdrew a short distance, leaving the torpedoes behind.

7. As the O.C., Raiding Party realised that surprise was now impossible, he withdrew his party to the West of the Sunken road.

8. It was then determined to make an effort to regain the torpedoes and the carrying party advanced to do so, upon which fire was opened on them. Very Lights were shown.
The German patrol mentioned in para:6 had also interposed themselves between our patrol and the torpedoes.

9. As by now it was clearly impossible either to carry out the raid, or regain the torpedoes, the order to withdraw was given and the N.C.O. in charge of the Power Buzzer was ordered to send the prearranged signal for no operations (N.G) from ANGLE Banks.
Unfortunately, owing to a bad 'Earth', the message was not received and hence the delay in warning the Artillery and other covering troops that the raid would not take place.

10. The whole raiding party was back in our line a little after 1.a.m. having suffered one casualty,- slightly wounded.

11. The Right Defensive Flank retired as a right rear-guard to the raiders without incident.

12. The Left Defensive Flank during its withdrawal, came across a party of some 30 of the enemy, who were immediately attacked, and who retired at the double, but wheeled round and opened fire which was at once replied to, and the enemy made off. During this little scrap, Lieut: YATES, commanding the party, was hit in the shoulder (slightly at duty), and one Indian Officer and 2.O.R.I. wounded (all slightly).

SECRET.   B.M.O. 800   8th July, 1917.

To/

The 5th Cavalry Division.

Taking advantage of a pre-arranged Artillery Barrage, last night, (7th/8th), three troops, 7th Dragoon Guards carried out a raid on XI TREES, in order to 'round up' any enemy in that vicinity.

The three troops paraded as ordered, South of the TUMULUS, on the BELLENGLISE Road at 10.pm, and when moving off, "A" Troop unfortunately had four casualties from shell-fire, which delayed the preliminary advance for a few minutes, as the casualties had to be evacuated by the Stretcher-bearers, who were going with the raiding troops.   However, all the troops reached their respective positions five minutes before Zero hour, and communication from ANGLE BANK was established immediately by metallic circuit to CRESSY TRENCH.

The wire-cutting party in front of "A" Troop moved up and cut through the concertina and loose wire which they found in a few minutes, and reported to Lieut: HASTINGS, "A" Troop, who advanced at once through the Gap, and worked according to instructions.

Only 5 men were found in the XI. TREES in a rifle pit at the Northern end, four of whom ran away before the troop could get up to them: one man who refused to surrender in the rifle pit was bayonetted, and identifications were taken.

The troop worked round lefthanded to ANGLE BANKS, followed by the N.C.O. and four men who acted as rearguard.

R............

II

2. "C" Troop, under 2/Lieut: GILMAN, got into position to cover the right flank, and met with no opposition.

This troop remained in position until the rockets went up to withdraw.

3. "B" Troop under 2/Lieut: MACBEAN, covering the left flank, met with considerable opposition from a patrol of about twenty men, and a Machine Gun, who were lying up in the sunken road in G.33.a.5.4., who opened rifle and M.G.fire as the troop advanced. 2/Lieut: MACBEAN ordered the troop to lie down and return the fire, while he, accompanied by his Sergeant and one man worked round the enemy's left flank, and after getting to within 15 to 20 yards of them, bombed the enemy out of the sunken road, which the troop immediately occupied, finding three German dead.

The Troop held this position until the enemy were reported to be working round their left flank, when Lieut: MACBEAN brought back his left flank, and moved his Hotchkiss Rifle to bring fire to bear on them.

The enemy apparently withdrew, as they showed no further activity.

Shortly afterwards the signal to withdraw went up.

Identifications were taken, and the troop withdrew via SOMERVILLE WOOD.

As all three troops withdrew, the Germans put up a very moderate barrage in the ACENSION VALLEY.

All troops leaders testify to the very accurate shooting of our Artillery.

.Captain,
for G.O.C., SECUNDERABAD CAVALRY BRIGADE.

Copy No. _____

SECUNDERABAD CAVALRY BRIGADE OPERATION ORDER NO: 47.

---------oOo---------   7-7-17.

1. The Brigade will be relieved in the Line by the 16th Battalion, ROYAL SCOTS, 101st Brigade on the 9th July, and night 9th/10th July, in accordance with the attached Tables.

2. (b) <u>13th & 14th M.G. Squadrons</u> will be relieved by details of the 101st M.G. Company.

   (c) Units on completion of relief will proceed to Bivouacs.

2. All details of reliefs will be arranged by the Os.C.concerned.
    No troops will be withdrawn until the Commander relieving is satisfied that all is correct.
    Patrols will be pushed well out, and will not be withdrawn until the relief is complete, or they have been replaced.

3. All movement East of a North and south line through Q.30. central will be conducted in small parties equivalent in size to a troop or platoon, 200 yards distance being maintained between parties, and no transport will move East of this line before 9.30. p.m.

4. Advanced parties of at least one Officer per Company and one N.C.O. per platoon will be sent forward.

   (a) For Front Line Units, on the evening of 8th instant,
   (b) For other Units, on the evening of 9th instant.

5. Guides will be provided by the outgoing Units for each company, platoon or post.

6. All maps, air photographs, and trench stores will be handed over and receipts obtained.
    Duplicate forms will be made out, and the actual handing over should, as far as possible, be done in daylight.

7. Reliefs will be completed by 2.a.m. 10th instant.

    Commands pass on completion of reliefs, which will be reported by the code word 'MOUNT'.

8. Administrative Instructions attached.

9. Report Centre opens at TREFCON at   2.30 AM 10th.

10. ACKNOWLEDGE.

signature
Captain,
Brigade Major, SECUNDERABAD CAVALRY BRIGADE.

Issued by N.R.-

   Normal O.O. distribution.
   Copy No. 15. - C.R.H.A.
      "   16.   14th M.G. Sqdn.
      "   17 - M'how I.C.F.A.
      "   18 - R.E. Liaison Officer.
      "   19 - French Liaison "
      "   20 - 101st Inf. Bde.

RELIEF TABLE ISSUED WITH SEC'BAD CAVALRY BRIGADE

OPERATION ORDER NO: 47.

---oOo---

Date of Relief.	Outgoing Unit.	Incoming Unit.	Relief to commence at	Relieved Unit will march Dismounted to
9th.	XXth Deccan Horse.	10th Bn. Lincoln Regt ~~1 Company, 16th Bn. ROYAL SCOTS.~~	4.30.pm.	TREFCON.
9/10th	34th Poona Horse.	1/2 Bn 16th Royal Scots ------do------	10.~~30~~.pm	R.21.a.
9/10th	7th Dragoon Guards	------do------	11.~~30~~.pm.	R.21.a.
9/10th	Details of 13th & 14th M.G. Squadrons.	1 Section 101st M.G. Company.	11.30 pm ~~12.midnight~~	R.21.a.

Serial No: 119

Secunderabad Cav: Bde

War Diary

From 1st August 1917
to 31st August 1917

Army Form C. 2118.

3rd/4th Cavalry Brigade

WAR DIARY
INTELLIGENCE SUMMARY.
(Erase heading not required.)

Instructions regarding War Diaries and Intelligence Summaries are contained in F.S. Regs., Part II. and the Staff Manual respectively. Title pages will be prepared in manuscript.

Place	Date	Hour	Summary of Events and Information	Remarks and references to Appendices
MONCHY CAYEUX -ANVIN -EPS -	1/8/17 to		Brigade remained in billets as per margin. Training carried out on mounted and dismounted work.	REF MAP LENS 1/10000
HERBEVAL HESTRUS	31/8/17			

G.H. Howell Capt.
Brigade Major
for G.O.C. Secunderabad Cavy Bde

Army Form C. 2118.

WAR DIARY

Seaforth ~~Security~~ Brigade.

INTELLIGENCE SUMMARY.

Page 1.

(Erase heading not required.)

Place	Date	Hour	Summary of Events and Information	Remarks and references to Appendices
MONCHY — CAYEUX — ANVIN — EPS — HERBEVAL	1/8/17 31/8/17		Brigade renewed on trellers as per margin. Training. Reg'l sports & Horse shows. Very wet month.	REF MAP. LENS 1/100000

G.M.H.
1-9-17.

Confidential

Serial No. 119.

War Diary

Secrad Cavalry Brigade

From 1st September 1917
  to 30th September 1917

Confidential

19

War Diary

Secunderabad Cavalry Brigade

From 1st October 1917
To 31st October 1917

Vol I

Army Form C. 2118.

WAR DIARY

Staff Captain. Brigade

or

INTELLIGENCE SUMMARY.

(Erase heading not required.)

Instructions regarding War Diaries and Intelligence Summaries are contained in F. S. Regs., Part II. and the Staff Manual respectively. Title pages will be prepared in manuscript.

Place	Date	Hour	Summary of Events and Information	Remarks and references to Appendices
MONENT ETAPLES	1/4/17		Brigade remained in Billets as per margin	Ref Map Étaples 1/10,000
AMIENS - EU -	2/4/17		Training Cadres. Reft. Mounted and dismounted work	Ref Map 1/100,000
HAZEBROUCK	3/4/17		Received orders from Brigade would move N.E. on 6th	
HESTRUS	4/4/17	1 P.M.	Brigade marched to BOESEGHEM and via WESTREHEM - ST HILAIRE - ARE - Brigade left billets BOESEGHEM arrived about 1.30 pm	Ref Map HAZEBROUCK 1/100,000 Appx. "A"
BOESEGHEM	5/4/17	Night	March continued to HATOU close via HAZEBROUCK - STEENVOORDE	Appx. 19 Appx. "B"
			Brigade troops Cavalry - WATOU arrived about 4.30 pm Very wet and windy	
HATOU	7/4/17		Situation unchanged. Wet and stormy.	
	8/4/17		Received orders for return march.	
HATOU	9/4/17	push	Brigade marched via REMIRSBORE area via STEENVOORDE - CAESTRE - BAVINCHOVE - arrived about 3pm Beaumont Centre - RENESCURE	Appx "C"

P.T.O.

WAR DIARY
INTELLIGENCE SUMMARY

Army Form C. 2118

2nd Cavalry Bde.

Place	Date	Hour	Summary of Events and Information	Remarks and references to Appendices
RENESCURE	16/4/18		March continued to FAUQUEMBERGUES via FRUGES — MIZERNES — CLERY. Arrived about 1 p.m. Bde went billeted "D" HERVARRE Camp.	Ref. Map 1/100,000
HERVARRE	17/4/18		Brigade marched by regiments, to arr FRUGES — COUPIELLE VIEILLE — WAILLY — ORSAUY — TORCY — ROJON — OFFIN — LIBIEZ — LOISON — HESMOND. Arrived about 2 p.m. Brigade HQrs Castle — FRUGES. Units billeted as follows:— N Battery R.H.A. FRUGES 7th Dragoons — COUPIELLE VIEILLE — WAILLY — ROLLEZ Royal Horse — CRECQUY — TORCY — SAINS le FRESSIN Queens Bays — ROJON — OFFIN — LIBIEZ — LOISON 13 m Sqdn. & Cossackie HEUSE — QUESNOYNGE.	Apx I Ref Maps Sheets 5a, 11, 13 & 14 1/100,000
FRUGES	18/4/18 to 30/4/18		Situation unchanged. Fine and cold. Training carried out on the usual lines and reconnaissance work.	

G. A. Hull Capt
Brigade Major

SECRET.   Apx "A"   Copy No 13

SECUNDERABAD CAVALRY BRIGADE OPERATION ORDER NO; 53

Ref: Map 1/100,000 - LENS & HAZEBROUCK.   5th October 1917.
----

2. The Brigade and attached troops will march North on 6th and 7th Inst.

B. Route. WESTREHEM - ST HILAIRE - AIRE.
    Destination. BOESEGHEM area.
    Starting point. HEUCHIN church (N exit of HEUCHIN)
    Units will pass starting point as under :-

	Divl.Hd.Qrs.)	
	Signal Squadron)	9.15 A.M.
	Hd.Qrs.17th Bde.R.H.A.)	
	Brigade Hd.Qrs.)	
	Signal Troop.)	9.30 A.M.
	7th Dragoon Guards.)	
	34th Poona Horse.	9.45 A.M.
	XXth Deccan Horse.	10. A.M.
	"A" Echelon of above.	10.10 A.M.
To march (	"N" Battery R.H.A.	10.25 A.M.
under Senior (	13th M.G.Sqdn.	10-35 A.M.
Officer making (	S.C.F.A.	10-45 A.M.
their own pace.(		
	"B" Echelon.	10.50 A.M.

3. A distance of 500 yards will be maintained in rear of Regiments, Batteries and similar units.
    Normal Advanced Guard 7th Dragoon Guards.
    Normal Rear Guard, behind "A" Echelon, XXth Deccan Horse.

4. "A" Echelon will come under orders of Captain A.HIATT, 7th Dragoon Guards at the starting point.
    "B" Echelon will come under orders of B.T.O. at starting point and follow the Brigade. It will remain brigaded till arrival in forward area on 7th inst.
    Cyclists will rendezvous at starting point at 11 A.M. and march under Sergt. WALLING, 7th Dragoon Guards.

5. Dismounted Reinforcements will rendezvous at the Present Supply Dump at 3 P.M., 7th Inst and march under Major O.H.DYKE, to GAUCHIN - VERLOINGT where they will report to Lt.Col YOUNG, Royal Canadian Dragoons.

6. Billeting parties to meet Staff Captain at the five cross roads ¾ mile west by south of A of AIRE at 10-30 A.M. D.H.Q., Signal Squadron and H.Qrs, 17th Bde.R.H.A., will be billeted at STEENBECQUE by Canadian Cavalry Brigade.

7. Brigade will continue the march on 7th inst leaving billets at about 10-30 A.M.

8. Reports to head of Column.

9. Railhead 7th & 8th inst. THIENNES.   G. K. Howell
                                             Captain,
                                    Brigade Major, SECUNDERABAD CAVALRY BDE.

1 - 18 Normal O.O.Distribution.
19.   D.H.Q.Unit.
20.   C.R.A.
21.   5th Signal Squadron.

Issued to Signals 8 P M

SECRET.   Apx 'B'   Copy 13

SECUNDERABAD CAVALRY BRIGADE OPERATION ORDERS No.54.

Ref. Map 1/100,000.   6th October 1917.
----

1. The Brigade and attached units will march to WATOU area to-morrow 7th Inst -

2. Route.- HAZEBROUCK - STEENVOORDE.

   Starting point - Junction of St. VENANT - HAZEBROUCK and
                          AIRE - HAZEBROUCK roads.

   Units will pass starting point as under :-

   "B" Echelon.   11.15 A.M.
   Divl. H.Qrs.   )
   Signal Squadron   )   11.30 A.M.
   H.Qrs, 17th R.H.A. Bde.   )
   Bde. H.Qrs.   )
   Signal Troop.   )   11.45 A.M.
   34th Poona Horse.   )

   7th Dragoon Guards.   12. 5 P.M.
   XXth Deccan Horse.   12.25 P.M.
   "A" Echelon of above.   12.45 P.M.

To march under (13th M.G. Sqdn.   1.   P.M.
Senior Officer ("N" Bty, R.H.A.   1.10 P.M.
making their   (S.C. Field Ambce.   1.20 P.M.
own pace.   (

   Normal advance guard - 34th Poona Horse.
   "   rear guard.   - XXth Deccan Horse. behind "A" Echelon.

3. A distance of 500 yards will be maintained between Regiments Batteries, and similar units.

   A distance of 200 yards will be maintained between Squadrons and groups of not more than 10 vehicles.

   Units are reminded that they are marching accross the general trend of traffic, and must give way to that crossing them.

4. "A" Echelon will come under the orders of Captain A. HIATT, 7th Dragoon Guards at the starting point. They will not pass "B" Echelon on the march.

   Rug Wagons will join "B" Echelon at the starting point at 11.15 5 A.M. ready to move off at 11.15 A.M.

   Cyclists will rendezvous at the starting point at 12.45 P.M. and march under Sergt. WALLING, 7th D. Guards.

5. Billeting parties to meet Staff Captain at Area Commandant's Office at WATOU at 12.50 P.M.

6. Reports to head of column.

                            (Signed) G. Simson, C a p t a i n,
           for Brigade Major, SECUNDERABAD CAVALRY BRIGADE.

Nos. 1 - 18. Normal O.O. Distribution.
No.19 D.H.Q. Unit.
   20 C.R.A.
   21 5th Signal Squadron.
      Issued to Signals   P.M.

ADMINISTRATIVE INSTRUCTIONS Issued with O.O.
7th October 1917.

Ref. Map Sheet 37. 1/40,000.　　　　　VATOU AREA.

1. Camps are allotted as under :-

    "N" Battery R.H.A.　　K.3.c.9.2.
    7th Dragoon Guards.　K.5.d.6.6.
    Poona Horse.　　　　　K.5.b.3.6.
    XX Deccan Horse.　　　K.4.d.5.4.
    13th M.G.Sqdn.　　　　K.5.d.7.4.
    Brigade H.Q.　　　　　notified later.
    Signal Troop &
    Post Office.　　　　　K.4.d.3.9.
    M.V. Section.　　　　 K.5.c.3.6.
    Sec'bad C.F.A.　　　　K.4.c.r.r.

2. **Rations.** The Brigade Supply dump is at K.4.b.4.0. It is probable that units will have to draw rations from this dump.

3. **Water.**　(a) Drinking water points are in VATOU and at K.3.c.3.3.
   (b) Water points are at Regimental billets with the following exceptions :-
   7th Dragoon Guards and Sec'bad C.F.A. will water at K.5.central.
   13th M.G. Squadron will water at K.5.c.3.3.

4. Tents and Trench Covers.
   Will be issued as soon as available.

5. **Sanitation.** Litter will be dumped at manure dumps.
   All tins will be burnt at Incinerators.

6. **Pumps & Troughs.** On leaving this area units will take forward as many pumps and troughs as possible up to 1 per squadron.

7. **Transport.** Instructions for the return of A.H.T. wagons will be issued later.

Captain,
Staff Captain, SECUNDERABAD CAVALRY BRIGADE.

Apx "C"

SECRET-   Copy No 13.

SECUNDERABAD CAVALRY BRIGADE OPERATION ORDER No: 54.

Ref:Map 1/100,000 N HAZEBROUCK.   14th October 1917.

1.   The Brigade, "N" Battery R.H.A. and Sec'bad C.F.A. will March West on 15th, 16th and 17th Inst.

2.   Route.- STEENVOORDE - OXELAERE - BAVINCHOVE.
        Destination 15th Inst. - RENESCURE.
        Starting point. Road junction 1 mile N of B in
                        BEAUVOORDE.
        Units will pass the starting point as under :-

        Brigade Hd.Qrs.   )
        Signal Troop.   ) 9.45 A.M.
        XXth Deccan Horse.   )
        34th Poona Horse.   10.5 A.M.
        7th Dragoon Guards.   10.25 A.M.
        15th M.G.Squadron.   10.45 A.M.
        "N" Battery R.H.A.   10.55 A.M.
        "A" Echelon in order of units. 11.5 A.M.
        Sec'bad C.F.A.   11.15 A.M.
        M.V.Section.   11.25 A.M.
        "B" Echelon in order of units. 11.35 A.M.

        Normal Advanced Guard XXth Deccan Horse.
        "   Rear   "   7th Dragoon Guards.

3.   A distance of 300 yards will be maintained between Squadrons and groups of not more than 10 vehicles.

4.   "A" Echelon will come under the orders of Capt.A.HIATT, 7th Dragoon Guards at the starting point.
        "B" Echelon will come under the orders of the B.T.O. at the starting point. It will remain brigaded until morning of 17th Inst.
        Cyclists will rendezvous at starting point at 11-30 A.M. and march under Sergt. WALLING, 7th Dragoon Guards.

5.   Billeting parties will meet the Staff Captain at the church RENESCURE at 10-15 A.M. 15th Inst.

6.   The Brigade will continue the march on 16th Inst., leaving billets at about 8.15 A.M.

7.   Railhead. October 16th. LUMBRES.
                   October 17th. HESDIN.

8.   Reports to head of column.

                                          G.B. Howls
                                          Captain,
               Brigade Major, SECUNDERABAD CAVALRY BRIGADE.
Normal C.O.Distribution.

SECRET.   Copy No_____

Apx "D"

SECUNDERABAD CAVALRY BRIGADE OPERATION ORDER No; 56

Ref; Map 1/100,000 - HAZEBROUCK.   15th October 1917.

1.   The Brigade, "N" Battery R.H.A. and Sec'bad G.F.A., will continue the march to-morrow.

2.   <u>Route.</u>- ARQUES - WIZERNES - CLETY.
      <u>Destination.</u>   FAUQUEMBERGUES area.
      <u>Starting point.</u> Junction of ARQUES - CAMPAGNE and ARQUES - RACQUINGHEM Roads.

      Units will pass starting point as under:-

      Brigade H.Q.   )
      Signal Troop.   )   7.45 A.M.
      7th D.Guards.   )

      XXth Deccan Hse.   8. 5 A.M. (not to pass through CAMPAGNE)

      13th M.G.Squadron.   8.15 A.M.
      "N" Battery R.H.A.   8.35 A.M.
      "A" Echelon.   8.45 A.M.
      Sec'bad G.F.A.   8.55 A.M.
      M.V.S.   10.5 A.M.
      "B" Echelon.   10.5 A.M.

34th Poona Horse (Fighting Troops only) marching via HELFAUT, will join the column behind XXth Deccan Horse at road junction ½ mile N of P in PIHEM.

Their transport must join their respective echelons at the brigade starting point.

      Normal Advanced Guard 7th Dragoon Guards.
      "   Rear   "   behind "A" Echelon 34th Poona Horse.

3.   A distance of 300 yards will be maintained between Squadrons and groups of not more than 10 vehicles.

4.   "A" Echelon will come under the orders of Capt.A.HIATT, 7th Dragoon Guards at the starting point.

      Rug wagons will join "B" Echelon at starting point.

      <u>Cyclists</u> will rendezvous at the cross roads in CAUCHIE D'ECQUES at 10 A.M. and march under Sergt.WALLING, 7th Dragoon Guards via THEROUANNE and COYECQUE.

5.   Billeting parties will meet the Staff Captain at FAUQUEMBERGUES church at 10 A.M.

6.   The Brigade will continue the march on 17th Inst., leaving billets at about 6 A.M.

7.   Reports to head of column.

                              G.B.Howell. Captain,
                        Brigade Major, SECUNDERABAD CAVALRY BRIGADE.

Normal O.O.Distribution.

ADMINISTRATIVE INSTRUCTIONS ISSUED WITH O.O. No. 56.

1. 2nd BLANKETS. Lorries will be sent out to 7th Dragoon Guards and XXth Deccan Horse at 6 A.M. and will rendezvous at H in CAMPAGNE at 7.30 A.M.

   (b)   O.C. Poona Horse will detail lorry to be at church BLENDECQUES at 8 A.M.

   (c)   The Brigade H.Q. lorry will pick up 13th H.C. Squadron blankets at CAMPAGNE at 6.15 A.M., "N" Battery blankets at RENESCURE at 6.35 A.M. and Brigade H.Q., Signal Troop, M.V. Section blankets at Brigade H.Q. at 7.10 A.M.

   (d)   The O.C. Sec'bad C.F.A. will send blankets to T raod at W in WARDRECQUES by 7.30 A.M.

2. HORSE RUGS. A.H.T. Wagons carrying horse rugs will join "B" Echelon transport at the starting point.

3. GUIDES. Units must detail guides to meet A.H.T. wagons and conduct them to billets in the New Area. This was not done to-day.

4. BILLETTING. Certificates will be given to the Maires of communes.

Captain,

Staff Captain, SECUNDERABAD CAVALRY BRIGADE.

Apx. 'E'

SECRET.   Copy No. 13

SECUNDERABAD CAVALRY BRIGADE OPERATION ORDER NO; 57

Ref; Map 1/100,000 - Sheets 5a,11,13 & 14.
                                                    16th October 1917.
---

1.   Brigade will march to FRUGES area to-morrow in accordance with attached march table.

2.   "A" Echelon & Cyclists will accompany units.

        "B" Echelons will join units when they pass through FAUQUEMBERGUES with the exception of that of 7th Dragoon Guards which will march with the Poona Horse "B" Echelon as far as VAILLY Halte.

3.   2nd Blankets. Lorries will report to units at 7 A.M., and will proceed direct to new area under unit arrangements.

        (b) The Brigade H.Q. lorry will pick up Blankets of "N" Battery R.H.A. at 6.30 A.M. and afterwards those of Brigade H.Q. etc., S.C.F.A., and 13th M.G.Squadron. It will then proceed to FRUGES.

        (c) Immediately on arrival in new area lorries and A.H.T. wagons will return to FRUGES and will report to Staff Captain.

4.   Horse Rugs. A.H.T. wagons carrying horse rugs will accompany units.

5.   Billetting Parties. of units billetting in FRUGES will meet the Staff Captain at the church, FRUGES at 8.0. A.M.

6.   Report centre moves with Brigade Headquarters.

                                    [signature]
                                                    Captain,
                    Brigade Major, SECUNDERABAD CAVALRY BRIGADE.

Normal O.O.Distribution.

March table issued with Sec'bad Cav.Bde. O.O.No.57.

	Starting Point.	Time.	Route.	Destination.	Remarks.
Bde.H.Q. & Sig.Troop	Junction of HERVARRE FAUQUEMBERGUES & VILLAMETZ - FAUQUEMBERGUES Roads.	9.30 A.M.	Main Road.	FRUGES.	
"N" Battery R.H.A.	Northern entrance to FAUQUEMBERGUES	10.A.M.	Main Road	FRUGES.	Not to enter FAUQUEMBERGUES till after tail of L.G.Sqdn.
7th Dragoon Guards.	Southern exit THIEMBRONNE	9.45 A.M.	RUMILLY- VERCHOCQ.	COUPELLE VIEILLE WAILLY.	Not to enter VERCHOCQ till 10.30 A.M.
34th Poona Horse.	As for B.H.Q.	9.A.M.	FAUQUEMBERGUES MONTEVILLE WAILLY Halte.	CREQUY TORCY	
XXth Deccan Horse.	Road Junction ½ mile S of FAUQUEMBERGUES Church.	9.A.M.	VERCHOCQ - HERLY-EMBRY	ROYON OFFIN LEBIEZ LOISON HESMOND	To be clear of VERCHOCQ by 10.30 A.M.
13th M.G. Squadron.	As for B.H.Q.	9.35 A.M.	Main Road.	FRUGES	
S.C.F.A.	As for B.H.Q.	10.10 A.M.	Main Road.	FRUGES.	
M.V.Sectn.	As for B.H.Q.	10.15 A.M.	Main Road.	FRUGES.	

Army Form C. 2118.

WAR DIARY
or
INTELLIGENCE SUMMARY
(Erase heading not required)

8th Cavalry Bde — November 1917

Instructions regarding War Diaries and Intelligence Summaries are contained in F.S. Regs., Part II. and the Staff Manual respectively. Title pages will be prepared in manuscript.

Place	Date	Hour	Summary of Events and Information	Remarks and references to Appendices
BOVES COURCELLES ALLY- OLGERY - RAINON COURCELLE HEUDE	1/11/17		The Brigade remained in billets as per previous message.	
	to 8/11/17		Training carried out on dismounted and dismounted work.	
			Brigade received orders to move South.	
	9/11/17		Brigade marched South to OUTREBOIS area. Route: WESTOUTRE - THIEVRES - HESDIN - LABROYE - AUXI-LE-CHATEAUX - BOUQUEMAISON.	
	10/11/17 6.30a		March continued to CONTY area. Route: CANDAS-LE-MEILLARD-NAMPONT-RUSSEMONT-MOLLIENS AU BOIS - 1300 Saint Leger. QUERRIEUX	
	11/11/17 4p		March continued to BRAY area - 4th day on LANEUVILLE-VAUX-EN-SOMME SAILLY LAURETTE - MORLANCOURT - BUIRE-SUR-SERRE - MERICOURT.	
	12/11/17		Gen Allen the ESTREES - BAIZIEUX - BAISIEUX	
	20/11/17		A state of warning to be in readiness to marched	
	23/11/17		Brigade marched to area around MERICOURT.	

MERICOURT

Army Form C. 2118.

WAR DIARY
or
INTELLIGENCE SUMMARY.

(Erase heading not required.)

Sec'd. .....War Bee....... No. 11

Instructions regarding War Diaries and Intelligence Summaries are contained in F.S. Regs., Part II. and the Staff Manual respectively. Title pages will be prepared in manuscript.

Place	Date	Hour	Summary of Events and Information	Remarks and references to Appendices
MERICOURT	29/11/17		Brigade marched to TREFCON and via FAVIANCOURT - BRIE - ESTREES - EN CHAUSSEE - ROUPAUX - arrived at Billets TREFCON	Reference S/11/17 X App. G
TREFCON	29/11/17		Orders received to take over B.2 Subsector (See VERGUIER) on night of 1st/2nd Dec '17	
	30/11/17		Advanced parties went about to proceed to B.2 Subsector when at about 9.15am orders to turn out as quickly as possible for a move NORTH thousand were received. Report on operations on 30th is attached (appx "H")	App H

B Stuart Col
Comdg 2nd Wd Cdn Bde.

SECRET.   Copy No.

SECUNDERABAD CAVALRY BRIGADE OPERATION ORDER No: 58.

Ref.Map :-1/100,000.   8th November 1917.

---

1.   The Brigade and attached units will march South on 8th and 10th and 13th inst.

2.   Destination 9th. OUTREBOIS area.
        Route - Western outskirts of HESDIN - LABROYE - AUXI LE CHATEAU.
        Starting point - HESDIN station.
        Order of March.-
                Bde.H.Qrs & Signal Troop.
                XXth Deccan Horse.
                34th Poona Horse.
                7th Dragoon Guards.
                13th M.G.Squadron.
                "N" Battery, R.H.A.
                "A" Echelon in order of units.
                S.C.F.A.
                M.V.S.
                "B" Echelon.
        Head of column to pass starting point at 10-30 A.M.
        Normal Advanced Guard XXth Deccan Horse.
        Normal Rear Guard (behind "A" Echelon) 7th Dragoon Guards.

3.   "A" Echelon will come under the orders of Lieut.F.C.GUTHRIE XXth Deccan Horse at the starting point.
        "B" Echelon will come under orders of B.T.O. at the starting point, it will remain brigaded on the night of 8th/10th.
        Cyclists will rendezvous at the junction of JONTES - AUBIN ST VAAST and VALBERCOURT-AUBIN ST VAAST roads at 10-30 A.M. and march under Sergt.WALLING, 7th Dragoon Guards via LABRUS - TURTEFONTAINE - DOMPIERRE sur AUTHIE and South bank of river.

4.   The Brigade will water on arrival at AUTHIE River.

5.   Billeting parties will meet the Staff Captain at the Town Hall, AUXI LE CHATEAU at 12 noon.

6.   Reports to head of column.

                                        Captain,
                Brigade Major, SECUNDERABAD CAVALRY BRIGADE.
Normal O.O.Distribution.

ADMINISTRATIVE INSTRUCTIONS ISSUED WITH O.O.No.58.

6th November 1917.

1. **2nd Blankets.** (a) Lorries for the carriage of 2nd Blankets will join units as under to-day at 5 P.M.

   Brigade H.Qrs.   1.
   Regiments. each 1.   by 7. AM.

   (b) The Brigade Headquarter lorry will collect blankets of

   Sec'bad C.F.A. at 7 A.M.
   "N" Bty.R.H.A. at 7.15 "
   Signal Troop) at 7.30 "
   H.Q.Unit.   )
   13th M.G.Sqdn. at 7.45 "

   (c) Lorries less that of XXth Deccan Horse will rendezvous loaded at crossroads FRUGES – HESDIN and BEAZENCOURT – FRESSIN at 8-30 A.M.

   XXth Deccan Horse lorry will join the above at HURY St LEU at 8.50 A.M.

2. **Horse Rugs.** A.H.T.Wagons will march with "A" Echelon.

3. **Surplus Stores.** (a) Surplus Government Stores will be collected by D.A.D.O.S. to-day and taken to the new area. No Government Stores will be left in this area.

   (b) There will be no Brigade dump for officers kit.

   Captain,
   Staff Captain, SECUNDERABAD CAVALRY BRIGADE.

DISTRIBUTION OF BILLETS.

8th November 1917.

Brigade H.Qrs.)	
Signal Troop.)	
M.V.Section.)	LE MEILLARD.
Supplies.)	
Bde. "B"Echelon.)	

"N" Battery, R.H.A.   FROHEN LE PETIT.

7th Dragon Guards.   (AUTHEUX
                        (MACFER.
                        (MONPLAISIR.

34th Poona Horse.   (ST ACHEUL.
                        (HEUZICOURT.
                        (GREMONT.

XXth Deccan Horse.   BOISBERGUES.
13th M.G.Squadron.   MT RENAULT M.
Sec'bad C.F.A.   LE QUESNEL M.

Captain,
Staff Captain, SECUNDERABAD CAVALRY BRIGADE.

A."B"

SECRET.   Copy No. _____

SECUNDERABAD CAVALRY BRIGADE OPERATION ORDER No; 59.

Ref.Map :-1/100,000 LENS.   9th November 1917.
----

1.   The Brigade will continue the march to CONTAY area
to-morrow.

2.   Route - CANDAS - LE VAL DE MAISON - HERISSART. RUBEMPRE
        Starting point - Church FIENVILLERS. - MOULIENS AU BOIS
        Order of March -
                Bde H.Qrs.
                Signal Troop.
                7th Dragoon Guards.
                XXth Deccan Horse.
                34th Poona Horse.
                13th M.G.Squadron.
                "N"Battery, R.H.A.
                "A"Echelon.
                S.C.F.A.
                M.V.S.
                "B"Echelon.
        Head of column to pass starting point at 8-30 A.M.
        Normal Advanced Guard 7th Dragoon Guards.
        Normal Rear Guard (behind "A"Echelon) 34th Poona Horse.

3.   "A" Echelon will come under orders of Lieut.F.C.GUTHRIE,
XXth Deccan Horse at Starting Point.
        Rug Wagons will march with "A"Echelon.
        Cyclists will rendezvous at 6 cross roads N of LL in
FIENVILLERS at 8-30 A.M. and march under Sergt.WALLING, 7th Dragoon
Guards via CANAPLES - TALMAS - RUBEMPRE.

4.   Billeting parties will meet Staff Captain at church
HERISSART at 10 A.M.

5.   The march will be continued on the 11th.

6.   Reports to head of column.

CONTAY   7 Bde.
QUERRIEU   D.H.
P.H   Captain,

                        Brigade Major, SECUNDERABAD CAVALRY BRIGADE.

Administrative Instructions issued with O.O. N° 59.

9th November. 1917

Horse Rugs & Blankets.

a. The Bde M.O. lorry will call at Units as under:-
13th M.G. Sqdn at 7.A.M. for 250 horse rugs.
N. Battery R.H.A. at 8.A.M. for 100 "
Jodhpur. C.F.A. at 8.45.A.M. for 50 "

b. The Bde A.S. AT wagon will also call at Jodhpur C.F.A. for 2" Blankets

c. Lorries will rendezvous at CANDAS at 9.30. A.M.

J Smison. Capt.
Staff Captain
Secunderabad. Cav. Bde.

SECRET.   COPY No. 12

SECUNDERABAD CAVALRY BRIGADE OPERATION ORDERS No:- 60.

Ref.Map :-1/100,000.   11th November 1917.
----

1.   Brigade and attached units will complete the move in accordance with attached march tables.

2.   "A" Echelon will come under the orders of Captain A. HIATT, 7th Dragoon Guards at the starting point daily.

        "B" Echelon will remain brigaded till completion of move.

        Cyclists will march under a British Officer per Regiment and H.G. Squadron.

        A.H.T. Wagons will march with "A" Echelon.

3.   A distance of 300 yards will be maintained between Squadrons and between Regimental Transport Echelons.

4.   Railheads -

                CONTAY area   CORBIE.
                BRAY area   LAFAUQUE.
                Final area   TINCOURT.

5.   Reports to head of column.

                                        Captain,
                Brigade Major, SECUNDERABAD CAVALRY BRIGADE.

O.O.Distribution.

SECUNDERABAD CAVALRY BRIGADE.

March tables issued with O.O.No :- 60.

11th November 1917.

Order of March.	Starting point.	Time.	Route.	Destination.	Remarks.
Bde H.Q.	Cross roads	4. P.M.	LA NEUVILLE-		
Signal Tp.	a mile South	4. P.M.	VAUX SUR SOMME-		
34th Poona Horse.	of P in PONT	4. P.M.	SAILLY LAURETTE - MORCOURT.		Notified later
7th D.Gds.	NOYELLES.	4.15 P.M.			
XXth Deccan Horse.		4-30 P.M.			
13th M.G. Squadron.		4-45 P.M.			
"N"Bty.R.H.A.		4-55 P.M.			
"A"Echelon in order of Units.		5- 5 P.M.			
S.C.F.A.		5-15 P.M.			
M.V.S.		5-20 P.M.			
"B"Echelon.		5-30 P.M.			

Normal A.G. 34th Poona Horse.
Normal R.G. under a British Officer behind "B" Echelon,
XXth Deccan Horse.

13th November 1917.

Order of March	Starting point	Time	Route	Destination	Remarks
Bde H.Q.	Cross roads	4-30 P.M.	ESTREES	Billets	
Signal Tp.	miles S	4-30 P.M	-BRIE -	from	
XX Deccan Horse.	of P in TROY.RT.	4-30 P.M.	VRAIGNES.	Staff Captain.	
34th Poona Horse.		4.45 P.M.			
7th D.Gds.		5 P.M.			
13th M.G. Squadron.		5.15 P.M.			
"N"Bty.R.H.A.		5-25 P.M.			
"A"Echelon in order of Units.		5.35 P.M.			
S.C.F.A.		5-45 P.M.			
M.V.S.		5-50 P.M.			
"B"Echelon.		5-60 P.M.			

Normal A.G. XXth Deccan Horse.
Normal R.G. behind "B" Echelon 7th Dragoon Guards.

ADMINSTRATIVE INSTRUCTIONS issued with O.O.No.60.

11th November 1917.

HORSE RUGS. (a) Lorries will rendezvous at cross roads QUERRIEU - CORBIE and PONT NOYELLES - VECQUEMONT at 12 noon 11th November, and proceed to MORCOURT. Regiments are responsible for informing drivers of these orders.

(b)   The Brigade Headquarter lorry will call at Units as under :-

    18th M.G.Squadron.   at 10 A.M., for 150 Horse Rugs.
    Sec'bad C.F.A.   at 10-45 A.M. for 50 Horse Rugs.
    "N" Battery, R.H.A. at 11-30 A.M. for 100 Horse Rugs.

1 Representative only from each unit will ride on lorries.

(c)   The Brigade A.H.T. wagon will not call at Sec'bad C.F.A. for 2nd Blankets.

Captain,
Staff Captain, SECUNDERABAD CAVALRY BRIGADE.

S.M.O.505

Headquarters Secunderabad Cavalry Brigade.
19th November 1917

To/

C.O. Distribution.

Continuation Operation Order No.1.

Head of Column will pass the starting point at :- Zero-4 hrs 50 mins

Route.   LONGAVESNES - LIERMONT - NURLU - EQUANCOURT
         Northern end of FINS.

No.1.A Echelon under an Officer per Regiment will rendezvous at junction of roads ¼ Mile N. of TINCOURT at Zero-3hrs 20 Mins and follow No.1.A Echelon of Canadian Brigade.

No.2.A Echelon will rendezvous at the same place at Zero-3hrs 10 Mins and follow No.2.A Echelon of Canadian Brigade.

B.S.O. and B.T.O. will accompany No.2.A Echelon.

Brigade B Echelon will be commanded by 2nd Lt. T. WOOD, 7th Dragoon Guards.

[signature]
Captain.
Brigade Major Secunderabad Cavalry Brigade.

S E C R E T.

SECUNDERABAD CAVALRY BRIGADE.   Copy No. 15

Operation Order No 61

15th November 1918.

Reference Map
1/100000

1. The Brigade and attached Units (less "B" Echelon and Dismounted Reinforcements) will march to a forward concentration area N.E. of F I N S on Y/Z night.

    Starting point, Church B O U C L Y.

    Order of March, 1 Squadron 7th Dragoon Guards,
                       B.H.Q. and Signal Troop.
                       7th Dragoon Guards. (less 1 Squadron)
                       1 Section 13th M. G. Squadron.
                       34th Poona Horse.
                       Field Troop R.E.
                       20th Deccan Horse.
                       13th M. G. Squadron (less 1 Section) with
                                  3 S.A.A. limbers
                       "N" Battery R.H.A.
                       Light Section Ammn Column.
                       Pack Sectn, S.C.F.A.

    Head of Column will pass starting point at a time and date to be notified later.

2. In moving to the forward concentration area, whenever possible, Squadrons will move off roads. All wheels will move by the roads only. Squadrons and wheels will move closed up.

3. On arrival in the forward concentration area there will be a halt of two and a half hours during which horses will be watered and fed.

    After feeding, nose bags will be refilled from forage dumps which have been prepared in this area.

    Arrangements will be made by units, in consultation with Staff Captain, for a hot meal to be ready in this area.

4. The Brigade will be ready to move forward from the F I N S area at Zero plus 3-1/2 hours.

5. Guides will meet units at N U R L U to direct them to their places in F I N S area.

6. "A" Echelon will be subdivided into No.1 "A" Echelon and No.2 "A" Echelon as under

No.1 "A" Echelon	No.2 "A" Echelon.
Signal Troop limber	Supply limbers
Brigade Tool limber	Mess Carts (3 Regts & B.H.Q. only)
Regt. & Sqdn S.A.A. limbers	Water Carts.
M.G. S.A.A. limbers (less 3)	Cook Carts.
	Technical Carts.
	Officers Pack horses (less proportion with Squadrons).

No. 2 "A" Echelon will be Divisionalised under Lt. G. R. H. BENNETT, Fort Garry Horse.

No. 3 "A" Echelon will be Divisionalised under Capt. A. HIATT 7th Dragoon Guards.

Orders for concentration of "A" Echelon will be issued later.

7. The Dismounted Reinforcements of all units and "B" Echelons, Divisionalised, will be assembled at B O U C L Y by 4 p.m. on Z day.

Major R. H. O'D. P A T E R S O N, 34th Horse will command the dismounted Reinforcements of the Division.

Capt F. H. W I L K E S, Royal Canadian Dragoons will command "B" Echelon, Divisionalised.

Duplicate nominal rolls of Officers and O.R's for dismounted reinforcements will be submitted forthwith.

8. Officers detailed as liaison officers and Gallopers with Divisional Hd.Qrs. will report at the G.S.Office at 2 P.M. on Y day.

Those for duty with Brigade Hd.Qrs will report to Brigade Major at starting point.

9. M.V.S. will march with and form part of No 2 A echelon

10. Acknowledge

[signature]
Captain.
Brigade Major, SECUNDERABAD CAVALRY BRIGADE.

Normal Distribution 1-17
Secbad CFA 18
5th Field Squadron RE 19

Issued to Brigade at 2 P.M.

ADMINISTRATIVE INSTRUCTIONS issued with O.O. No - of date.

18th November 1917.

Reference 1/100000.

1. FORWARD CONCENTRATION

(a) The following advanced parties will meet Staff Captain at B of B.DESSART, N.E. of FINS on Y day as stated below :-

UNIT	TIME	OFFICERS	O.R.	WAGONS.
"N" Battery	12.30 p.m.	1.	2.	1 L.G.S. / 1 Water Cart
13th M.G.Sqn.	12.50 "	1.	3.	1 L.G.S. / 1 Water Cart
7th Dragoon Gd	1.10 "	1.	2	ditto
Poona Horse	1.30 "	1.	4	ditto
XXth Deccan Hse	1.50	1.	4	ditto.
S.C.F.A.	2.10	1 N.C.O.	2.	1 L.G.S.
Field Troop	2.30	ditto	2	ditto
H.Q. Unit Signal Troop M.V. Section Supply.	2.50	ditto	ditto	ditto

(b) Staff Captain will allot areas and issue rations, fuel and soyers stoves.

(c) L.G.S. wagon will carry cooking pots for Officers and men.

(d) The route for advanced parties to the concentration area is optional, but parties must arrive at the times as stated above, and on no account must one unit's party proceed as a column immediately in rear of another unit's party.

(e) On arrival in the forward concentration area the Brigade will be formed in line of regtl masses, and on receipt of orders units will proceed to water. O.C.Poona Horse will detail 1 British Officer for duty at water points, who will report to Staff Captain at 3.30 p.m. on Y day.

(f) Advanced parties will take shovels for digging latrines and chloride of lime will be carried on water carts.

(g) Lieut.Pemberton B.T.O. will assemble the above wagons after the Brigade has moved forward.

Captain,
Staff Captain Secunderabad Cavalry Brigade.

SECRET.   Copy No:

SECUNDERABAD CAVALRY BRIGADE

Operation Order No. 63.

Apx 'E'

Reference Map
1/200,000 and
1/40,000.   Dated 19th November 1917.

1.   On "Z" day a surprise attack is to be made on a front of 13,000 yards, from a point 1,000 yards E. of GONNELIEU to a point 1,000 yards E. of HERMIES.

The attack will be made by five Divisions out of the line and by part of two Divisions holding the line, assisted by 360 Tanks.

2.   The object of the operation is to break the enemy's defensive system by a coup de main - to pass the cavalry through the break - to seize CAMBRAI and BOURLON WOOD and the passages over the SENSEE River and to cut off the troops holding the front line between HAVRINCOURT and that River.

3.   As soon as the Infantry has secured MARCOING and MASNIERES and the BEAUREVOIR - MASNIERES line, the Cavalry will push forward with the following objectives :-

5TH CAVALRY DIVISION.

(a) To isolate CAMBRAI from the E., N.E., and N. by :-

(i) Seizing the high ground NIERGNIES to CAUROIR and the high ground TILLOY - CUVILLERS - THUN LEVEQUE commanding the crossings over the CANAL L'ESCAUT at ESWARS and MORENCHIES.

(ii) By blocking all exits from the Town.

(iii) By destroying the following Railways :-

1. LE CATEAU - CAMBRAI.
2. SOLESMES - CAMBRAI.
3. SOLESMES - HASPRES - VALENCIENNES - DOUAI - CAMBRAI.
4. LOURCHES - CAMBRAI.

2.

(B) Seize the crossings over the SENSEE RIVER between PAILLENCOURT and AUBENCHEUL AU BAC (both inclusive) and, as soon as the situation admits, the crossing over the SENSEE at PALLUEL.

4. The 1st Cavalry Division to isolate CAMBRAI from West and North-West.

5. The 2nd Cavalry Division follows the 5th Cavalry Division objectives.

(a) To take over the crossings over the canal L'ESCAUT at ESWARS and MOENCHIES from the 5th Cavalry Division, commencing by relieving the troops holding the high ground at NIERGNIES and AWOINGT.

(b) To push patrols E and N.E. in the area ESNES, WAMBAIX, ESTOURNEL, CARNIERES, AVESNE, IWUY.

(c) When relieved by the infantry, to push forward N.E. extending its left to IWUY and LIEU ST AMAND, and blocking the crossing over the canal L'Escaut at BOUCHAIN.

5. When the Cavalry is ordered to advance, the Division will move forward as under:-

(a) ADVANCED GUARD. CANADIAN CAVALRY BRIGADE

ROUTE:-
GOUZEAUCOURT - LA VACQUERIE - MASNIERES
(VIA KAVANAGH ROAD from Q.30.b.5.3.)

OBJECTIVES

(i) To seize the high ground NIERGNIES to CAUROIR and the high ground TILLOY - CUVILLERS - THUN LEVEQUE commanding the crossings over the canal L'ESCAUT at ESWARS and MORENCHIES.

(ii) To block all exits from CAMBRAI.

(iii) To destroy the following railways:-
1. LE CATEAU - CAMBRAI.   2. SOLESNES - CAMBRAI.
3. SOLESMES - HASPRES - VALENCIENNES - DOUAI - CAMBRAI.
4. LOUCHES - CAMBRAI.

The Canadian Cavalry Brigade and Sec'bad Cavalry Brigade will each detail one squadron for a special mission. The Commanders of these squadrons will report at Divisional Headquarters at noon on "Y" day for instructions.

In the advance to its objective the Canadian Cavalry Brigade will be responsible for the protection of both flanks.

The right flank guard of the Canadian Cavalry Brigade will be taken over by troops of the 5th Cavalry Brigade (2nd Cavalry Division) as soon as those troops can get up.

The left flank guard will remain in position and cover the exits from CAMBRAI and the left flank of the Division until relieved by the 4th Cavalry ~~Division~~ Brigade (2nd Cavalry Division).

In the advance from Masnieres all telegraph and telephone lines will be cut.

On gaining the crossing over the L'ESCAUT CANAL at MORENCHIES, touch will be obtained with 1st Cavalry Division in the neighbourhood of TILLOY.

4.

(b) MAIN BODY. order of March as in margin, will advance at the same time.

Sec'bad Cav: Bde Group.
Divisional H.Q. Group
Ambala Cav: Bde Group.
No 1 'A' Echelon Group.

ROUTE:-
Track from Q.32.d.3.3 - QUEENS CROSS - Q.23. central - VILLERS PLOUICH - MARCOING RAILWAY BRIDGE.

(c) The Sec'bad Cavalry Brigade after crossing the canal at MARCOING will march on NIERGNIES and, when the Canadian Cavalry Brigade has gained the crossings at MORENCHIES and ESWARS, the Secunderabad Cavalry Brigade will cross at ESWARS and advance with the following objective:-

ADVANCED GUARD
Lt Col R. SPARROW
C.M.G.
7th Dragoon Gds
Sec'n "N" Bty R.H.A.
1 - 13th M.G. Sqdn
Main Body.
Poona Horse
20 Deccan "
13 M.G. Sqdn
"N" Bty R.H.A. less 1 sec'n
Field Troop R.E.
Pack Sec'n S.C.F.A.
Light Sec'n Amm. Col.
REAR GUARD.
1 Troop 20th Deccan H.H.
under a British officer

OBJECTIVE:-

Seize the crossing over the River SENSEE between PAILLENCOURT and AUBENCHEUL AU BAC (both inclusive) and, as soon as the situation admits, the crossing over the SENSEE at PALLUEL.

7. Consequently on receipt of orders to move forward the Brigade and attached units (order of march as per margin) will cross the enemy's trench system and, under the protection of Detachments supplied by the Advanced Guard (in position on the ridge W of NIERGNIES and between that village and the MASNIERES - CAMBRAI road) will concentrate in the valley of the GRAND RIOT stream S.E. of the line NIERGNIES - AWOIGNT when orders for the further advance will be issued.

As soon as the Brigade is concentrated these detachments will be withdrawn.

The Section of "N" Battery R.H.A. will not join the advanced guard until the enemy trench system has been crossed.

8. The O.C. 7th Dragoon Guards will detail a patrol of 1 officer and 4 despatch Riders for liaison with the attacking infantry. This patrol will report to the Brigade Major at Zero hour for instructions.

5.

9. No 2 "A" Echelon will follow the same route as the Main Body of the Division. after 2nd Cav Div have passed

10. Medical arrangements are contained in Medical Operation Orders No 12 issued direct to Medical Officers of Regiments. Other units will make themselves acquainted with the contents of and initial the copies in possession of Medical Officers, in whose charge they are.

11. Prisoners of War will be sent to Divisional Report centre where the A.P.M. will form a collecting station. As soon as Division leaves FINS the Divisional Report centre will move to Rq.b.88 N.E. of VILLERS PLOUICH.

12. Reports to head of Main Body

R. R. Shuttl. Captain
Brigade Major Secunderabad Cav: Bde.

Issued by D.R. at 5.45 P.M
O.O. Distribution 1-17.
S.C.F.A. 18
Field Troop R.E. 19.
Canadian Cav: Bde 20.

Appx F

Diary of Events.

Sicunderabad Cavalry Brigade.

20/22 Nov 1917

12.45 a.m.	Brigade left VRAIGNES ahead and marched to concentration area N.E. of FINS arriving at 5.0 a.m.
5.0 a.m.	where horses were fed and watered, off saddled, and men had a hot meal.
8.50 a.m.	Brigade was saddled up and ready to move. Patrols were sent out from 7th Dragoon Guards to connect with the Infantry and report on progress of the attack.
10.25 a.m.	Report timed 9.15 a.m. received from contact patrol with the Infantry that 2nd objective had been reached. Report forwarded to Division.
12.10 p.m.	Orders received to advance. Situation on front MASNIERES — MARCOING not clear. Patrols sent forward to discover situation from Infantry leaders and personal reconnaissance.
12.15 p.m.	Vanguard Squadron (CAPT FRIEND) moved. Advanced Guard 7th Dragoon Guards and 1 Sectn 13 MG Sqdn.
1.15 p.m.	GOC joined Advanced Guard commander.
1.35 p.m.	Message received from advance Patrol that MARCOING was clear of enemy and bridges at that place over canal DESCAUT were intact.
2.0 p.m.	Main Guard reached MARCOING. GOC met staff officer of 29th Divn who informed him that situation NORTH and EAST of canal was uncertain. Vanguard squadron crossed canal by bridge East of railway bridge and found Infantry hung up in railway cutting by snipers and machine guns. Squadron extended the right flank of the Infantry which was in the air up to and including the lock bridge between MARCOING and MASNIERES.
2.10 p.m.	Above situation reported to Division (B M 4).
2.15 p.m.	Main body assembled south of MARCOING in L 28 C td.
2.45 p.m.	Officers patrol despatched to enquire situation in front of Canadian Brigade. Reported at 3.10 p.m. that Bridge over canal at MASNIERES had been broken by a tank. Vanguard squadron reinforced by one squadron (CAPT ANSDELL).

2.0 pm	One Squadron of Dragoon Guards (CAPT LANE) sent forward to cross canal at NOYELLES SUR L'ESCAUT in order to work round right flank of enemy holding up our Infantry N.E. of MARCOING. Copy of Capt Lane's report attached.
3.20 pm	Division asked (BM 6) whether if Brigade could cross at NOYELLES it should do so.
4.0 pm	Our Infantry in front of MARCOING held up by M.G. fire from direction of RUMILLY and were digging in. Report (BM 7) sent to Division that break through was unlikely.
4.45 pm	Infantry situation was, Infantry held up by BEAUREVOIR – MASNIERES line which was heavily wired and apparently strongly held. Infantry holding canal bank near lock bridge between MASNIERES and MARCOING asked for dismounted support on their right otherwise they feared they would lose ground. As doing this would have necessitated the abandonment of the idea of a mounted advance the question was referred to the Division (BM 8).
5.30 pm	Three advanced squadrons were withdrawn.
6.10 pm 6.30 pm	G.O.C. received an ikky to which Infantry situation was explained BM 9 and it was stated that owing to that situation it was doubtful whether the necessary support could be given to the proposed attack by the Canadian Cavalry Brigade.
6.45 pm	Permission received to give dismounted support to the Infantry. Capt Lane's squadron (dismounted) was therefore sent forward to report to the Infantry Commander at NOYELLES SUR L'ESCAUT. The Squadron held the bridge over the canal at that place and during the night beat off two hostile counter-attacks.
6.50 pm	Brigade withdrawn half a mile to R.3.a.
8.0 pm	G.O.C. went to report to Divisl HQ where he was informed that orders had just been issued for a withdrawal to FINS area.
9.45 pm	Orders cancelling the withdrawal were received and the Brigade bivouacked for the night.

21st Nov.
6.0. am.   As the position taken up by the Brigade in the dark the previous evening seemed somewhat exposed the G.O.C. decided to move the Brigade back to a more covered position in R 2 d.

6.20 am.   Liaison Officers were sent forward to H.Q. of 87th & 88th Brigades and Canadian Cavalry Brigade.

8.45 am.   Liaison Officer with the 87th Brigade reported that the Infantry would attack at 11.0. am. This was confirmed by the G.O.C. 29th Divn whom the Brigadier met just outside bivouac at 8.50. am.

10.30 am   Orders were issued for the Brigade to saddle up and remain ready to move.

12.45 pm. G.O.C. went forward to H.Q. 87 Brigade. Information received that 88th Brigade was being heavily counter-attacked on its right flank, result of which was then unknown.

           The attack of the 87th Brigade was only partially successful and its Commander informed the

2.15 pm.   G.O.C. that unless tank attack could be reorganised he intended occupying the Infantry positions of the previous night.

2.45 pm.   Ambala Brigade was transferred to 1st Cavalry Division and Brigade was ordered to prepare to withdraw should orders to that effect be received.

6.0. pm.   Brigade withdrew to the area previously occupied by Ambala Brigade. Most of the night was spent in watering the horses.

G. B. Howell Capt
Brigade Major.

B.M.2   21.11.17

To Secunderabad Cavalry Brigade

Herewith report from Capt Lane. Ref 1/100000

At about 2.0 pm on the 20th I was ordered to take my squadron and make good the village and crossings at NOYELLES SUR L'ESCAUT.

Lt DAWKINS and 1 Troop was detailed as Advance Guard. They advanced rapidly to point B.M.647 where we were held up by rifle and M.G. fire.

I decided to gallop the village with Troops at 40 yards distance.

The M.G. fire was high and did no damage.

Village was captured at 2.45 pm and the advance was successful. Total capture – 15 prisoners, subsequently 10 others were found in hiding.

Identifications are being forwarded under separate cover.

Prisoners were handed over to the Infantry who came up later in support.

Telegraph lines were cut leading to CAMBRAI – CANTAING and CANTIGNEUL. The main bridges over the L'ESCAUT were blown up and I discovered 3 small wooden bridges (trestle) still standing over the L'ESCAUT and held them against possible enemy enterprise.

At 4.30 pm a bridge was found standing over the canal de L'ESCAUT. The Bde could have been crossed but the branch line to the N.W. of the canal was occupied by the enemy, my patrols were heavily fired on and made to retire.

I determined to hold the crossings in case they should be required. I was reinforced by the Infantry at 4 pm and got in touch with the 4th D. Guards on my left rear at 5.0 pm.

In consequence of orders from the Brigade I evacuated the village and returned to my Regt.

When sent back dismounted I reported for duty to

OC. 2ⁿᵈ Royal Fusiliers. I was placed on outpost duty at NOYELLES SUR L'ESCAUT and established communication with 11ᵗʰ D.Gds on my left, also the Middlesex on my right.

I was relieved by the 18ᵗʰ Hussars at 5.0. a.m. Night uneventful except for spasmodic bombing along the canal.

Certified True Copy.

G.H. Howell Capt.
Brigade Major.

SECRET   Ap 'G'
                          Copy No. ......

Secunderabad Cavalry Bde

Operation Order No. 63

Ref. Map
1/100000   Dated 26-11-17

1. Brigade will march to TREFCON area to morrow.
   Starting Point - Western entrance CHUIGNES.
   Order of March - B.H.Q. & S. Troop.
                     34th Poona Horse
                     7th D.Guards.
                     20th D.Horse
                     13th M.G.Sqdn.
                     "N" Bty. R.H.A.
                     Lt. Sect. Amm. Col.
                     "A" Echelon in order of units.
                     S.C.F.A.
   Head of column to pass S.P. at 9 a.m.
   ROUTE - FOUCAUCOURT - BRIE - ESTREE - EN -
                     - CHAUSSEE.

2. Normal Advance Guard - 34th Poona Horse.
   --- Rear --- (behind "A" echelon) -
                     - 20th Deccan Horse.

3. "A" Echelon will come under orders of Capt. A. HIATT. 7th D.Guards at S. Point.
   "B" Echelon will rendezvous at FOUCAUCOURT at 9 a.m. and march under B.T.O.
   M.V.S. will march with 'B' Echelon.
   Brigade is to be clear of ESTREE-en-CHAUSSEE by 1.30 p.m.

4. Cyclists will rendezvous at the F.m FROISSY at 9.30 a.m. & march via CAPPY - HERBECOURT - PERONNE under Sgt WALLING, 7 DGds.
   Reports to head of Column.

                          G. B. Howe Captain
                          Brigade Major, S'bad Cav. Bde.
Issued at 9.30 p.m.
OO Distribution 1-17.
S.C.F.A.   18
Lt. Sect. Amm Col 19.

Ap. H

Secunderabad Cavalry Brigade
Diary of Events

30th November 1917
9.15 a.m. Orders received to act as quickly as possible for a move north.
11.0 a.m. Brigade ready to move.
10.15 a.m. moved off.
2.0 p.m. Brigade was concentrated N.E. of VILLERS FAUCON.
2.20 p.m. Brigade left VILLERS FAUCON in following order:- 7th Dragoon Guards, 1 Section 13th M.G. Sqdn., N Bty R.H.A., 20th Deccan Horse, 34th Poona Horse, 18th M.G. Sqdn (less 1 Sect) (Advanced Guard Lt. Col. R. SPARROW C.M.G. 7th Dragoon Guards, 1 Sect 13 M.G. Sqdn) with orders to work on the outer flank of the Ambala Brigade which was advanced Guard to the division on the line GOUZEAUCOURT - GONNELIEU.

3.15 p.m. On arrival of the advanced Guard EAST of REVELOU from the Ambala Brigade moved to the attack on GAUCHE WOOD. As the left of the Ambala Brigade was in touch with the right of the 5th Cavalry Brigade the advanced Guard was directed on GOUZEAUCOURT and the main body halted in W.5.
At this period of the advance the Brigade came under considerable shell fire which fortunately caused but few casualties.

3.30 p.m. Advanced Guard arrived at GOUZEAUCOURT and found the situation as follows. 5th Cavalry Brigade (with whose Commander I/OC. had spoken en route) held up on Southern edge of village by heavy M.g. fire from GONNELIEU and ridge south of that village GOUZEAUCOURT had just been occupied by two Battalions 1st Guards Brigade whose left flank was in the air at the station. One squadron was pushed forward to extend their left flank and get into touch with nearest Infantry on left. Right of 20th Div. was found to rest on sunken road R.25.b.
Patrols were pushed forward to reconnoitre GONNELIEU with a view to a mounted attack on that place but it was found to be considerably wired and defended by many machine guns.

4.8 p.m. Report sent to Division. B.M.2.
5.0 p.m. A staff officer was sent to O.C. 1st Guards Brigade who expressed himself satisfied that he could maintain his position so long as his left flank was secure.
6.25 p.m. Left of Guards Brigade was in touch with right of 20th Divn. advanced Guard was withdrawn to W.5 and Division informed. (B.M.3)
11.55 p.m. G.O. 6 G received Brigade will move into Divisional Reserve E. of arriving at 1.30 a.m. 1st Decr.

2/

1st December
9.30 a.m. — As the Guards attack had been held up on the QUENTIN RIDGE the 7th Dragoon Guards were placed at the disposal of G.O.C. Ambala Brigade.

10.15 a.m. — As there appeared a possibility of the Brigade acting dismounted the necessary preliminary arrangements were made.

2.5 p.m. — On demand from 7th Dragoon Guards extra ammunition and stretcher bearers were sent forward.

6.0 p.m. — Orders received to relieve Ambala Brigade and Infantry holding the line from CHAPEL CROSSING (excl.) to North-Eastern Corner of GAUCHE WOOD
Relief was completed by 5.20 a.m.
Delay was due to difficulty in getting position of Guards Brigade to hand over their positions as they had no information regarding relief.
Eventually the position of the Brigade was as shown on sketch attached to B.M.2/7 of 2nd inst.

8.0 p.m. — G.A. 630 was received and M.G. barrages were arranged accordingly, the barrages being stiffened by 6 guns of 14th M.G. Sqdn.

9.?? p.m. — Brigade Headquarters were established at W.10.d. Telephone wires were laid to Hd.Qrs. of all three regiments.

1.30 a.m. — G.A. 634 (warning of an expected counter-attack) was received, and orders for action to be taken should the attack come off were issued. The attack however did not materialise.

7.0 a.m. — 8th Hussars and 6 guns 14th M.G. Sqdn moved up into Brigade reserve W.10.d.

9.45 a.m. — As no attack had developed G.O.C. went forward to see and reorganise the front line which was held as it had been taken over in the dark from elements of various units.

11.0 a.m. — News of massing of German troops round VILLERS GUISLAIN was received by G.O.C. returned to Brigade Hd.Qrs.
The 6 reserve guns 14th M.G. Sqdn were posted in position to cover the approaches from VILLERS GUISLAIN towards CHAPEL CROSSING and GAUCHE WOOD.

12.0 noon — G.O.C. had personal interview with Brigade Commander 86th Infantry Brigade. The latter agreed to support any counter-attack of the Brigade but considered his troops too tired and his units too weak to take part in the counter-attack itself.
The arrangements for counter-attack were given verbally to a Staff Officer of the Division and confirmed in writing (B.M.16)

2.25 p.m. — Orders for relief by 1st Cav. Divn. received.

5.0 p.m. — Report received that large numbers of enemy were moving towards right flank of Poona Horse from direction of

3

VILLERS GUISLAIN. At this juncture telephone communication with front line was interrupted by shell fire. Connection however was maintained by lamps and runner. The enemy advance was brought to a halt by rifle and Hotchkiss fire before it had really developed. A party of about 10 enemy succeeded in getting into the wood of whom only two succeeded in getting back.

6.30 pm All quiet reported to Division.
After the failure of the counter-attack our positions around GAUCHE WOOD were heavily shelled.

8.0 pm Relief by 1st Cavalry Division commenced and command passed at 12 midnight. One section of 13th M.G. Sqdn remained in reserve to 1st Cav Divn till 12 noon 3rd

12 midnight Brigade Hd Qrs moved to HEUDECOURT SUCREVIE.

A Gregory
Br. Genl.
4th Dec' 1917. Comdg Sec'bad Cav. Bde.

Army Form C. 2118.

H.Qrs. 7th Cav. Bde.

WAR DIARY
or
INTELLIGENCE SUMMARY.

(Erase heading not required.)

December 1917.

Instructions regarding War Diaries and Intelligence Summaries are contained in F. S. Regs., Part II. and the Staff Manual respectively. Title pages will be prepared in manuscript.

Places	Date	Hour	Summary of Events and Information	Remarks and references to Appendices
Village S. of HEUDECOURT	1.XII.17	1.A.M.	The Brigade marched from GOUZEAUCOURT to valley 1000 S.E. of HEUDECOURT	
		9.30am	7 Dragoon Guards were placed at disposal of G.O.C. 178th Inf. Bde.	
		A.M.	Orders received to be prepared to relieve Cheshire Cav Bde in GAUCHE WOOD (S.of N. of VILLERS GUISLAIN.	
		7.P.M.	The Bde (6th & 7th D.Guards, marched to relieve Cheshire Cav Bde. (7th DGuards see Appendix H attached to War Diary for November 1917)	
	2.XII.17	9.P.M.	The Brigade less village were relieved in the line by the 1st Cavalry Division and marched back to HEUDECOURT.	
SOREL-LE-GRAND.	3.xii.17	11.30 am	Brigade marched to bivouac 1 mile S.W. of SORELECOURT and remained in state of readiness below by day and 1 hour by night.	
	6.XII.17		State of readiness changed to 1 hour's notice only	
	8.xii.17		Brigade marched to bivouac at COURCELLES and 32nd Route Lignes-Bivouacs at TINCOURT. Orders for COURCELLES being unavoidable, but the Route March and XIV Divnal Stores had to continue. The march was practice to bivouac. DEVISE marching via MONS EN CHAUSSEE.	

A.5834. Wt. W4973/M687. 750,000 8/16 D. D. & L. Ltd. Forms/C.2118/13.

Army Form C. 2118.

WAR DIARY or INTELLIGENCE SUMMARY.

(Erase heading not required.)

Place	Date	Hour	Summary of Events and Information	Remarks and references to Appendices
SE DENISE	9.xii.17		Reconnaissance of the 2nd line North and East of Fremicourt was carried on to cover of the Brigade being made to act mounted in reply to a threat of enemy attack.	
	10.xii.17	6.30 AM – 8 AM	The Brigade in position. Horses had not access to water to be kept.	
TREFCON	7.xii.17		Brigade marched to permanent winter quarters at TREFCON. Horses of squadrons to mine at Thorin where were billeted.	
	18.xii.17		Brigade Head Quarters Horses billeted to mine in Hamlet of MERS near Roupy. H.Q. 2nd line from R. OMIGNON to a point E. of VENDELLES. (R 2 x 07)	Wire 5.2.2.52
	20.xii.17		For long see to park in ak or time to three brew for months.	

J. Gregory, Brig General
Commanding 5th Cav. Bde.

Army Form C. 2118.

119

WAR DIARY ~~or~~ **INTELLIGENCE SUMMARY.**

H.Q. M. Seumaaban Cavalry Brigade

January 1918. *(Erase heading not required.)*

Place	Date	Hour	Summary of Events and Information	Remarks and references to Appendices
TREFCON	1/1/18 to 7.1.18		Brigade remained at TREFCON as mobile Reserve on 1 hour notice.	1/16000 ST QUENTIN 1/40000 63c
	7.1.18 to 24.1.18		Brigade found working parties daily	
	25.1.18		Dismounted Col Brigade relieved 2nd Mounted Bde as Reserve Bde to "7" Sect.	
			H.Q. Squadron — VADENCOURT	
			7/9 Lancers — LE VERGUIER	
			34th Hors — VADENCOURT	
			20 Huss — " "	
	26.1.18		Relief completed 7am.	
	27.1.18		Quiet day, nothing to report.	
	28.1.18		" " " "	
	29.1.18		" " " "	
	30.1.18		" " " "	
	31.1.18		" " " "	

J Mitchell Capt
for G.S.O.
Secunderabad Cavalry Brigade

Confidential

War Diary

Sec'ond Cavalry Brigade

1st to 28th Feby 1916.

Army Form C. 2118.

WAR DIARY
2nd Indian Cavalry Brigade
INTELLIGENCE SUMMARY.

(Erase heading not required.)

Instructions regarding War Diaries and Intelligence Summaries are contained in F. S. Regs., Part II. and the Staff Manual respectively. Title pages will be prepared in manuscript.

Place	Date	Hour	Summary of Events and Information	Remarks and references to Appendices
TRÉFCON	1st		2nd Indian Cav. Bde. and Divisional Bde. marched from TRÉFCON area to GUIVRYCOURT area and arrived at 8 P.M.	
	2nd		The march continued at 9 A.M. and the Brigade arrived in the new area as under at 3.40 P.M. Bde Hq. BELLOY SUR SOMME. Hq. 7 Dragoon Guards. Mr. ST. SAUVEUR - LA CHAUSSEE - TILLOY - ARGOEUVRES Poona Horse. HAVERNAS - MIRAUMES - NAOURS. XX Deccan Horse. ST. OUEN - BETHENCOURT - BERTRANCOURT les DAMES. 13 M.G. Sqdn. FLESSELLES.	
BELLOY-SUR-SOMME	3rd – 8th		Nothing to report	
	9th		Definite orders received that the following units would proceed overseas:— Indian Cav. Bde. Staff. Poona Horse. XX Deccan Horse. 13 Machine Gun Sqdn. Indian Cav. Field Ambulance. Indian M.V. Section.	
	12th		Orders received that 14 Machine Gun Sqdn. would accompany Brigade overseas.	

Army Form C. 2118.

WAR DIARY of Sialkot Cavalry Brigade
INTELLIGENCE SUMMARY.
(Erase heading not required.)

Instructions regarding War Diaries and Intelligence Summaries are contained in F. S. Regs., Part II. and the Staff Manual respectively. Title pages will be prepared in manuscript.

Place	Date	Hour	Summary of Events and Information	Remarks and references to Appendices
BELLAH June Summer	12.		and that the 13th Hussars have light wheel be borrowed H.P.	
	13.		Clipping of all animals and underclothing with material to bring repaired forwarded work.	
	14.		Orders received that draught horses showed be transferred between the Divisions for draught mules.	
	16.		Stated Divisional Brigade repairs, and arrived to pickets at 7.30 p.m.	
	18.		Instructions received that British and Italian units have prisons as our Resourcements Part VII As and Part XVII respectively also 10½ annual of all classes.	
	21.		Transfers of draught animals completed also native woodwork.	
	22nd	3 P.M.	Inspection of units preceding moves by Major General Sir C.T. McM. KNANAGH. K.C.B. CVO. DSO. Chief Cavalry Corps.	
			Indian RHA. drawn returned to the Base for duty with BAC's.	
	23.		No further alarms today, detail as under, concerted by Major IFA HILDSARMD Pura Horse entrained at Saidux at 4 P.M. for Toranto	
			6 B.O.s. 10 I.O.s and 100 O.R.s	

Army Form C. 2118.

Sialkot Cavalry Brigade

WAR DIARY or INTELLIGENCE SUMMARY.
(Erase heading not required.)

Place	Date	Hour	Summary of Events and Information	Remarks and references to Appendices
BELLOY EN SANTERRE	24th		The 2nd advanced party, start at noon, arrived at SAILLEUX at 11 P.M. for TARANTO.	
	25 & 26		7. B.O.J. — 5. I.D.V. — 2. O.R.B. — 15. G.R.I. Sick and unsuitable horses were evacuated and remounts have taken over from the units in the Division to make up units full establishment. All units skill defence of gun as is being strongly established plus 15%. Both regiments fully established for 8 advanced party to proceed.	
	27th		Crews received and subsequently drilled on 28th.	
	28th		10 A.M. units for Brigade march independently to new billets on arrival to Brigade Grand and Battalion Granges. There will be billets of: AMBALA CAVALRY BRIGADE. Units will established as under at 2 P.M. BDE. H.Q. CREUSE. Portecture. PISSY — SEUX — ROUVRELLES. XX Dragoon Horse. SAINS en AMIÉNOIS — COTTENCHY — RÉMIENCOURT — GUIGNEMICOURT 1st Dragoon Guards. LONGPRÉ 18th Machine Gun Squadron. COCQUEREL	

Kirinmore Capt.
for O.C.
Secundrabad... Brig.

Army Form C. 2118.

Staff Bangalore Bde

March 1915

WAR DIARY
or
INTELLIGENCE SUMMARY.
(Erase heading not required.)

Place	Date	Hour	Summary of Events and Information	Remarks and references to Appendices
CREUSE	1st		The 3rd Advanced Party arrived at Marseilles & onward to Major C. TARNIS, M.C. entrained at SALEUX at 1 P.M. and 6 P.M. for TARNIS at 6 P.M. Detail A. B.O.I. 8. I.O.1. 9. K.B. 22. S.R.I. XX Decan Horse Mule & Bhels Mass rations as under — PROVEL. NEUVILLE. SUS LEVILLY. NAMPY. PLACHY BUYON.	
	2nd – 6th		Nothing to report.	
	7th		Units now completed Establishment of animals with auto from the 8th Inance.	
	8th		Approx. 2 squadrons Poona Horse and all Bangalore transport less horse cart entrained at SALEUX for MARSEILLES. Train left at 10 A.M., 12.30 P.M. and 2.30 P.M.	
	19th		Bangalore, remainder of Poona Horse and 3 sqdns. XX Decan Horse entrained at SALEUX for Marseilles.	
	25th		Remainder of XX Decan Horse, Apex Troop and M.V. Section entrained at SALEUX for MARSEILLES.	
	21st & 22nd		Poona Horse and XX Decan Horse, Bangalore, Signal troop and M.V. Section arrived MARSEILLES.	
	30th		Embarkation on HT. MENOMINEE and PANCRAS complete. Ships remained at anchor to 31st inst.	

Army Form C. 2118.

WAR DIARY or INTELLIGENCE SUMMARY.

(Erase heading not required.)

Instructions regarding War Diaries and Intelligence Summaries are contained in F.S. Regs., Part II. and the Staff Manual respectively. Title pages will be prepared in manuscript.

Place	Date	Hour	Summary of Events and Information	Remarks and references to Appendices
AT SEA.	April 1st		H.T. MENOMINEE and PANCRAS sailed from MARSEILLES.	
	5 & 6		arrive MALTA. Owing to engine trouble the "MENOMINEE" was delayed and animals were consequently transferred to CAMP RICASOLI. H.T. PANCRAS sailed on 6th for ALEXANDRIA.	
	10		H.T. PANCRAS arrived ALEXANDRIA.	
	11		H.T. MENOMINEE moved from MALTA and arrived ALEXANDRIA on 15th inst.	
TEL EL KEBIR.	11 - 16		Unit arrived at TEL EL KEBIR and camped at N.N.W. corner of Re-camp.	
EGYPT.	20		Orders received for the POONA HORSE and xx Deccan Horse to proceed to join the 7th Mounted Brigade at BELAH. (PALESTINE).	
	22		POONA HORSE and xx Deccan Horse marched to KANTARA, leaving at QASSASSIN at night 22/23, ISMAILIAH at night 23/24, EL FERDAN at night 24/25 and arrive KANTARA on 25th inst.	
	26		Jebad. C.T.A and M.V. Jethu arrive TEL EL KEBIR. POONA HORSE entrained for BELAH, and arrived on 26th inst.	
	27		xx Deccan Horse — — — — — — — — — — — — 27th inst.	
	28 & 29		Jebad. C.T.A and M.V. Jethu marched to KANTARA.	
	30		The break up of the Secunderabad. Cav. Bde. was complete.	

1917-1918
5TH CAVALRY DIVISION
SECUNDERABAD CAV. BDE

'N' BATTERY R.H.A.
JAN 1917-FEB 1918.

Army Form C2118.

WAR DIARY
INTELLIGENCE SUMMARY N Battery R.H.A.

JAN 1917

Place	Date	Hour	Summary of Events and Information	Remarks and references to Appendices
BEAUCHAMPS	1st to 31st		In the field. Orders received to re- Arm E.A. Batteries attached E.169th Sheet in Same Sheets	

INTELLIGENCE SUMMARY   FEB 1/17

Place	Date	Hour	Summary	Remarks
BEAUCAMPS			Do not think Battery Groups Reserve Battery was firing. Gun arrivals. No. 1 + 2 L.G. Vaughan E.X Battery. No. 11 B.9 received from reserve with men. 2/Lt. G.W. Towell posted to the Battery 26/1/17 from A.170 R.F.A. went to R.H.A. School, Lerdy Capt. 26/1/17. Temp. Captn. F.S. Aarons promoted to Capt 4/1/17 & stood a time in Reserve Artillery School	

J. B. ——
Maj. Adj. A
Coy. N. Battery. R.H.A.

"N" Battery R.H.A. WAR DIARY or INTELLIGENCE SUMMARY

March 1917.

Army Form C. 2118.

Place	Date	Hour	Summary of Events and Information	Remarks and references to Appendices
BEAUCHAMP	19th & 20th	mid day	Marched to VILLERS:- wasted oc 17 AM CHA	A99/607 A99/607
VILLEROY	20.	8.30 am	Marched to ST AUBIN.	
ST AUBIN	21.	–	Marched to TACNIL. water supply Ex: hrs Rv: Rv.	
TACNIL	22.	–	Marched to LE HAMEL.	
LE HAMEL	23.	–	Rested at LONGUEAU. (horses & men not on train)	
LE HAMEL	24.	?	Marched to a bivouac near TROIE.	
BIVOUAC (near TROIE)	25.	–	Rested. Reconnaissance to O.M.Rs. to TREMONT horses.	
do	26.	7am	Marched to ALBECOURT & HARRT. to CATTEAU & WEST ENCAMPMT. Battery came into action just to S. of NURLU at A & S.D.A. north of Avelun. At 9pm. fired 390 rounds at SOREL on PRUD'COURT. Pulling into a forward camp with casualties in the Pickets of VILLEROY + VILLER FAUCAN - MEZNIERES to MALLE. At 3am. 27th (on Canada) for very heavy shelling of known hostile works & Railways)	
HALLE	27.	–		

WAR DIARY
INTELLIGENCE SUMMARY

March 1914

Place	Date	Hour	Summary of Events and Information	Remarks
ARRAS	28th	3 pm	Marched to ARRAS from CLERY.	
CLERY	29th	3 pm	Marched to ARRAS via HEM.	
HEM	30th	11.30 am	Marched to HEM via BRAY-VILLERS.	
NESLE	31.			
	12		MAJOR T.V. FRENCH R.H.A. relinquished command of the 2nd R.H.A. Battery	
	14?		MAJOR E. LT. SPEARER SMITH took on command of "N" Battery	
			R.H.A. on 14th March 1917. Leaving from the Artillery ?	
			41 Sn. Div.	

M.Spencer Smith — Major R.H.A.
N. R.H.A.

Serial No. 22.

Confidential

War Diary

"N" Battery R.H.A

From 1st April 1917
To 30th April 1917

Army Form C. 2118

"N" Battery
R.H.A.

WAR DIARY
or
INTELLIGENCE SUMMARY
(Erase heading not required.)

Instructions regarding War Diaries and Intelligence Summaries are contained in F. S. Regs., Part II. and the Staff Manual respectively. Title Pages will be prepared in manuscript.

Place	Date	Hour	Summary of Events and Information	Remarks and references to Appendices
BAYONVILLERS	1st to 13th	—	Rested at BAYONVILLERS. Ordinary Routine Work	
-do-	14th	—	Marched under C.O.C. See'bd Cav Bde to the vicinity of TREFCON and Bivouaced	
	15th	—	Marched 1 mile east to bivouacs	
Near TREFCON	16th to 30th	—	Rested. Ordinary Routine work & Officers Reconnaissances Dull Orders & Brigade Field days & training in all technical instruments, Signalling etc.	

M.A. Pomeroy Collin

Army Form C.
WAR DIARY
or
INTELLIGENCE SUMMARY

"N" Battery R.H.A. May 1914

A/99/18/3

Instructions regarding War Diaries and Intelligence Summaries are contained in F.S. Regs., Part II. and the Staff Manual respectively. Title Pages will be prepared in manuscript.

(Erase heading not required.)

Place	Date	Hour	Summary of Events and Information	Remarks and references to Appendices
TREFCON	1st		Rested my Battery near TREFCON (Colony having not left TREFCON) orders still pending with ---- and training in all technical movements	
	5th		There were visits of T.H.A. 5 + 6 Bgs Dum is bivouacs	
HAMELET	8th		on it	
	9th		Rested my Battery to be reviewed by C.O.C. III Corps	
			to go into firing L.O. + Subaltern reconnoitred position	
	10th	11am	Orders received to form Section & our Bn at once near TREFCON Battery marched into bivouacs near TREFCON	
TREFCON	11th		Rested near TREFCON	
		9pm	One section went into action on to the right of Railway B/75 R.H.A. Remainder of Battery in this section	
	27/5 3.15am	Bayonets for 30 mins to assist Infantry to make a raid on enemy's lines which proved successful. Rounds expended from mid-night-mid-night 1200.	

M. Ottmeadwith
Major R.H.A
Cmg "N" Battn. R.H.A

INTELLIGENCE SUMMARY

(Erase heading not required.)

Place	Date	Hour	Summary of Events and Information	Remarks and references to Appendices
Lecluse	5/6	—	In action near La Bergere & the 3rd & 5th the battery in action was fairly heavy, but only 2 men wounded. Single wounds.	a.4.
	12	—	Any gun detachment was sent to a forward position for the purpose of trying many angles and trajectories during the night and experimentally changing the mouth of the dial sight occasionally to enable the men to rest.	
	18.19.20.21	—	The battery bombarded enemy front line to assist the Canadians (Div. Pet.) to extend its trenches, which proved very successful.	
			During the month dug outs were made & gun pits were improved. The total ammunition expended during the month was 4,335 rounds.	

M.G.Greenhill
Major RHA
O.C. "N" Bat, RHA

Army Form C. 2118.

WAR DIARY
or
INTELLIGENCE SUMMARY

(Erase heading not required.)

Instructions regarding War Diaries and Intelligence Summaries are contained in F. S. Regs., Part II. and the Staff Manual respectively. Title Pages will be prepared in manuscript.

"C" N Battery R.H.A.   July 1917

Place	Date	Hour	Summary of Events and Information	Remarks and references to Appendices
Ferquier	1st	—	In action near Le Ferquier	Q47
"	4th	11:45	Bombarded enemys front line for 15 minutes to support Sec'n Can Car Bde to make a raid. This small raid was successful	
"	8th	11:45	Bombarded enemys front line to assist Canadian Car Bde to raid enemys positions. This raid was most successful. Over 30 O.P.'s, machine gun emplacements and dugouts dealt with. Battery was thanked & complimented for support given by C.O.C. Can. Cav. Bde.	
"	10th	10:30pm	One Section was relieved by V Battery R.H.A. Also a section of C.295 Bdy. R.H.A. took over our guns, whilst we relieved V Battery	
"	11th	10:30pm	Remainder of Battery relieved by W Bty R.H.A. and C.295 Bdy R.H.A. Rounds expended from 1st to 11th 2845	
	13th	—	Rested in bivouacs till 15th	
	15th	—	Battery proceeded under orders of C.R.H.A. 3rd Cav. Divn. to Cappy & rested for the night	
	16th	—	Marched from Cappy to Domart	
	17th	—	Marched from Domart to Amplier	
	18th	—	Marched from Amplier to Willeroval in the vicinity of St Pol and rested for the day.	
St Pol.	19th	—		

WAR DIARY

"N" Battery R.H.A.

July 1917 (continued)

A.A.Q.

Army Form C. 2118.

INTELLIGENCE SUMMARY

Place	Date	Hour	Summary of Events and Information	Remarks and references to Appendices
Savincourt	21st-26th		Marched from bivouacs near St. Pol to a small village called Savincourt. Billets at Savincourt till 26th. Ordinary routine work and training of all Specialists.	
	27th	11:00am	Came under orders of I.C.R.H.A. and marched to Gouvaix Legal and relied for the night.	
	28th	8:0am / 10:15	Marched from Gouvaix Legal to Bully - bivouaced awaiting orders to be used by G.O.C. 2nd Canadian Divisional Artillery to go into action. Went into action near Givin and came under orders of O.C. 5th Cdn. Field Artillery Bde.	
Givin	29th		Registered all targets on enemy's front and support gun-positions. Registered more targets & took part in a small preliminary bombardment on enemy front line.	
	30th		Remained quiet all day.	
	31st		Total number of rounds expended from 29th to 31st 646	

Wellesmith
MAJOR R.H.A.
Commanding N. Battery R.H.A.

Army Form C. 2118

"N" Battery R.H.A. WAR DIARY August 1917

INTELLIGENCE SUMMARY
(Erase heading not required.)

Place	Date	Hour	Summary of Events and Information	Remarks reference Appx
LIEVIN	1st		In action was been attached to II Canadian Division	
"	2nd		Received a letter from G.O.C. III Corps stating that the area from which the 3 how. Gun was worked was the best defence works that he had seen and congratulates all ranks of the division with holding that front.	
"	4th	3.45	Bombarded enemy's defence for raid to assist 11th Canadian Inf. Bde to raid enemy's trenches, this attack proved successful	
"	8th		Gen H.F. Mercer C.B. M.G.R.A. 1st Army visited N Battery R.H.A. Brig-Gen Gregory C.O.C. 2nd Ind H.A. Bde visited Battery R.H.A	
"	15th		Attack on German French system to N. of LENS by Canadian Corps all objectives on German line gained by 11 am. 1st Canadian Div were heavily counter-attacked but in all places our men held their ground enemy losses were severe. In immense amount of ammunition was brought up during the night 15/16	
"	16th		Enemy gun counter-attacked without success the withdrawal of N & X Batteries from action with Canadians unfruitfully performed	

Army Form...

"N" Battery R.H.A. WAR DIARY Aug 1914

INTELLIGENCE SUMMARY. (continued)

(Erase heading not required.)

Place	Date	Hour	Summary of Events and Information	Remarks reference Appendices
NERY	18	—	Orders received for "N" & "X" Batteries to be transferred to H.Q. 1st Cav. Div. Arty. remaining on present positions to form a group with 463rd & 365 R.F.A. To be commanded by Major E.M. SPENCER-SMITH D.S.O. R.H.A. to be known as SPENCER-SMITH'S GROUP. 2nd Lt BOND [?] i/c armrs of 2 nd [?] FENTON R.H.A.	9.50
	1		We attacked ALOOF + CINNABAR trenches, "N" Battery covering the 30th Battn Bom Inf. 2nd Lt F.A. MITCHELL R.H.A. represented the group as Liaison Officer with The Battalion. Very heavy shelling the straggle for ALOOF trench going on all day at B-40 pm Bhurte [?] were having been reported Lt Col ALOOF trench was full of Germans "N" Battery were ordered to fire + the most intense fire was directed on it for about 15 minutes. When the trench was taken on 23rd inst. it was found to be choked with German dead. A message of congratulation on this shooting was received from the Canadian Divn on our left & from our own Infantry & from S.O.S. + intense burst of fire were	

Army Form C. 2118

"N" Battery R.H.A.

WAR DIARY
or
INTELLIGENCE SUMMARY.
(Erase heading not required.)

Aug 1914 (Continued)

Place	Date	Hour	Summary of Events and Information	Remarks references to Appendices
NERY	31	—	Called but during the night	a 51
		—	Capt. MITCHELL was dead with great sorrow during all this time. His actions heard most splendidly commented upon by Commanders. It was recommended for a Military Cross.
	23		Attack on AlOOF trench was successful. Firing all these days the supply of ammunition was most difficult. As many as 500 rounds of wagons being sent up nightly to the Batteries. Ammunition returned to the dumps he did did not use due to the defending of
	24		GREEN GRASSIER was captured but lost again. From now onward the Artillery had constant calls for S.O.S., fired many rounds during the night harassing the enemy's approaches.
	25		During the night there were many occasions on which gas rockets went up on account of the premature of gas shells

WAR DIARY

N Battery R.H.A.   Aug 1914 (continued)

INTELLIGENCE SUMMARY

Place	Date	Hour	Summary of Events and Information	Remarks
MEIN	30th	—	"N" Battery was heavily shelled. During the month the Battery fired 15, 160 rounds. The undermentioned had the honour to receive the Military Medal. Bdr OAKLEY J, J McDonnell, Gr Conway J, Lineman, Dr WALLACE H. The O.P. situated in the BOIS-de-FIANMENT was constantly shelled. It had very little cover. The devotion to duty shown by the Battalion officers, telephonists & linemen was beyond all praise.	452

Gus Alexander
MAJOR R.H.A.
Commanding N Battery R.H.A.

"N" Battery R.H.A. WAR DIARY. September 1914

Army Form C. 2118.

INTELLIGENCE SUMMARY.
(Erase heading not required.)

Place	Date	Hour	Summary of Events and Information	Remarks and references to Appendices
LEVIN	1st	—	In action under 1st Canadian Divl Arty & 1st SPENCER-SMITH'S Group. One gun was moved forward to a specially prepared position for the purpose of enfilading the battery was engaged in harassing the enemy's approaches especially at night.	463
	8th	10:30 am	The battery was relieved by 60th Bty C.F.A. & went to wagon lines between AIX-NOULETTE - BULLY - GRENAY.	
	9th	—	" did " above	
	9th	—	Marched under C.T.H.A. to Bois Dum to OURTON.	
	9th	—	Marched to HESTRUS coming under C.O.C. T.H.A.	
	10th	—	The G.O.C. See had Bois Bde was Bde useful battery — went round horse lines. he expressed himself as being pleased with the condition of the horses.	
	13th	—	The horses of the battery were inspected by Maj-Gen MacANDREW bonds st Bois Drin. The G.O.C. T.H.A. the D.A.A.G. comments the G.O.C. Divn & G.O.C. T.H.A. both complimented the B.C. on the condition turnout of	

"N" Battery R.H.A. WAR DIARY September 1914 (continued)

WAR DIARY or INTELLIGENCE SUMMARY

Place	Date	Hour	Summary of Events and Information	Remarks references to Appendices
HESTRUS	13		Forces & appearance of the men etc. It was disappointing that it appeared to be a cold & showery afternoon, which rather spoilt the turn out.	954
	14		Divis: remainder of month being rested, work consisting of training of signallers, telephonists, learning & overhauling all ranges & equipment etc.	
	15		The following appeared in Divnl. Orders 10.16.16 dt- 26-9-14. The G.O.C. has much pleasure in publishing the following extract of the good work done by 4th Bde R.H.A. while	
	30		attached to the Canadian Forces during the recent operations :— The G.O.C. II Canadian Division wishes to express to Major 15th Bde 15th Bde R.H.A. & the Batteries R.H.A. etc his appreciation & thanks for the work of his division for the magnificent support which was given them throughout the recent operations. The obstinate nature of the fighting & the repeated German counter-attacks called for the	

A.(850) W. W.Co.Lid.39gs. 50000. 4/17 Sch. 8a. Forms/C.2111/14.

"N" Battery R.H.A. WAR DIARY Sept 1914 (continued)

Army Form C. 2118

Instructions regarding War Diaries and Intelligence Summaries are contained in F.S. Regs., Part II. and the Staff Manual respectively. Title pages will be prepared in manuscript.

INTELLIGENCE SUMMARY. (Erase heading not required.)

Place	Date	Hour	Summary of Events and Information	Remarks references to Appendices

HESTRUS

the greatest efforts on the part of the Artillery, the successes gained were largely due to the splendid way in which N + X Batteries R.H.A. bombed to eveny call of their excellent shooting particularly when the detachments were exhausted by long hours of continuous firing.

R.H.A. had the honour of being mentioned in the Canadian Corps Orders in connection with the work done by them while the battery was attached to the Canadian Corps.

26 - 1 Dr. 13-9-14 Left Letters R.H. Canadian Corps 16.30 / done especially good work during recent operations: -

Major C. M. SPENCER-SMITH D.S.O. R.H.A.

Lieut F. A. MITCHELL R.H.A

Dec 14-9-14.

Major C. M. SPENCER-SMITH D.S.O. R.H.A.

3894 Br. DOBBS H.

N Battery R.H.A. Sept 1914

WAR DIARY

INTELLIGENCE SUMMARY. (continued)

Army Form C. 21

Place	Date	Hour	Summary of Events and Information	Remarks references to Appendices
HESTRUS			Added to this, complimentary letters were received from the G.O.C. Commander Canadian Corps & from the C.R.A. 1 Canadian Divisional Artillery	95f

M Alexander
Major. R.H.A.
Commanding N Battery R.H.A.

N Battery R.H.A. WAR DIARY October 1914.

Army Form C. 2118
E/99/3372

Place	Date	Hour	Summary of Events and Information	Remarks references to Appendices
HESTRUS	1st		In billets at HESTRUS	467
-do-	2nd		Brig-General C. GREGORY. C.O.C. Sec'nd Cav Bde inspected battery and stated that it was very pleased indeed with turn out of both men & horses	
-do-	3rd		Brig-Gen J. SELIGMAN D.S.O. R.H.A. G.O.C. R.H.A. Cav. Corps inspected the battery	
-do-	4th		Ordinary Routine work, consisting of Drill Orders & Training of all Specialists	
-do-	5th		Marched to NEUFPRÉ met G.O.C. Brigade en Rte	
-do-	6th		Marched to WATOU and received warning orders to go into action during the night. the weather was very wet and cold	
WATOU	7th		Marched from WATOU to RENESCURE & billeted in the night	
-"-	8th		Marched from RENESCURE to BOUT DE LA VILLE Yr battery was inspected on the line of march by Maj Gen H.A. MACANDREW D.S.O. 5th Cav. Div. and was complimented on the turn out and condition of the horses	

Army Form C.

"N" Battery R.H.A. **WAR DIARY** October 1914.

Instructions regarding War Diaries and Intelligence Summaries are contained in F. S. Regs., Part II. and the Staff Manual respectively. Title pages will be prepared in manuscript.

(Erase heading not required.)

Place	Date	Hour	Summary of Events and Information	Remarks references to Appendices
BOUT DE LA VILLE	19		Marched from Bout-de-la-Ville to FRUGES	95
	20		Billets at FRUGES. Ordinary Routine work, consisting of Stable Duties, Billet Parades, Gun Drill & cleaning of all Scurra Bits	
	22		Brig Gen C. GREGORY G.O.C. Second Cav Bde inspected all the mules in Stables, and the horses in Stables, he informed himself himself with the condition of the horses	

Milfoenewith
MAJOR R.H.A.
Commanding "N" Battery R.H.A.

Army Form C. 2118

WAR DIARY
INTELLIGENCE SUMMARY

November 1914

Place	Date	Hour	Summary of Events and Information	Remarks
FRISES	1st 2nd 3rd		On Lines at Frises G.O.C. See had Car fetched — wrote letter to the Gen'l that he was officer offg Car Pour that...	
	5th		O.C. H.A. officer ...	
	8th		Capt. F.G. ANDERSON, R.H.A. was ordered to St Paul only and Capt. G.A. FENTON R.H.A. was ordered to ... in command of Battery by authority of G.O.C. R.H.A. Cavalry Corps	
	9th	9.30am	Marched under orders of G.O.C. See had Bns Bde to MOHEN-LE-PETITE — rested for the night.	
	10th	8.30am	Marched from MOHEN-LE-PETITE to PONT-NOYELLES.	
	11th	9.00am	Marched from PONT-NOYELLES to LA NEUVILLE-LEZERY.	
		3.00pm	Marched from LA NEUVILLE to BUSLE	
BUSLE	12th .. 19th 20th	MID-NIGHT 12-noon	Rested at BUSLE awaiting orders to be received by G.O.C. VII Corps to whom ... attached Marched from Buscle to Bois DEBATT near FINS Marched forward through VILLERS-PLOUCH to MARCOING ... that morning ... unable to advance ...	

N. Batty. R.H.A. WAR DIARY November 1914.

Army Form C. 21

Instructions regarding War Diaries and Intelligence Summaries are contained in F. S. Regs., Part II. and the Staff Manual respectively. Title pages will be prepared in manuscript.

INTELLIGENCE SUMMARY.
(Erase heading not required.)

Place	Date	Hour	Summary of Events and Information	Remarks references to Appendices
near MARCOING	20		Arrived at 2 a.m. and started at 11am for Gonnelieu	760
	22		Travelled from MARCOING to ENS and billeted for the night	
LA NEUVILLE	23		Marched from ENS to LA-NEUVILLE and billeted for the night	
TREFCON	24		Marched from LA-NEUVILLE to TREFCON + rested till 30—	
	30	10am	Orders received from 5th Cav. Bde. to entrain and march at once to join Gough's column near VILLERS GUISLAIN and co-operate with 9th Division. Marched via in motor cars to railway station just south of TEVELON. Marched to billets and entrained. No Casualties	

Ja Morris South
MAJOR R.H.A.
Commanding N Battery R.H.A.

WAR DIARY

"N" Battery R.H.A.

December 1914

Place	Date	Hour	Summary of Events and Information	Remarks and references to Appendices
MAZE? RUBEMPRÉ	6th	4.30am	Moved into action near VAUCELETTE FARM. Subjecting infantry and Dismounted cavalry who was holding same position until	
	7th	8.0am	Remainder of day. Captain G.A. FENTON T.H.A. wounded & England & overseas Artillery Course. 2 Lieut. W.ILL drew in from action and wounded to hospital near SAULCOURT.	
SAULCOURT	8th	4.30pm	Retired to SAULCOURT & during the day received orders to go into action on the 8th	
	9th		Moved into action, but section remaining in action took command to CARPENTER'S WOOD in the 2nd Lieut. V. BRAMMEL was sent to Division from H.Q. 14th Brigade T.H.A. 1st section retired from the position as ordered	
	10th		2nd Lieut. G.M. SPENCER-SMITH D.S.O. R.H.A. took over temporary command of the Battery on the 10th was attached to the Cavalry Corps for duty.	
	25th		Command of the Battery taken on Lieut. G.W. YOWELL M.C. T.H.A. Total number of rounds expended during month 1,342.	

[signature]
LIEUT. R.H.A.
Commdg "N" Battery R.H.A.

WAR DIARY / INTELLIGENCE SUMMARY

Army Form C. 2118.

N Battery R.H.A.   January 1918

Place	Date	Hour	Summary of Events and Information	Remarks and references to Appendices
T/C 1.3	1		1. Section in action in CAUBRIETIS WOOD & the remaining 5 sections above will further report. By Sec. lots c. 1. 40,000	A27
	2		Nothing to report	
	3		Captain G.A. FENTON R.H.A. joined from Overseas Artillery Course & took over command of the Battery.	
	4		Nothing to report.	
	5		During the night fired at intervals	
	6		Lieut. E.A. MITCHELL R.H.A. proceeded on leave to the United Kingdom.	
	7		Nothing to report	
	8		Lieut. V.B. CAMMEL R.H.A. joined from leave in the United Kingdom.	
	9		Nothing to report	
	10		Major G.M. SPENCER-SMITH D.S.O. R.H.A. proceeded on leave to the United Kingdom (on leave) Lieut. R.H. LLOYD R.F.A. was attached to R.H.A. by authy of A.G. G.H.Q. ¶ A.G. 382/14 ¶ dt. 10.1.18	
	11		Nothing to report	
	12		2/Lt. T.H.C. MILLARD R.F.A. (Sanby atd. to Battery) joined from Hall Rd. R.F.A. & Lt. R.H. LOYD R.H.A. proceeded in R.H.A. Brigade at Cav. Corps.	
	13		Nothing to report	
	14		2/Lt. J.B. SMITH R.F.A. proceeded on Equitation Courses at Cav. Corps	

(2449) Wt. W.4957/M90 750,000 1/16 J.B.C. & A. Form/C.2118/12.

Army Form C. 2118.

"N" Battery R.H.A. WAR DIARY January 1918

INTELLIGENCE SUMMARY.
(Erase heading not required.)

Ref. Sheet 62 C, 1:40,000

Place	Date	Hour	Summary of Events and Information	Remarks and references to Appendices
962	30		Lieut. V.B. CAMMEL temporarily attached to Head Quarters C.V.B. Brigade R.H.A.	
	31		Lieut. E.A. MITCHELL R.H.A. rejoined from leave to the United Kingdom	
			Total number of rounds expended during month 394	

C. Bruce
Captain R.H.A.
Commanding "N" Battery R.H.A.

"N" Battery R.H.A. WAR DIARY

February 1918

Ref Sheet 62c 1/40,000

Place	Date	Hour	Summary of Events and Information
R.q.C.15	1st		In action, one section in CAUBRIES WOOD & the remaining sections about a mile back.
	2nd		Nothing to report
	3rd		Lieut G.W.PYE R.F.A. rejoined 1st R.H.A. Bde Ammn Column
	4th		Nothing to report
	5th		
	6th		
	7th		Lieut R.L.LLOYD R.H.A. rejoined from R.H.A. Course at Cavalry Corps
	8th		Nothing to report
	9th		
	10th		
	11th		
	12th		
	13th	1.15am	Two enterprises were carried out (a) Main raid by Royal Canadian Dragoons near BUISSAIN-GAULAINE FARM (G.21.c.) Subsidiary by 18th (K.G.O.) Lancers on trenches near ST HELENE. The howitzer sections took part in Bde barrage in connection with these operations – some 100 rounds on LING VALLEY (G.24.a) Both raids were entirely successful – tribute was paid by the raiding parties to the accuracy & effect of the artillery
	14th		Nothing to report
	15th		Major G.M. SPENCER-SMITH D.S.O. R.H.A. returned from leave & Overseas Artillery Course. "U" Battery section was relieved by a section of "U" Battery R.H.A.
TREFCON	16th		Remaining 3 sections were relieved by "U" Battery R.H.A. and marched to wagon line
	17th		
	18th		Lieut V.B. CAMMEL R.H.A. rejoined from H.Q. 14th Brigade R.H.A.
	19th		
	20th		
	21st		
	22nd		
	23rd		Ordinary routine were consisting of training of young gunners in laying a sight setting
	24th		
	25th		Lieut G.W. TOWELL R.H.A. rejoined from leave
	26th		
	27th		
	28th		

[signature]
MAJOR R.H.A.
Commanding "N" Battery R.H.A.

1917-1918
5TH CAVALRY DIVISION
SECUNDERABAD CAV. BDE

7TH DRAGOON GUARDS
JAN 1917-FEB 1918.

SERIAL NO. 14

Confidential
War Diary
of

7th DRAGOON GUARDS.

FROM 1st January, 1917 TO 31st January 1917

Army Form C. 2118.

WAR DIARY

or

INTELLIGENCE SUMMARY.

(Erase heading not required.)

Vol VII
of 4th Dragoon Guards
for January 1917

Instructions regarding War Diaries and Intelligence Summaries are contained in F. S. Regs., Part II, and the Staff Manual respectively. Title pages will be prepared in manuscript.

Hour, Date, Place.	Summary of Events and Information	Remarks and references to Appendices.
FEUQUIERES 1.1.17.	Situation unchanged.	Ref. Map. ABBEVILLE 1/100,000
3.1.17.	Pioneer Battalion rejoined from XIV Corps.	
14.1.17.	Three Officers and 10 NCOs and men to Divisional School. Corps Commander attended Church Parade and saw Regt. march past.	
19-31.1.17.	Hard frost and occasional snow. Individual training and musketry daily.	

R.W. ——— Lt Colonel
Comdg 4th Dragoon Guards

Serial №: 74

7th Dragoon Guards.

From 1st to 28th February 1917.

Army Form C. 2118.

7TH (PRINCESS ROYAL'S) DRAGOON GUARDS.

No..................
Date..................

Instructions regarding War Diaries and Intelligence summaries are contained in F. S. Regs., Part II, and the Staff Manual respectively. Title pages will be prepared in manuscript.

WAR DIARY
or
INTELLIGENCE SUMMARY.

(Erase heading not required.)

of 7th (P.R.) Dragoon Guards for February 1917.

Hour, Date, Place.	Summary of Events and Information	Remarks and references to Appendices.
FEUQUIERES 1-2-17 to 7-2-17	Situation unchanged. Hard frost continues.	Ref. Map. ABBEVILLE 1/100,000.
8-2-17	H.Q. details of Pioneer Battalion left by lorry for XIII CORPS.	
10-2-17	Pioneer Company left by lorry. 5 officers 254 O.R.	
11-2-17 to 28-2-17.	Situation unchanged. Thaw commenced on the 16th.	

R.M...... Lt Colonel.
CmdG 7th Dragoon Guards.

Serial No: 14.

Confidential

War Diary
—
1st March 1917
—
1st W Guards
—
Staff Cov: Bde

Vol IX

Army Form C. 2118

WAR DIARY
or
INTELLIGENCE SUMMARY.

of 4th Dragoon Guards

for March 1917.

(Erase heading not required.)

Instructions regarding War Diaries and Intelligence Summaries are contained in F. S. Regs., Part II, and the Staff Manual respectively. Title pages will be prepared in manuscript.

Hour, Date, Place.	Summary of Events and Information	Remarks and references to Appendices.
FEUQUIERES		
1st	Situation unchanged.	
6th	Major HURT, Duke of Lancaster's Yeomanry & Capt WARD, Wilts Yeomanry, attached to us for training.	
7th	Parade of Regiment for presentation of decorations by G.O.C. Bde.	
12th	Three Officers to Divisional School for a course.	
5 pm	Received orders for Regt. to be prepared to move at 48 hours notice.	
13th	Major HURT to Gun school.	
14th	Pioneer battalion arrived at rail head 5.30 am Transport of battalion, marching by road, arrived 4.30 pm	
15th	Capt WARD rejoined his unit. G.O.C.'s inspection of transport of Bde.	
19th	8 am Received notification that division would move East tomorrow, details & instructions to follow.	

Army Form C. 2118

WAR DIARY
or
INTELLIGENCE SUMMARY.
(Erase heading not required.)

of 1/7th Blagown Princes
for March 1917 continued

Hour, Date, Place.	Summary of Events and Information	Remarks and references to Appendices.
20th	Received orders at 3.15 am to move of the Pt. gage	Rd. Mat. ARRAEVILLE DIEPPE } 1 AMIENS } 100.000
LE QUESNE.	Regt. Paraded 9 am and marched in Bde via OISEMONT - AUMATRE - ANDAINVILLE to LE QUESNE. Arrived 1 pm Regt. billeted in LE QUESNE, ARGUEL and ST AUBIN RIVIERE weather cold Monday, march to be continued tomorrow	
21st	Regt paraded at 10.15 am and marched in Bde via HORNOY - THIEULLOY L'ABBAYE - FRICAMPS - QUEVAUVILLERS to NAMPS au MONT. Arrived 1.15 pm	
NAMPS au MONT.	Regt billeted in NAMPS au MONT and NAMPS au VAL. Very cold Tuesday, one snow.	
22nd	Regt paraded 9.15 am and marched in Bde via ST SAUFLIEU - BOVES - VILLERS BRETONNEUX, and billeted in bivouacs Camp N.E. of HAMEL. Arrived 4 pm. Cold, lowering, snow. Officers & men under cover horses in open.	
near HAMEL.	6.30 am. Received orders that Bde will probably not move today, but to be prepared to do so at half an hour notice. 10 pm. Recd orders to effect that we move at 8.30 am tomorrow.	
23rd		

Army Form C. 2118

WAR DIARY
or
INTELLIGENCE SUMMARY

(Erase heading not required.)

Of 7th Dragoon Guards
for March 1917. Continued.

Instructions regarding War Diaries and Intelligence Summaries are contained in F. S. Regs., Part II, and the Staff Manual respectively. Title pages will be prepared in manuscript.

Hour, Date, Place.	Summary of Events and Information	Remarks and references to Appendices.
24th	Regt paraded at 8.30 am and marched to Bois ha MÉRICOURT — CHUIGNES — CAPPY — HERBECOURT and bivouacked immediately N.E. of Bois de MEREAUCOURT. Arrived 1 p.m. Weather fine but very cold.	Ref. map AMIENS 1: 100,000.
Bois de MEREAUCOURT 25th	B echelon transport bivouacked yesterday and marched to HERBECOURT. 7.30 am. Received orders to be prepared to move at 3 hours from 10 am.	
26th	Situation unchanged. Continual showers.	
27th	4 am. Received orders that Regt would move today. Regt paraded at 1 p.m. and marched to HERBECOURT and TRACHES to bivouac at HALLE.	
HALLE	Arrived 1.30 p.m. Men under cover, horses in the open. Snow and showers of rain.	
28th	Regt paraded at 3 p.m. and marched to Bois to a bivouac at CLERY. Arrived 3.45 p.m. Very bad bivouac. Continual showers of rain and very cold.	
CLERY.		

Army Form C. 2118

WAR DIARY

of 4th Dragoon Guards

or

INTELLIGENCE SUMMARY.

for March 1917. Contd.

(Erase heading not required.)

Instructions regarding War Diaries and Intelligence Summaries are contained in F. S. Regs., Part II, and the Staff Manual respectively. Title pages will be prepared in manuscript.

Hour, Date, Place.	Summary of Events and Information	Remarks and references to Appendices.
29th	Regt paraded at 3 pm and marched to bivouac immediately N of HEM. Rain all day. 6 am Received orders that Bde would move to-day.	Reference Map. AMIENS 1:100000
30th	Regt paraded at 11.30 am and marched in Bde to BAYONVILLERS via FRISE - CAPPY - PROYART. Arrived 4 pm. All men and horses under cover.	
BAYONVILLERS 31st	Situation unchanged.	

R. Mumon Lt Colonel
Comdg 4th Dragoon Guards

Confidential Serial No. 46.

War Diary
7th K.O. Guard

From 1st April 1917 to 30th April.

Army Form C. 2118.

WAR DIARY
or
INTELLIGENCE SUMMARY.

of 7th Dragoon Guards. for April 1917.

(Erase heading not required.)

Instructions regarding War Diaries and Intelligence Summaries are contained in F. S. Regs., Part II, and the Staff Manual respectively. Title pages will be prepared in manuscript.

Hour, Date, Place.		Summary of Events and Information	Remarks and references to Appendices.
BAYONVILLERS	1st.	Situation unchanged. Wet and very cold	Ref. Map. AMIENS 1:100,000
	6th.	Brigade Scheme Co-operation with aeroplanes.	
	7th.	Situation unchanged. Frost and snow	
	11th.	Division ordered to move East. No definite orders to the Regiment until 10.40 pm. at 10.45 pm the move was cancelled.	
	12th.	Situation unchanged. Snow and very cold	
	13th.	Division ordered to move East. Orders received at 6.30 pm for march the following day.	
	14th.	The Brigade marched at 9.a.m. Starting point AARBONNIERES Church — via LIHONS — CHAULNES — MARCHELEPOT — ST CHRIST — ENNEMAIN across country to TREFCON. Regiment arrived at 4.30 pm Trois and hence were moved a good bivouac.	Ref Map. ST QUENTIN. 1:100,000.

Army Form C. 2118.

WAR DIARY
or
INTELLIGENCE SUMMARY.

of the 7th Dragoon Guards (Continued)

for April 1917

(Erase heading not required.)

Instructions regarding War Diaries and Intelligence Summaries are contained in F. S. Regs., Part II, and the Staff Manual respectively. Title pages will be prepared in manuscript.

Hour, Date, Place.	Summary of Events and Information	Remarks and references to Appendices.
TREFCON. 15th	Situation unchanged, fine but rain later.	Ref. map. ST QUENTIN 1:100,000.
17th	Ordered to carry out reconnaissance daily for Officers and N.C.O.s in the direction of BELLICOURT – LE TRONQUOY – CASTRES – SERAUCOURT – ARTEMPS.	
18th	Situation unchanged. Rain and stormy.	
19th	" " Fine and windy.	
25th	Brigade Scheme.	
26th	Situation unchanged. Weather improving.	
30th	" " Very fine.	

R. Mann Lt.Col.
Comdg. 7th Dragoon Guards.

Confidential. Serial No. 94.

From 1st May to 30th June 1917

War Diary for month of May 1917

From 1st — 31st May 1917

1st Dragoon Guards

Vol. XI

Army Form C. 2118.

WAR DIARY
or
INTELLIGENCE SUMMARY. of the 7th Dragoon Guards for May.

(Erase heading not required.)

Hour, Date, Place.	Summary of Events and Information	Remarks and references to Appendices.
TREFCON. 14.	Situation unchanged. Very fine and hot.	ST QUENTIN. 1:100,000
8th.	Wind veins changed to fine.	
11.45	Took Army Commanders Inspection of the Brigade 4m N.E. of BEAUVOIS.	
12h.	Situation unchanged.	
14h.	Very hot, some rain later.	
	Orders for Trench Party received. Total number Officers 17. O.Rs 292. 2 officers partly to Recommoitré cross country route up to hunch line. 4 officers and 30 O.Rs. went up 24 hours in advance to take over the line from the 2/4 LINCOLNS.	
16.15	Regiment proceeded by troops and headed across country to the valley immediately S.W. of LE VERGUIER and arrived about 9.45 p.m. Distribution. 2 Squadrons in the outpost line and 2 Squadrons in Support. Approximate extent of front 1200 yds.	1:20,000 BELLENGLISE Sheet IV

1/2 m S.E. of LE VERGUIER.

WAR DIARY
or
INTELLIGENCE SUMMARY.

(Erase heading not required.)

Army Form C. 2118.

of the 7th Dragoon Guards.

for May 1917.

Instructions regarding War Diaries and Intelligence Summaries are contained in F. S. Regs., Part II, and the Staff Manual respectively. Title pages will be prepared in manuscript.

Hour, Date, Place.	Summary of Events and Information	Remarks and references to Appendices.
½ S.Eq. LE VERGUIER		Refmap. 1:20,000. POEUILLE ENGLISE Sheet IV
16.	Situation normal. After shells dropped round ASCENSION FARM about 8 a.m. Trenches shaken and very little wire in front.	
17.	C.O's Conferences at Bde Hqrs. at 12 noon and early the further orders. Intermittent shelling on left during. Visibility poor.	
18.	Enemy artillery more active: Enemy patrols seen entering their lines opposite (G.27.c.) at 4.10 a.m. & at 9.30 p.m. 30 Huns came out of the same gap in the wire. Front Officer patrols sent out forward our advanced enemy posts at G.26.c. Post was held but could not ascertain in what strength.	
19.	1 Officer & 4 men from 9th HODSON'S HORSE came up to take over. Quiet day. 1 Officer & 4 O.Rs per Sqdn went to take over line from C/o N.Horse Relief Complete at 11.5. p.m.	
20.	Regiment billeting the individuals live running S from the E edge of LE VERGUIER village. About 150 shelters Alpha around D Sqn. Reveler at Northern end of the line	

Army Form C. 2118.

WAR DIARY
or
INTELLIGENCE SUMMARY.

(Erase heading not required.)

of 7th Dragoon Guards for May 1917.

Instructions regarding War Diaries and Intelligence Summaries are contained in F. S. Regs., Part II, and the Staff Manual respectively. Title pages will be prepared in manuscript.

Hour, Date, Place.		Summary of Events and Information	Remarks and references to Appendices.
In S.W. of LEVERGUIER.	25.	Situation unchanged. Previous nothing particular every night for both in the support and front line. Very fine weather, quite good	Ref. Map. 1:20,000 BELLENGLISE Sheet IV.
	26.	Situation unchanged.	
	26.	1 officer, 1 x sqdn and 1 NCO per post sent up to 12th wer from 9th Hussars	
	27.	Relief completed 12 midnight. About 700 Shells dropped around ASCENSION FARM.	
H2 S.E. of LEVERGUIER.	28.	The Enemy harass their front. Constantly we have men Nos 1 and 4 No 2 post li Laundren Are No 7.8.9. to 34th P. Horse.	
	29th	Relief completed at 2 am. Intermittent shelling day and night. Very fine weather.	
	29/5.	Such Officers patrol sent out to enemy wire for about 500x E. of ASCENSION FARM. Found their unoccupied histories. Made from the rear in their way back. Very wet weather.	
	30.	20 Germans seen to enter pits in G.26.C. at 10. pm. No movement observed during rest of the night.	
	31	Situation unchanged. Very fine.	

R. Mignon Lt Col.
Comdg. 7th Dragoon Guards.

War Diary
1st Dragoon Guards.

June 1st to June 30th 1917

Army Form C. 2118.

WAR DIARY of 7th Dragoon Guards.

INTELLIGENCE SUMMARY. for June.

(Erase heading not required.)

Instructions regarding War Diaries and Intelligence Summaries are contained in F. S. Regs., Part II. and the Staff Manual respectively. Title pages will be prepared in manuscript.

Place	Date	Hour	Summary of Events and Information	Remarks and references to Appendices
1/2 mile S.E. of LE VERGUIER	2nd		Enemy artillery activity increased.	BELLENGLISE Sheet IV 1:20,000.
	3rd		Own artillery concentrated on enemy lines at civilian. At 9:30pm a report was received stating that the enemy had evacuated their trenches in front of the Squadron and that the trench on the right. At 10:45pm a patrol of 2 officers & 40 men went out in the direction of G.26. to ascertain the accuracy of this report. (Patrouilla reached the trenches in G.32.a and reached, the enemy were found in strength. (Patrouilla at 60 mtrs.) Enemy opened considerable amount of fire on our patrol, who were at a disadvantage of finding the enemy lying up in the banks. Reinforcements were heard coming down the slope from the HARGICOURT SWITCH to our own patrol withdrew.	
	4th		Situation unchanged. Very warm and weather settled.	
	6th		Nos 1 and 2 Posts shelled during the afternoon. Little damage done.	
			Patrol Lieut. SOMERVILLE went at 9:30pm and worked left handed up to the German wire and returned by ASCENSION FARM. Enemy heard working in front of their trenches but no patrols seen or encountered.	
	7th		Patrol 1 Offr. & 30 men went out and found enemy in rifle pits in G.26.c. but did not get close enough to attack enemy by surprise.	
	8th		Rams, 1 Offr & 30 men went on patrol in the same direction as in the 6th inst. No sign of enemy movement heard or seen.	
	9th		2 Officers & 30 men patrolled towards the rifle pits in G.26.c. but no enemy found. Situation normal.	
	10th		2 Officers & 30 men went out to the trenches in G.32.a. Enemy they reached the trench, heavy artillery put a barrage on tps of them and then lifted to between them and our front line.	

A.5834 Wt.W4073/M687 750,000 8/16 D&D. & L. Ltd. Forms/C.2118/13.

WAR DIARY or INTELLIGENCE SUMMARY

Army Form C. 2118.

Instructions regarding War Diaries and Intelligence Summaries are contained in F.S. Regs., Part II. and the Staff Manual respectively. Title pages will be prepared in manuscript.

(Erase heading not required.)

Continued. Page II. of the 7th Dragoon Guards for June.

Place	Date	Hour	Summary of Events and Information	Remarks and references to Appendices
1½ m S.E. of LEVERGUIER.	9th		A telephone line was then found at the top of the Bank running in a Northerly direction; this was immediately cut. Heavy artillery continued shelling between the Banks and on our own. An S.O.S. signal was put up by the Regiment on our right, and shortly afterward an S.O.S. went up from the S.O.S. lines to this patrol's, & leaving the German trenches. Our guns opened on this. After hearing come through both barrages, NOK and then returned by ASCENSION FARM, after hearing no signs of the enemy. Patrol Off. Officer and 3.0. men went out patrol, & saw no signs of the enemy.	BELLENGLISE. Sheet IV. 1:20,000.
	10th		Heavy activity around. At Marieguil; an our guns were used to fire on these S.O.S. lines, hostility N. who went on our front did not shoot was an unbusy reconing parts were out. A number of shells dropped that around ASCENSION FARM. The same time the Germans dropped open trench shells round ASCENSION FARM, - no material damage was done. Activity normal. Patrol found a small party of Germans in the Rifle pits at G.25.c. but the enemy withdrew and they before our own patrol could get close enough, and no further signs of them could be found. Heavy Hindenburg German artillery shelled our area most of this afternoon without any particular object; no damage done.	
	11th			
	12th		Orders for relief received. Royal Canadian Dragoons with 12th are from us, 7 Officers & 9 NCOs came up to take over.	
	13th		Relief completed by 12 midnight. Squadron marched back respectively to TREFCON. Arrived at 2.30 a.m.	
TREFCON	14th		The Corps Commander (Gen. Kavanagh) inspected the horses of the Brigade at 11.0 a.m.	ST QUENTIN. 1:100,000.
	15th			
	16th		Situation unchanged. Squadron Training. Very hot.	
	17th			
	18th			
	19th		ditto. Thunderstorm during the night.	

Army Form C. 2118.

WAR DIARY of the 7th Dragoon Guards.
INTELLIGENCE SUMMARY. for June

Instructions regarding War Diaries and Intelligence Summaries are contained in F.S. Regs., Part II. and the Staff Manual respectively. Title pages will be prepared in manuscript.

(Erase heading not required.)

Place	Date	Hour	Summary of Events and Information	Remarks and references to Appendices
TREFCON.	20th		Brigade Tactical Exercise. Rkutzyme. 4m. N. of BEAUVOIS. Fine day. Squadron practised night patrolling	ST. QUENTIN. 1:100,000.
	21st		Regimental Drill. Rain in the afternoon.	
	22nd		Fires for Horses kindly received. Situation unchanged.	
	23rd		Rain. Squadron paraded at 5 hrs & marched onwards commencing at 9.0 p.m. and marched up to X road at BIHECOURT, where the led horses were sent back from. Relieved the 8B Hussars and join in to the trench on our right. During the Rue d'OMIGNON, Right Coupure at 11.45 p.m. 2 Squadron in outpost line 1 Squadron in support 1 Squadron in Reserve.	BELLENGUISE. Sheet IV. 1:20,000.
VADRICOURT	24th		Heavy machine. Patrol sent to reconnoitre ST HELENE Trench which was found unoccupied. Situation normal.	
	25th		Bellin Observation with Sector. Patrol sent out to ST HELENE and again to the junction with INK ALLEY. Tasting and important head in INK ALLEY but no opposition met with.	
	26th		Very fine. The Trench Owen right relieved.	
	27th		Thunderstorm in the afternoon and Evening. Situation normal.	
	28th		Arrangements for a raid undertaken. 1 officer and 20 men per squadron start a course of training. ST HELENE Trench patrolled and found unoccupied.	
	29th		Situation normal. Dull and some rain.	
	30th		Dull and windy. Patrol sent out to reconnoitre ground between XI Trees and FILTER Redoubt. Enemy found to be holding the XI Trees, about 20 strong. Patrol could not get round beyond.	

[signature] Major
Capt. of 7. Dragoon Guards

Serial No: 74.

War Diary

7th Dragoon Guards

From 1st July 1917 to 31st July 1917.

(Vol I)

Army Form C. 2118.

Instructions regarding War Diaries and Intelligence Summaries are contained in F. S. Regs., Part II. and the Staff Manual respectively. Title pages will be prepared in manuscript.

WAR DIARY
of the 7th Dragoon Guards

INTELLIGENCE SUMMARY.
for July

(Erase heading not required.)

Place	Date	Hour	Summary of Events and Information	Remarks and references to Appendices
VADENCOURT. ½ N of MAISSEMY.	1/2/3/4		Patrol of 1 Officer and 25 men went out and saw parties of the enemy working in the XI Trees. Situation unchanged. Raiding party of 4 Officers and 80 other ranks carried out a rehearsal in a "open air" kind of STIRENCOURT. Rehearsal went very well.	BELLENGLISE 1:20,000 Sheet IV
	5/6	10.0pm	Raiding party who "Wiped Bangalore Torpedoes, which at went according to programme. and were carried out with Lot £2. At 9.30pm the party had were carried out along the BELSH POSS road preceded by a hump of "C" Sqd who were to protect their right flank at the ANGLE BANKS. Party reached the weapons at in the Sunken road in 6.33.a.5.4 without incident. Several parties of the enemy were heard working and moving about infront of the enemy was not seen or heard from front trees, always moving his time in front of FLUER REDOUBT, his party carrying forward toward trench parties of the enemy were moving about why else between. The least forward was about 50% of the German wire. When the Bangalore Torpedoes had been fired. Suddenly when the torpedo party were within about stops, when lying in his cover, a few Germans came right into his party and my party had got within— they gave away his return fired. Two Germans were shot and the remainder rushed with the bayonet. This gave away his return to infant, which might have been affected and consequently into the trench, party had to return in no man's land and weather improved to get up to the German trenches rather other than had been given, and consequently his program was not able to be carried out. A party was sent back with the temperature of the dead German, but by that time a thing party of the enemy was forming to be holding the Sunken road in G.33.a.5.4.	
			Three Officers of the 18th Royal Scots came up to look at the line, preparing to taking over from us later.	
	6/7	10.0pm	A trench raid worked in conjunction with a Divisional Artillery shoot was carried out when XI Trees and the immediate vicinity with the object of gaining identifications, though 1 Officer and 80 other trained men entered successfully Udemphlin. War wash was crossed the Officer in left Regiment took,	

Army Form C. 2118.

WAR DIARY

Page II (continued) of the 7th Dragoon Guards.
for July

INTELLIGENCE SUMMARY.
(Erase heading not required.)

Instructions regarding War Diaries and Intelligence Summaries are contained in F. S. Regs., Part II. and the Staff Manual respectively. Title pages will be prepared in manuscript.

Place	Date	Hour	Summary of Events and Information	Remarks and references to Appendices
VARENCOURT	7	10.0 pm	by the watering party much hope that with protect the left flank. Weather unchanged. Heavy artillery activity increased.	BELLEN 8.1.15. 1/20,000. Sheet IV
	8.			
	9.		Enemy shells VARENCOURT from 2.0 pm to 9.0 pm. 13th. 8.5. rs.g shells. Very little damage done. Relief commenced at 11.0.45 p.m. and completed by 10.0 p.m. officer other of the Royal Scots has previously come up to take over.	
TREFCON	10th		Situation normal. Arrangements being made for the French kiosks. Division here in the vicinity of St Pol in every stages as the horses are fit and not at all fit.	ST QUENTIN 1/100,000
BUIRE	14th		Brigade marched by Regiment at intervals of 500 yds Subaltern parties preceded the Regt and kept a days march ahead. Regiment marched at 1.30 pm via CARTIGNY to BUIRE. Subaltern party rendezvous at the Outcry - LASIGNE and an 9.0 by train to the new area.	LENS 1/100,000
SUZANNE	15th	6.0 a.m.	Regiment marched via HEM PERONNE - CAPPY to SUZANNE, and arrived at 10.30 a.m.	
VILLE sur CORBIE	16th	7.30	Regiment marched via BRAY to VILLE sur CORBIE and arrived at 10.0 a.m. Good billets and village unchanged during the afternoon.	
SARTON	17th	6.0 a.m.	Regiment marched via TOREUVILLE and LONGUEVOST to SARTON and arrived at 2.0 pm after the first long march.	
BRYAS	18th		Regiment marched via LUCHEUX - IVERGNY - BONNEVILLE to BRYAS, and arrived at 1.45 pm after the last march yet. Bivouacks party rejoined from St Pol. and head.	
	19th		Rain and cooler. Situation unchanged.	
ANVIN & PETIT	20th	2.45pm	Owing to the shortage operated at BRYAS (1 pond) the Regiment moved into bivouac at ANVIN LE PETIT. Good accommodation for men and horses.	
	21st		Fine and warm.	
	22nd		Situation unchanged.	
	23rd		Individual Training and parades for Regimental Sports.	

Army Form C. 2118.

Page III continued

WAR DIARY of the 7th Dragoon Guards
INTELLIGENCE SUMMARY for July

(Erase heading not required.)

Place	Date	Hour	Summary of Events and Information	Remarks and references to Appendices
ANVIN & PETIT..	24. 25. 26.		Situation unchanged. fine " hot " fine. Aeroplane communication scheme during which aeroplane left Hesdin.	Report. LENS. 1:100,000.
	27.		" " duties of 26th repeated.	
	28. 29. 30. 31.		W.A. situation unchanged.	

Stewart Lt.
Adjutant, 7 Dragoon Guards.

Serial No. 44.

War Diary

1st Dragoon Guards)

From 1st August 1917
to 31st August 1917

10

Army Form C. 2118

WAR DIARY of the 7th Dragoon Guards.
INTELLIGENCE SUMMARY. for August.

(Erase heading not required.)

Instructions regarding War Diaries and Intelligence Summaries are contained in F. S. Regs., Part II, and the Staff Manual respectively. Title pages will be prepared in manuscript.

Hour, Date, Place.	Summary of Events and Information.	Remarks and references to Appendices.
ANVIN. Aug: 1st	Weather unsettled.	LENS. 1:100,000.
7th	Fine	
9th	Bde Aeroplane scheme, for signallers.	
11th	Weather unchanged. Regimental Sports. Weather still unsettled.	
15th	Divisional Horse Show.	
16th	Fine	
20th	Weather unchanged. Divisional Commander inspected the Brigade in marching order at the junction of the roads 2.00 W. of CREPY.	
21st	Reviewing and bridge building over the river.	
22nd	Wind and rain. Weather very unsettled.	
25th	" "	
28th	Stormy	
30th	weather still unsettled	

C. P. Chapper. Major
Comdg. 7th Dragoon Guards.

Army Form C. 2118.

WAR DIARY

of the 7th Dragoon Guards

-OR-

INTELLIGENCE SUMMARY.

for August

(Erase heading not required.)

Instructions regarding War Diaries and Intelligence Summaries are contained in F. S. Regs., Part II, and the Staff Manual respectively. Title pages will be prepared in manuscript.

Hour, Date, Place.	Summary of Events and Information.	Remarks and references to Appendices.
ANVIN. Aug. 1st.	Situation unchanged. Weather unsettled.	LENS 1:100,000.
7th	"	
9th	Bde Recontre scheme for Squadrons	
11th	Situation unchanged. Regimental Sports. Bathing 5Kh unsettled.	
15th	" Divisional Horse Show.	
16th	Bde Tactical Exercise. True.	
20th	Situation unchanged. Divisional Commander inspected the Brigade in	
21st	marching order & the practice of the roads used by afcrew.	
22nd	Pouring and bridge building over the river.	
26th	Wind and rain.	
28th	Situation unchanged. Weather very unsettled	
30th	" Stormy	
	" Weather still unsettled	

C.L.K. ..... Major
Comdg 7th Dragoon Guards.

Confidential.

Serial No. 4.

War Diary

1st Cavalry Brigade

1st Dragoon Guards

From 1st to 30th Sept 1914

VOL. I.

Army Form C. 2118.

WAR DIARY of the 7th Dragoon Guards

INTELLIGENCE SUMMARY for September 1917.

(Erase heading not required.)

Instructions regarding War Diaries and Intelligence Summaries are contained in F. S. Regs., Part II, and the Staff Manual respectively. Title pages will be prepared in manuscript.

Hour, Date, Place.	Summary of Events and Information.	Remarks and references to Appendices.
ANVIN.	Situation unchanged. Fine. Cavalry Corps Horse Show RAIMECOURT.	Ref map.
1st.	" " Squadron Training.	LENS. 1:100,000.
3rd.		
8th.	'A' & 'B' Sub-Squadrons finishing scheme. Weather unsettled.	
11th.	Regimental scheme.	
16th.	Inspection of Horses return by the Corps Commander.	
15th.	Regimental Tactical exercise. Fine.	
19th.	Situation unchanged. Tactical exercise against the Canadian	
20th.	Cavalry Brigade, at which the Corps Commander was present.	
22nd.	Regimental Orders. Situation unchanged.	
25th.	" "	
23rd.	" "	
30th.	Situation unchanged.	

R. Mumm. Lt Col.
Cmdg. 7th Dragoon Guards.

(114)

Confidential

War Diary
7th Dragoon Guards.

From 1st October 1914
To 31st October 1917

Army Form C. 2118.

Instructions regarding War Diaries and Intelligence Summaries are contained in F. S. Regs., Part II. and the Staff Manual respectively. Title pages will be prepared in manuscript.

WAR DIARY
or
INTELLIGENCE SUMMARY.
(Erase heading not required.)

VOL 1. of the 7th Dragoon Guards.
for October 1917.

Place	Date	Hour	Summary of Events and Information	Remarks and references to Appendices
ANVIN	1st 2nd 3rd 4th 5th		Situation unchanged. Squadron Training. Regimental Drill. Fine. Brigade Tactical Exercise. Rain in the afternoon. Squadron Training. Received notification that the Brigade would probably move N.E. next day. Received orders for next days march at 9.0pm.	Ref LENS 1:100,000
	6th	9.30am	Brigade marched via WESTRHEN – ST HILAIRE – AIRE to BOESINGHEM area. Starting point HEUCHIN Church. Regiment detailed advance guard to the Bde. Arrived at BOESINGHEM at 1.30pm. Rain and wind. A few horses were under shelter. Received orders for next days march at 7.50pm.	Ref HAZEBRN 1:100,000
BOESINGHEM	7th	11.30am	Marched via HAZEBROUCK – STEENVOORDE to WATOU. Regiment proceeded at the X road (on the AIRE – HAZEBROUCK road) ½ N of the 2nd E in BOESINGHEM. 'B' echelon preceded the Brigade. Very wet and windy. Arrived at WATOU at 4.30pm. and bivouaced in field W of WATOU, in an old artillery horse lines. A certain number of stab. were round at 8.0pm. Very heavy rain in the night. Water then came into lines at mid-night.	
WATOU.	8th 11th 12th		Situation unchanged, very wet.	
			Ambulance Brigade arrived in this area.	
			1st Cav. Div. marched to back area.	
	14th		Rain and stormy. Received orders for return march at 4.0pm.	
	15th	10.25am	Bde. marched via STEENVOORDE – OXELAERE – BAVINCHOVE to RENESCURE area. Fine and cold. Regiment arrived at CAMPAGNE at 2.45pm after a very slow march owing to the paveé roads. All the horses under cover. Orders received for next days march at 8.15pm	
CAMPAGNE.	16th	8.25am	Brigade marched via ARQUES – WIZERNES – CLETY to FAUQENBERG area. Regiment arrived	

Army Form C. 2118.

WAR DIARY of the 7th Dragoon Guards
or
INTELLIGENCE SUMMARY. for October 1917.

(Erase heading not required.)

Instructions regarding War Diaries and Intelligence Summaries are contained in F. S. Regs., Part II. and the Staff Manual respectively. Title pages will be prepared in manuscript.

VOL 1.

Place	Date	Hour	Summary of Events and Information	Remarks and references to Appendices
THIENBRONE	17th	9.45am	The Brigade marched by Regiments to new area. The Regiment passed at the Southern exit of the village and marched via RUMILLY – VERCHOCQUE to WAILLY and COUPELLE – VIEILLE. A very trying billeting area. Poor accommodation for men or horses. Received orders to send 3 officers and 6 N.C.Os to the 6th Cav. Div. Pioneer Battalion at BAILLEUL.	Ref HAZEBROUCK 1:100,000.
COUPELLE – VIEILLE	26th		Situation unchanged. Fine and cold. Seven Corporals transferred to R.F.A. as Bombardiers.	
	22nd		Squadron Training.	
	24th	9.15am	Commanding Officers Mounting Order parade outside Squadron billets.	
	28th		Situation unchanged. Fine.	
	29th		'B' and 'C' Sqd. rehearsed Field Firing Scheme.	
	30th	9.15am	Regimental Tactical Exercise.	
	31st		The 'A' 'D' Sqdns rehearsed Field Firing Scheme. Situation unchanged.	

R. Munro Lt. Col.
Commanding 7th Dragoon Guards.

WAR DIARY or INTELLIGENCE SUMMARY

Army Form C. 2118

Vol. 1.   7/4th Dragoon Guards
                           1st October 1917.

Place	Date	Hour	Summary of Events and Information	Remarks and references to Appendices
ANNIN	1st		Musketry. Lewis gun. Squadron Training.	
	2nd		Drill. Fire	
	3rd		Brigade Tactical Exercise. Rain in afternoon.	
	4th		Squadron Training.	
	5th		Received notice that the Brigade was on 2 hours notice from 9.0 p.m. Received orders for next days march at 9.0 p.m.	
	6th	9.30am	Brigade marched via WESTRHEM – ST HILAIRE – AIRE to BORSINGHEN area. Starting point HEUCHIN Church. Regiment detailed advance guard to the Bde. Arrived at BOESINGHEM 1.30 p.m. Rain and wind. A few horses were under shelter. Received orders for next days march at 7.30 p.m.	
BOESINGHEM	7th	11.30 am	Marched via HAZEBROUCK – STEENVOORDE via WATOU (via AIRE – HAZEBROUCK road) ½ N of Pt 2nd E in BOESINGHEM. Regiment paraded at the XRDS (N of BOESINGHEM) & below followed in Brigade. Very wet and windy. Arrived at WATOU at 4.30 p.m. and bivouacked in front W of WATOU, in an old artillery horse lines. A certain number of tents bivouacs at types. Very heavy rain in the night. Wet. Situation unchanged – very wet	
WATOU	8th		" " " Australian Brigade arrived in the area.	
	9th		" " " 1st Div. Div marched to back area.	
	12th		Rain and strong. Received orders for return march at 4.30 p.m.	
	14th			
	15th	10.25 am	Bde. marched via STEENVOORDE – OXELAERE – BANNONVE to RENESCURE – BANNONVE to CAMPAGNE at 2.45 p.m. After a very slow march owing to the bad roads. All too were under cover. Orders received for next days march at 8.15 p.m.	
CAMPAGNE	16th	8.25 am	Brigade marched via FIQUES – WITZENES – CIETY to FAUQUEMBERG area. Regiment arrived at THIEMBRONNE at 1.15 p.m.	

Army Form C. 2118.

WAR DIARY
or
INTELLIGENCE SUMMARY.

of the 7th Dragoon Guards

for October 1917

Vol. 1.

(Erase heading not required.)

Instructions regarding War Diaries and Intelligence Summaries are contained in F. S. Regs., Part II. and the Staff Manual respectively. Title pages will be prepared in manuscript.

Place	Date	Hour	Summary of Events and Information	Remarks and references to Appendices
THIEMBRONNE	17th	9.45a.m	The Regiment marched by Regiments to new area. The Regiment passed the Southern Exit of the village and marched via RUMILLY – VERCHOCQUE to WAVRY and COUPELLES–VIELLE area. Poor accommodation for men & horses. Received order to send 3 Officers and 6 NCOs to the 5th Can. Div. Pioneer Battalion at BAILLEUL.	Ref. HAZEBROUCK. 1/100,000
COUPELLE–VIEILLE	20th		Situation unchanged. Fine and cold. Seven Corporals transferred to R.F.A. on request.	
	22nd		Squadron Training	
	24th	9.15a.m	Commanding Officers watching the purse advise squadron drills	
	28th		Situation unchanged. Fine	
	29th		"B" and "C" Sqd. observed Field firing scheme.	
	30th	9.15a.m	Regimental Tactical Scheme.	
	31st		Fine "A" Sqd. observed Field firing scheme. Situation unchanged.	

R. Wynn/ Lt. Col.
Commanding 7th Dragoon Guards

Army Form C. 2118.

WAR DIARY
of
INTELLIGENCE SUMMARY.
(Erase heading not required.)

of the 7/th Dragoon Guards.
for November.

Instructions regarding War Diaries and Intelligence Summaries are contained in F.S. Regs., Part II. and the Staff Manual respectively. Title pages will be prepared in manuscript.

Place	Date	Hour	Summary of Events and Information	Remarks and references to Appendices
COUPELLE VIEILLE	1st	3.0pm	Regt Outpost scheme at AZINCOURT at by Bn. Scheme watched by Div. Commander at LEULIEZ Branch.	LENS
	3rd	7.30am	Field Scheme carried out by "A" and "B" Sqdns.	Liberated also
	5th		Cold and dull. Dismt. Parl. by Lt. Bhr & WD. Whitby to have 5 F=	ABBEVILLE CALAIS HAZEBROUCK
	7th			
	8th			
	9th		Men for Div. reviewed.	
		8.30am	Regt paraded and marched via FRUGES - MESOULT - LABROYE - AUV - LE CHAUSSE to AUTHEUX. Regt arrived at 7.30pm. Bivs received at 7.0 p.m. for next day's march.	
AUTHEUX	10th	9.10am	Regt marched via TENVILLERT - LANDAS - MOLLIERS-aux-BOIS to GUERBIER arrived at A. 12.30 pm	AUTHEUX
GUERBIEU	11th	11.0pm	Regt marched via CORBIE - MERICOURT to CAPPY arrived about 10.30 pm	
CAPPY	12th	4.0pm	Regt paraded and marched via FAYRESCOURT - BRIE - ESTREES - on - CHAUSSEE to BOUVAINCOURT. Warily at horses under cover. Scheme watched Carried out 12.30 pm	
BOUVAIN COURT	15th		Afterwards in case of a wire found. Foggy but fine	
	19th		Yday. halted at 11.0 am	
	20th	12.30am	Regt marched via BEAUMETZ - TINCOURT - MOREU - FINS to the BOIS du DESSART. Where the	
BOIS du DESSART	21st		Bn. was bivouacked. Regt arrived at 5.50 am 9th Division walked under. Zero hour 6.20 am	VALENCIENNES BAPAUME
		12.30pm	Informed received that the "Infantry had taken FLESQUIERES. Squadron first of MARCOING nil clear. Regt ordered to move forward. 2nd Sqd advance guard to the Regt.	
MARCOING		about 2.0pm.	Village reached by MARCOING which was reached at 2.0pm. The MARSIERES - BEAUREVOIR line had not been reached by MARCOING bridges were intact. 8 to 10pm turned to the attack. Myself & also X forward MARCOING bridges were intact. Coy hard turned to the attack. Myself also X forward held by heavy M.G fire. Another turned to the finish road, to dismount for action and lent pickets to gain touch with Cav. Bde forward MARSIERES, where they were unable to move	
		2.20pm	Main body of the Bde. crossed just W of MARCOING.	
		2.0pm	"D" Sqd were ordered forward to MASNIERES Village, and ascertain if it was possible to cross by the bridge there.	

A 5834 W.t W.4973/M687. 750,000 8/16 D.D. & L. Ltd. Forms/C.2118/13.

WAR DIARY
or
INTELLIGENCE SUMMARY

Army Form C. 2118

The 7th Dragoon Guards Page II
for November 1917.

Place	Date	Hour	Summary of Events and Information	Remarks and references to Appendices
MARCOING	20th	2.25 p.m.	D' Sqd. galloped the village of NOYELLES taking 25 prisoners without any casualties and passed L'ESCAUT and been blown up about later 3 other troops (1 from each and 2 of the men) the evening was served out and held until 10 p.m. when the 4th Dragoon Guards and our right withdrew. Sqd. shortly afterwards they were ordered up to line. At 3.0 p.m. they were to rejoin the Brigade. Shortly afterwards they were ordered up to the firing line to support the infantry when they remained till 6 a.m. when 21st having been relieved by the 1st Division themselves the Rgt. had moved about a mile to a point along the MARCOING-NEURNIL road to bivouac just before and bivouaced in houses nearby.	NOYELLES
	21st	8.30 a.m.	Regt. moved to valley south east of GOUZEAUCOURT and remained standing to all day.	
		6.40 p.m.	Sqd. received orders to move to another bivouac. Whole horse lines off captured trenches near VILLERS-PLOUICH	
Inde W. of VILLERS-PLOUICH	22nd	6.50 a.m.	Regt. moved via MAREGNY - PREGOURT - TINCOURT to PINS and drawn at 3.0 p.m.	
		8.30 a.m.	Regt. marched via EQUANCOURT - NURLU - HAUT ALLAINES - CARRY - SUZANNE to FROISSY Camp arrived at 3.0 p.m.	AMIENS
FROISSY	23rd	12.30 a.m.	Received orders to "stand to" at ½ hour notice after 8.0 a.m. which was cancelled	
	24th		Remained "standing to"	
	25th		B's Sqdrn trained in the afternoon. Remainder playing a bit till 12.30 p.m.	
	26th	1.0 p.m.	Received orders that the Regt. would march to TREFCON next day	
	27th	8.30 a.m.	Regt. paraded and marched via CHURNES - FOUCAUCOURT - BRIE - MONS en CHAUSSÉE to TREFCON arrived about 2.0 p.m. The camp is rather very rough but	ST QUENTIN

Army Form C. 2118

WAR DIARY
or
INTELLIGENCE SUMMARY.

of the 7th Dragoon Guards. for November.

(Erase heading not required.)

Instructions regarding War Diaries and Intelligence Summaries are contained in F.S. Regs., Part II. and the Staff Manual respectively. Title pages will be prepared in manuscript.

Place	Date	Hour	Summary of Events and Information	Remarks and references to Appendices
TOSPELLE	1st	3.0 pm	Regt Outpost scheme at AZINCOURT. att by Bde. Scheme unchanged.	LENS. 1/100,000 obs.
VEILLE	3rd		7.9am. Inspection by Bvt Commander at LEBIEZ church.	ABBEVILLE- CALAIS- HAZEBROUCK
	5th		Field day scheme carried out by 'A' and 'B' sqdns.	
	7th		Cold and dull. Warned that the Divi. was likely to move S.E.	
	8th		Orders for move received.	
	9th		Regt paraded and marched via FRUGES – HESDIN – LABROYE – AUX-LE CHATEAU to AUTHEUX. Regt arrived at 7.30pm. Orders received at 9.45pm for next days march.	AMIENS
AUTHEUX	10th	9.10 am	Regt marched via FIENVILLERS – CANDAS – MOLIENS au BOIS to GUERRIEU arrived at 1.30pm.	
GUERRIEU	11th	4.0 pm	Regt marched via CORBIE – MERICOURT to CAPPY arrived about 10.30pm.	
CAPPY	12th	4.0 pm	Regt paraded and marched via FAUCOURT – BRIE – ESTREES- en- CHAUSSEE to BOUVAINCOURT. Nearly all horses wet thro'. Scheme unchanged. [arrived at 9.30pm.]	
BOUVAIN- COURT.	15th		Arrangements in case of a move forward. Foggy but fine.	
	19th		½ day. Informed at 11.0 am.	
	20th	12.30 am	Regt marched via BEAUNETS, – TINCOURT – NURLU – FINS to the BOIS de DESSART, where the Bn: was bivouacked. Regt arrived at 5.50 am. Off-saddled. Watered. Sadd'ed. Zero hour 6.20 am.	VALENCIENN
BOIS de DESSART	21st	12.30 pm	Information received that the "Infantry" had taken FLESQUIERES. Situation in front of MARCOING not clear. Regt moved to move forward. 'C' sqd advanced guard to the Regt. and advanced via QUEENS CROSS – VILLARS PLOUICH to MARCOING which was reached at about 2.0 pm. The NINEVISIERES – BEARVOIR line had not been captured, Germans were still holding out at this tunnel west by MARCOING Station, also N towards NOYELLES. MARCOING bridges were unsafe. 'C' sqd tried to cross the tunnel road, to ammunition for action and sent patrols but by heavy M.G. fire further further north. Cav. Bde towards NAIRIVIERES, where they were unable to cross. To gain touch with Can. Cav. Bde towards NAIRIVIERES, where they were unable to cross. Main body of the Regt remained just W. of MARCOING.	
MARCOING		2.20 pm		
		2.15 pm	D sqd were ordered forward to observe NOYELLES village, and ascertain if it was possible to cross by the bridges there.	

WAR DIARY of the 7th Dragoon Guards
INTELLIGENCE SUMMARY for November 1917

Page II — Army Form C. 2118

Place	Date	Hour	Summary of Events and Information	Remarks and references to Appendices
MARCOING	20th	9.25 pm	"D" Sqd galloped the village of NOYELLES taking 25 prisoners without any casualties, and pushed on until the CANAL DE L'ESCAUT had been blown up, but later 3 other tanks bridges were found intact. (Over the canal and 2 over the river.) The evenings the Regiment and the 4th Dragoon Guards and the Bde. Shortly afterwards they were ordered to rejoin the Bde. The main ridge over the L'ESCAUT had been held and immediately the Battalion after left took the 4th Dragoon Guards and the night with the Infantry. At 6.0 am they were ordered to rejoin the Bde. Shortly afterwards they were mixed up again with turn. Place dismounted by the 18th Hussars. Meanwhile the Bde. had moved about a mile back along the VILLERS – PLOUICH road to bivouac for the night and remained in horse wagon.	VALENCIENNES
1 mile W of VILLERS-PLOUICH	21st	6.30 a.m.	Regt. moved to valley S of the Bois de QUENNET and remained standing to all day	
		6.30 pm	Bde. moved across the road to another bivouac, where horses were off-saddled & watered at VILLERS-PLOUICH.	
	22nd	6.50 AM	Bde. reached via MARCOING – RIBECOURT – TREBESCOURT to FINS and arrived at 3.0 pm.	AMIENS
		9.30 am	Bde. reached via EQUANCOURT – MOISLAINS – HAUT ALLAINES – CLERY – SUZANNE to FROISSY Camp arrived at 3.0 pm.	
SY.	23rd	12.30 a.m.	Received orders to "Stand to" at ½ hours notice after 8.0 a.m. This line unchanged.	
	24th		Remained "Standing to"	
	25th		"B" Echelon joined us in the afternoon. Remained "Standing to" till 10.30 p.m.	
	26th	11.0 p.m.	Received orders that the Bde. would march to TREFCON next day.	ST QUENTIN
	27th	8.30 am	Regt. paraded and marched via CAHVIGNES – FAUCAUCOURT – BRIE – MONS a CHAUSSEE to TREFCON Regiment arrived about 2.0 pm. The camp in which we were quartered is very uncomfortable	
	28th		This line unchanged	

Army Form C. 2118

WAR DIARY
or
INTELLIGENCE SUMMARY. Of 7th Dragoon Guards for November

(Erase heading not required.)

Instructions regarding War Diaries and Intelligence Part II
Summaries are contained in F. S. Regs., Part II.
and the Staff Manual respectively. Title pages
will be prepared in manuscript.

Place	Date	Hour	Summary of Events and Information	Remarks and references to Appendices
TREFCON.	30th	9.40 am	Regt moved to take up at once. 11.30 am followed AMBALA Bde via VRAIGNES to vicinity of HEUDECOURT. German retired to heart through HEUDECOURT. Regt handed Advance Guard to Bde and advanced to GOUZEAUCOURT. 1 troop LOUVERVAL charged a pocket of Germans in the village Reking it. Grand Guard who took heard K.S.W. and found no situation. Regt moved up and dismounted in N.W. edge of village in support. Enemy shelled the village heavily. A troop followed later by 'B' Sqd to the GOUZEAUCOURT - TRESCAULT road and took up a defensive position, who patrols out in touch with infantry.	ST QUENTIN CAMBRAI. 1/100,000
		7.30pm	Regt moved back 1.5 km from Bde just N.E. of HEUDECOURT. Off-saddled 50% at a time.	

R. Munro Lt Col.
Cmdg. 7th D. Guards.

Army Form C. 2118

WAR DIARY
or
INTELLIGENCE SUMMARY.

Part II of 7th Dragoon Guards for Nivrewka
(Erase heading not required.)

Instructions regarding War Diaries and Intelligence Summaries are contained in F. S. Regs., Part II. and the Staff Manual respectively. Title pages will be prepared in manuscript.

Place	Date	Hour	Summary of Events and Information	Remarks and references to Appendices
TREFCON	30th	7.40 a.m	Regt ordered to reconnoitre up to & incl. vicinity of HEUDECOURT. German retired. Regt moved into ATTILLY & BRIE and charged a squadron of Germans in the village behind the K.S.LI. and found out situation. Regt met in support. Regt pushed thro' village the GOUZEAUCOURT—TRESCAULT road and wire but with infantry.	Sr QUENTIN CAMPAIGN. 1/100,000
		11.30 a.m	Enemy ARTILLERY & M.G. OPENED to have retired through at GOUZEAUCOURT. 1 troop GOUZEAUCOURT & infantry in GOUZEAUCOURT with 1 with Grand Guard takes N.E. corner of village and advanced to top of village heavily. A Sqn pushed later by B's to took up in different position not
			NE of HEUDECOURT S/P : taken 50% at LINE
		7.30 p.m	Regt went back to join a Bde just	

R.[?] Morris Lt.Col.
Cmdg 7 D.Guards

WAR DIARY
or
INTELLIGENCE SUMMARY

(Erase heading not required.)

Army Form C. 2118.

Page I.

Instructions regarding War Diaries and Intelligence Summaries are contained in F. S. Regs., Part II. and the Staff Manual respectively. Title pages will be prepared in manuscript.

of the 7th Dragoon Guards

for December 1917

Place	Date	Hour	Summary of Events and Information	Remarks and references to Appendices
GOUZEAUCOURT	1 XII/17	1.0 am	Regt moved back from Gouzeaucourt BOIZECOURT to S.N. of HEUDICOURT Station. Off saddled and bivouacked for the night	VALENCIENNES 1/100,000
		9.30 am	Regt placed at disposal of G.O.C. AMERICAN Bde. moved up approach to the sunken road E.S.N. of GOUZEAUCOURT	
		11.30 am	C Sqdn moved forward in support of 18th Lancers (IA) in GAUCHE WOOD.	ST. QUENTIN 1/100,000
		11.0 am	B Sqdn + D Sqdn moved up to the 9th between Gouzeaucourt and MELBOURNE WOOD. C Sqd on support line through	
			Regt and A Sqd moved to railway embankment W. of GAUCHE WOOD. O Sqd and support line through	
			the town. 1.45 pm heavy enemy shelling between front line and support line in sunken road (another)	
	4.30 pm		A Sqd moved up to support of D Sqd left flank which was weak.	
	9.0 pm		Orders received that Regt would be relieved by 1 Sqn PEMBROKE YEOMANRY and remaining byts by Gren ? &	
			Coldstream Guards Officer and 3 other ranks 13 other ranks wounded.	
2nd	3.45 am		Relief complete. Regt moved into Bois support in sunken road relieving 9th Norton Horse.	
	3.30 pm		Moved to Arusia as 0.C. Bora Horse reported enemy massing in front of GAUCHE WOOD	
	6.15 pm		Bois area as nothing happened.	
	9.0 pm		Regt relieved by 9th Lancers and marched back to Squentin to horses SW of HEUDICOURT STN	
3rd	11.30 am		Regt marched to bivouacs S.W. St SAULCOURT standing to at ½ hour notice by day and 1 hour	
SAULCOURT	4th			by night. Weather unchanged. Hard frost and very cold.
	5th			Weather unchanged. Hard frost and piercing N.E. wind.
	6th	6.30 pm		Orders received that we are placed on short notice any any old. Night sortie to keep horses light.
	7th			Dismal thaw. 9.0 pm orders by Messenger to stand to.
	8th	10.30 am		Alerts received for the march at 1.30 pm
	1.30 pm		Regt marched via RONSOY—LES—TINCOURT to BUIRE. Regt in the Premier place for taking and horses was further transferred	
			Regt moved at 3.15 pm	
	9th			Sick officer to hospital. Water line between TEMPIEUX to BUIRE and FRANCOURT	
BUIRE	10th	7.45 pm		Received orders to have to march from 6.30 am – 8.0 am ready to locate ? unwounded of the
			day at short notice. Very wet and raw. Situation unchanged	
	12th			Night generally ? Usual night fortie unchanged

A 8831 Wt W4973/M687 730,000 8/16 D. D. & L. Ltd. Forms/C.2118/13.

Army Form C. 2118.

WAR DIARY
or
INTELLIGENCE SUMMARY
of the 7th Dragoon Guards for December 1917

(Erase heading not required.)

Instructions regarding War Diaries and Intelligence Summaries are contained in F.S. Regs., Part II. and the Staff Manual respectively. Title pages will be prepared in manuscript.

Page II

Place	Date	Hour	Summary of Events and Information	Remarks and references to Appendices
BUIRE	16th	9.30 a.m.	Church Parade. 7.30 pm Received orders that the Regt. would march to TREFCON next day.	ST QUENTIN 1:100,000
	17th		Heavy fall of snow during the night	
		9.15 a.m.	Regt. paraded in snow and marched via BARTICOW — X road at BOIS DE BUIRE to TREFCON. and arrived at 10.45 a.m. Snow which covers and conceals was never further than state of standing to firm. 6.30 a.m. – 8.0 am parcelled. Regt. sick at 1 hour extra.	
TREFCON	18th		Hard frost and wintry. Roads blocked by drifts. Transport very difficult.	
	19th		Wind subsided. Let the snow and frost still remained.	
	23rd		Private 300 men for wiring and digging in the trench line S.S.W. of HARGICOURT draft of 44 ORs joined from the Base.	
	25th		Xmas Day. Weather unchanged.	
	27th		Starting to a thaw with rain.	
	28th		At noon that of OR than snow out of the 3.9 km trench around BINSECOURT.	
	29th		Thawing to a stiffest frost which ate 12 noon Jan 1st 1918	
	31st		Weather unchanged. Slight thaw but snow still lying about	

R. Munro Lt. Col.
Comdg. 7th Dragoon Guards.

WAR DIARY
or
INTELLIGENCE SUMMARY of the 7th Dragoon Guards for January 1918.

Army Form C. 2118.

Page I

Place	Date	Hour	Summary of Events and Information	Remarks and references to Appendices
TREFCON	1st		Situation unchanged. Cold and fine. Standing to at 1 hours notice to act as mounted	ST QUENTIN 1:100,000
"	3rd		Digging bomb-proof walls round all huts and stables. Hard frost.	Leave
"	7th		Providing working parties for 24th Division. Heavy rain and frost later.	
"	10th		Thaw set in. rain. Situation unchanged.	
"	13th		Handing to Brow reserve trenches through BIHECOURT in case of eventualities. Tom St Quy	
"	16th		in the trenches cancelled for the 14/15th as the Indian Troops are going East. All the frost out of the ground and temperature going up considerably.	
"	17th		Providing working parties daily digging and wiring reserve lines W of BIHECOURT	
"	19th	3.0 pm	Distribution of Medal ribbon by the Regt Commander at MERAUCOURT at 3.0 pm	
"	22nd		Working parties daily. Situation unchanged.	
"	24th		Orders for Trench party issued. Regt. hands 7 officers and 216 ORs exclusive potatoes	
"	25th		Lgts rode up independently arriving at JEANCOURT at 5.30 pm took over LEVERGUIER trs from the 9th Lancers	
LEVERGUIER	26th		Fine and warm. Forded working parties on the trails from 9 a.m – 2.0 pm Situation unchanged	
"	29th		Situation unchanged. Enemy Aircraft raided the trench area (5 casualties 8th Hussars)	
"	30th		Enemy balloon brought down in flames. 2nd life Guard arrived and relieved party of 1st life Guard	
"	31st		at TREFCON to take over the camp. Frosty. Artillery activity on both sides.	

R.G. Roberts. Capt.
for Lt. Col. Comdg. 7th Dragoon Guards.

Army Form C. 2118.

Page 1

WAR DIARY
or
INTELLIGENCE SUMMARY.
(Erase heading not required.)

of the 7th Dragoon Guards
for February 1918.

Place	Date	Hour	Summary of Events and Information	Remarks and references to Appendices
TREFCON	1st	8:30am	The Regiment less the trench party (215) paraded in camp and marched via TERTRY – ESTREES en CHAUSSÉE – BRIE – FOUCAUCOURT to BAYONVILLERS and arrived at 2:30pm after approx 17 miles. Passed via 7th Cav: Bde on the road marching 6–7 miles over our old camp.	Ref Map. 1/100,000 ST QUENTIN
BAYONVILLERS	2nd	8:30am	Paraded at T roads N of BAYONVILLERS and marched via AMIENS (Northern boulevard) – LONGPRÉ to ARGŒUVRES (A + B) LACHAUSSÉE (C + D) ST SAUVEUR (HQrs) arriving at 2:15pm. Bivouac in both days areas at 3:40pm.	AMIENS
ST SAUVEUR	3rd		Trench party high over the lines in front of BELLENGLISE AMBALA Cavalry. Whole line quite unchanged.	
" (VERNAND)	14/15		Regiment relieved by part of the Queens Bays and 11th Hussars and went into huts and tents at VERNAND and remained up as a working party under the Corps. Hqrs A + B Sqns had to move to PICQUIGNY in trucks room for RGA in ST SAUVEUR and ARGŒUVRES.	
ST SAUVEUR	15th			
PICQUIGNY	26th		H.R.H. PRINCESS ROYAL'S BIRTHDAY. Sent up 36 OR's in relief of trench counter with the French party.	
"	23rd		Indian Regiment 9th & 5th Cav: Div: hard training.	
"	25th		Situation unchanged. Warned that the Regiment will move to LONGPRÉ – LES – CORPS SAINTS	
"	28th	11:0am	Regiment paraded on the BELLOY road Sear of LACHAUSSÉE and marched via BELLOY – L'ETOILE LENS to LONGPRÉ. On completion of move via Regiment Course under the orders of the AMBALA – CAV – BDE.	ABBEVILLE
LONGPRÉ				

R/Mun Lt Col
Comdg: 7th Dragoon Guards

1917-1918
5TH CAVALRY DIVISION
SECUNDERABAD CAV. BDE

20TH DECCAN HORSE

JAN 1917-FEB 1918

TO EGYPT
GHQ TROOPS
7 MTD BDE

SERIAL NO. 120.

Confidential

War Diary

of

20th DECCAN HORSE.

FROM 1st January 1917 **TO** 31st January 1917

Army Form C. 2118

Vol VII
20 Deccan Horse

WAR DIARY
or
INTELLIGENCE SUMMARY
(Erase heading not required.)

Instructions regarding War Diaries and Intelligence Summaries are contained in F.S. Regs., Part II. and the Staff Manual respectively. Title Pages will be prepared in manuscript.

Place	Date	Hour	Summary of Events and Information	Remarks and references to Appendices
HARCELAINES	JANUARY '17			
	1st 2nd 3rd		Capt. C. Jarvis reported his arrival from Pioneer Coy. (GaZette 31.12.'16) The following Officers and men reported their arrival from Divl School. Lieut. V.W. Murray, Lieut. L.A. Glascock, Lieut. H.F. Hallifax, 4 R.N.I.C. recd. The Pioneer detachment reported its arrival.	ORI. 9 3.10.S. 20215
	7th 8th		Lieut. J.R. Collins. 4. 105. O.R.s 2. ORI. 195 Jellums 5 Inoli Ool 3 GS. L nagows Lieut. A.S. Godfree. 1 SAS. NCOs 30 Towns 9. Ammoh 22 1 GS. nagows Lieut. J.D.H. Armstrong reported his departure to Divn Hqrs. as Intelligence Officer. The following promoted to Bde attack Gazette of Indian dt. 1.12.'16 - Tiks. Lieutenant. E.E. Lanford - 30. July. '15. L.A. Raymen. 30 Aug 15. L.A. Glascock 2.12.'15. J.C. Gulieve 2.11.12.'15. The following NCOs are confirmed. P.S. Swayn he. Lieutenant 4.5. May 16 to be 26. Oct '15 F.H. Ruck — — — do — — 30. Aug. 13 to be 30. July. '16.	
	11		Risaldar Major Argatia Ram awarded order of British India 2nd class. (G.G. No.1342) T/Major. A. Chamberlayne reported his arrival.	
	12			
	13 14 15		Lieut L.A. Raymen v BB ORs reported their arrival on return from ROUEN. Stores received. Lieut E.E. Lanford reported his departure to Divl School. The following men received orders to follow by drivlion hands Trophies - 1. O.M. 2nd class. 2923. Surf. Nihal Singh. 1.D.S.M. Risaldar Konsal Singh. No.546. Dar. Cassim Khan 3192.L.D. Multiya Singh. Ali Shah Khan. 658 Lut. Mug'd Zaman Khan. (London Gazette Hazura Singh. 340 S.Mar. Syed Ghulam Mahbub. (29.12.'16)	(London Gazette 29.12.'16)
	17th		Capt. C. Jarvis awarded Military Cross. 'T/Lieut. A/Maj. WORGAN awarded D.S.O and men leaving department "2 Jan. '17." 368 T. Zahur Muh'd appointed Trumpet Major with effect from 10.12.'16 - Lieut. V.W. Murray reported his departure to Div. School. L/Cpl 3. Ationo reported his departure to Divl School. Major A. Chamberlayne appointed Sq An Commr. vice Capt. C. P. Gregson retired with effect dt. 1.1.'17 (AO 1363) L/Cpl 9. Aceon, Lieut. Murray, 2/Lieut. A.S. Godfree reported their arrival from Divl School.	
	19th 20th 21st 24th 26th >			

[signature]
Lt. Colonel.
Commanding IV Deccan Horse

Serial No: **120**.

20th Deccan Horse.

From 1st to 28th February 1917.

Daily list of

in Adjutant

Issued to Section _____

From whom.	No. and date of letter received.

WAR DIARY or INTELLIGENCE SUMMARY

Army Form C. 2118

Place	Date	Hour	Summary of Events and Information	Remarks and references to Appendices
	FEBRUARY '17			
	6.		T/2nd Lt. H.W. BARROW posted to Regt. Lieut. antd. 5th April 1915. (Supplement London Gazette 19.1.17) Lieut. H.W. BARROW reported his arrival from Regiment on duty.	
	8th		The Pioneer Coy departed —	
			Major Syke	Lieut Rayment	3. ORs Capt Gregor	Lieut Murray		
	9th		Jem. Gunga Bihary	Jem. Yusuf Ali Khan I	243 ORs. Jem. Zafar Yab Khan	9 Drivers.	
	11th		The following joined Rur? School. Lieut Salusan. Jem. Dalip Singh II	Jem. Syed Ahmad on General course. Lieut Cornie. Jem. Rahim Shir Khan + 2 NCOs on Hotchkiss gun course.	
	14th		2 R.M.G. received —	
	15		Lieut Lapshore antd as Lieut from 30.7.15. Ind. Army. Supt notification No 10448 dated 1.12.16 — The following joined Div. School in Hotchkiss rifle course. Jem. Nihal Singh + 2 NCOs. The following rejoined from Rur? School. Jem. Rahim Shir Khan + 2 NCOs.	
	18.		Lieut Hamber reported his arrival from Signalling Course — Lieut Murray Evacuated sick from Pioneer Coy 15.2.'17 —	
	1		2. Pack Horses received —	
	21st		The following rejoined from Div. School. Jem. Nihal Singh + 2 NCO's —	
	23rd		Lieut Sachesen. (Flag. Yeo) promoted Captain antd 1st Sept. 1916. T/Lieut Collins promoted Lieut antd 2nd Apl. 1915. (3rd Supplement No 29934 18.12.17) Maj. Chamberlain is left for Div. School.	
	26th		Maj. Cresar reported his departure as O.C. Reinforcement's ROUEN.	
	27th		Lieut R.P.N. SWAYNE reported his arrival from duty. —	
	28th		Maj. Chamberlayne reported his arrival from Div. School. Jemadar Ram Singh + 3 ORs reported their departure to ROUEN (duty)	

E. Jarvis Capt.
Commanding XX Reconnaissance

Serial No: 120

Confidential

War Diary

fn March 1914

XX" Deccan Horse

Stad Cur-Bar

Vol IX

Army Form C. 2118

WAR DIARY
or
INTELLIGENCE SUMMARY
(Erase heading not required.)

Instructions regarding War Diaries and Intelligence Summaries are contained in F. S. Regs., Part II. and the Staff Manual respectively. Title Pages will be prepared in manuscript.

Place	Date	Hour	Summary of Events and Information	Remarks and references to Appendices
MARCH				
HARCELAINES	1st		Major A. Chamberlayne reported his departure to join 11th Border Regt.	
		1-10	left for Pigeon Coy. The following reported their arrival from Base School. Jemr. SHEIKH MOHIUDDIN + 50 O.R. 29 O.R.	
	2nd		Major OM Dyke reported his arrival from Pigeon Battn.	
	3rd		Lieut. H.J. Halifax evacuated sick.	
	5th		The following rejoined from Divl. School. 2.10s. and 20 O.R.	
	6th		The following left for Pigeon Coy. Lieut HSC Hamley. The following rejoined from the Divl. School. Capt. E.T. Salusin, 2/Lieut T.P. Henley -	
	7th		Capt C.D. Gregson appointed Sqn Commander, vice Capt. E.T. Salusin. Lieut T.P. Henley - Joining 20 O.R. 30 O.R. (offg)	
	8th		Capt C.D. Gregson reported his arrival from Pioneer Coy. 2nd March 1917. (D.O. 1398)	
	9th		3 O.R. rejoined from Signal Troop.	
	10th		2 pack animals received.	
	11th		The following rejoined from Divl. School. Risaldar GURDIAL SINGH + 10 O.R.	
	12th		The following left for Divl. School. Major OM. DYKE. Lieut S.R. Collins. Lieut W.W. BARROW. 3 O.R.s. 3 O.R.	
	14th		Pioneer Coy. rejoined. Lieut HSC Hamley. Lieut L.A. Rayman. Lieut K.N. Murray. 3 IOs. 20 NCOs. 250 O.R. 2 horses.	
	17th		Major OM. DYKE + 10 O.R. rejoined from Divl. School. 1 remount received -	
	19th		Lieut J.R. Collins, Lieut W.W. BARROW rejoined from Divl. School. 30 O.R. received -	
ANDAINEVILLE	20th		Regt left HARCELAINES at 10 am, and arrived in new area (ANDAINEVILLE) at 1 pm. Lieut R.P.H. SWAYNE evacuated sick -	
NEUVILLE - SOUS-LOEUILLY	21st		Regt continued the march and arrived in new area (NEUVILLE - SOUS - LOEUILLY, - MAMPTY - FOSSEMANANT) at 2.30 pm.	
HAMEL	22nd		Regt continued the march, and arrived in the Bois DE CROIX D'ACEROCHE. 3 pm.	
FEUILLERES	24th		Regt continued the march, and bivouached ½ mile S of FEUILLERES. 1.30 pm.	
"	25th 26th		9 reinforcements recd.	
MALLE	27th		Regt continued the march, and arrived at MALLE at 4 pm.	
CLERY	28th		Regt continued the march and arrived at CLERY (BRONZE) at 4 pm. -	
CURLU	29th		Regt continued the march and arrived at CURLU (BRONZE) at 4.30 pm.	
FRAMERVILLE	30th		Regt continued the march and arrived at FRAMERVILLE at 2.30 pm. 2 remounts rec'd -	
			Capt Salusin reported his departure to ROUEN on duty on 24/3/17 -	

Commanding 1st [illegible] Horse

Confidential Vol 10 Serial No. 120.

War Diary
of
20th Deccan Horse

from 1st April
to 30th April

Army Form C. 2118

WAR DIARY
or
INTELLIGENCE SUMMARY
(Erase heading not required.)

Instructions regarding War Diaries and Intelligence Summaries are contained in F.S. Regs., Part II. and the Staff Manual respectively. Title Pages will be prepared in manuscript.

Place	Date	Hour	Summary of Events and Information	Remarks and references to Appendices
APRIL				
FRAMERVILLE	2nd		Capt. J.R. Gilkon appointed Transport Officer with effect from 2nd April. Lt Col Mason relinquishes cmd & returns to 2nd Division HQRS from 2/4/17 (vice Wigram 24/12/16 to 2/4/17)	
	5th		Lt Col R.C.P. Burgoyne DSO proceeded for Captain from 24/11/16 (vide London Gazette 29/3/17) Capt (Tp Major) Lt Col C.H. Bean DSO apptd officer to be again commander vice Bt Col L. Vernant invalided. 4/11/14/16. vide I.A.O. 186 of 26/3/17.	
	6th		Lieut R.P.N. Swayne LAR joined Cadre Base before ROUEN from No 3 Sen. Hospital as a supernumerary class 'b' 26/3/17	
	10th		Regt Sergt FRAMERVILLE at 9AM and arrived at TREFCON at 3 PM.	
TREFCON	15th		12 reinforcements received.	
	18th		11 reinforcements received on 16/4/17 from Cav Base before ROUEN	
	25th		Major R.M. Ryde 21st Cavalry and Major W.S. Crocker 8th Cavalry. Rank of Major to be antedated to 1st Sept 1915 (vide without pay or allowance) Capts (Temp Majors) R.C. Ross DSO, and Bt Major R.B. Worgan to be Majors from 1st Sept 1915 but without pay or allowances before 1st Sept 1916. Authority London Gazette of 6/4/17	
			By Lieut. H.F. Holifax 2nd Res Regt Cavalry apptd Qtr for General service 4/4/17 & ordered to join Expeditionary Force on 19/4/17 and Report to ? O. Halton Cav Base Depot & ROUEN (vide Embark of Body Orders - posted 165 of 20/4/17	
	24th		Cml ORI received from ROUEN on 21/4/17	
	26th		Cml 30 (Brev P.C. GOTHIC) 70RI and Ord asst armourer, and eight motor drivers received from ROUEN on 25/4/17	
	30th		Lt Col Ladams to be Commandant vide Indian Army Order No. 274 of 26.6.17	
			Brev Major R.B. Worgan Tempty Lt Col 8th Sqdn Cornwlls vice Major Ladams appointed Commandant.	
			Lieut Murray JAR apptd officer ig/c ROUEN today - ? 1 O.R.B Transport from A.T.C.	
			Lieut F.C. Gates having resumed regt. resumed charge ? R.T.C. Transport from A.T.C.	

J. Mornf
Lt. Col. Cmdg XX?V

Serial No. 120

From 1st May to 30th June 1917.

Confidential

War Diary for month of May 1917.

From 1st – 31st May 1917

D/y Deccan Horse

Vol XI

Army Form C. 2118

WAR DIARY or INTELLIGENCE SUMMARY
(Erase heading not required.)

Instructions regarding War Diaries and Intelligence Summaries are contained in F.S. Regs., Part II. and the Staff Manual respectively. Title Pages will be prepared in manuscript.

Place	Date	Hour	Summary of Events and Information	Remarks and references to Appendices
62/L28a.	15/7		Signaller Coy left TREFCON Camp at 8.am., arrived at 10:15 a.m. Relief was completed at 12:30. Army I. L.T. Lt. Col. Adams Commanding, with Capt Gregson, Capt Mulloy, Capt Larkin, 2/Lt Lawford, Fgg. Gascoite, Lt Godfree, 10 Indian Officers, 1 Sub Ant Surgeon, 266 O.R.I., 9 O.R.B. + 3 Followers.	
	16/7		A sqdn in main line + defence, 30 men Ration Fatigue for PH + 70 men digging in trenches. B, C + D sqdns in reserve.	
	17/7		B sqdn in main line, 3 sqdns in support. 20 men Ration Fatigue for PH, 70 men making light gun emp't under RE direction.	
	18/7		C sqdn in main line, 3 sqdns in support. RE stores + wiring. Shrap Park in trenches. Co MO in trenches.	
	19/7		D sqdn in main line, 3 sqdns in support. 100 men Collecting + carrying RE stores. 8 men wiring Shrap Park in trenches. Continued. O.P. + L.2.B.a. RE mazril	
	20/7		A sqdn in main line, 3 sqdns in support. 20 men wiring + 100 men fitting + 100 men carrying	
	21/7		Relief of PH commenced at 10 a.m. Completed 21:30. PH. A + B sqdns on left under Capt Gregson — C + D sqdns on Right under Capt Mulloy, fielding trenches. no 1017 Sout. Kalka Singh no 972 Sowar Ram Singh I. took on issue + injuring Park.	left 23
	22/7		Situation Quiet — No followers, took bombed by a Sellaburst. No 1260 Sowar Shih Rezabuddin no 1602 Sowar Bharwan slightly wounded at duty.	
	23/7		Situation Normal. As followers. Patrol was sent out. 2/Godfree, Sowar Ram Singh 1265 Sowar Sarda Singh + 757 Sowar Lal Singh and B.O.R.I. G. Murray. Patrol successfully encountered with the enemy. 3 wounded and captured 72 enemy killed. Patrol returned Kathal Cassalline — Report returning 17.30.	App. 9
	24/7		Situation Normal — No followers. Bar. upriver. Time arrival at H.O. Patrol — Infantry — 2/Manley, Raynham + 2 left Robinson, took on unload — new Park. 2.O.R.I. enquired his unload. + Offered + dispatch to + pm C spsn.	
	25/7		Situation Normal. Patrol advances to the + Tomkinson 2/Russell + 2 O.R.I. proceed to Shrap Park — Concluded wiring Range + Shrap Park.	
	26/7		Situation Normal — Capt CD Gregson proceeds to England + 2 O.P.A. from Relieved by Capt James. The Patrol during night acquired useful information + security + zebilite (App. B)	APP 18

Army Form C. 2118

WAR DIARY
or
INTELLIGENCE SUMMARY
(Erase heading not required.)

Instructions regarding War Diaries and Intelligence Summaries are contained in F.S. Regs., Part II. and the Staff Manual respectively. Title Pages will be prepared in manuscript.

Place	Date	Hour	Summary of Events and Information	Remarks and references to Appendices
Field	28/5/7		Relief of 9 L.H.R. in Bde Reserve A.S.C. Commenced 9.10 p.m. complete 12.30 a.m.	
	29/5/7		2 Tunbridge 2nd Lieut Robinson reported departure Back area - Lt Burrows reported arrival of new ptn to half D Sqdn - Eff Str - Pay team employed to D Sqdn. Working parties of 200 O.R. under R.E. direction	
	30/5/7		Situation Quiet - working parties 140 O.R. under R.E. direction	
	31/5/7		Enemy helicopter reported overhead in Emone - 144 O.R. working under R.E. direction	

31st May '17

[signature]
Lt. Col.
Comd. 10 L. Horse Regt.

War Diary

20th Deccan Horse

1st June to 30th June 1917.

Army Form C.2118

WAR DIARY
or
INTELLIGENCE SUMMARY
(Erase heading not required.)

Instructions regarding War Diaries and Intelligence Summaries are contained in F.S. Regs., Part II. and the Staff Manual respectively. Title Pages will be prepared in manuscript.

Place	Date	Hour	Summary of Events and Information	Remarks and references to Appendices
Field	1.6.17		Regiment in Brigade Reserve. Situation Quiet.- 136 O.R. working nightly under R.E. direction. Wiring Trench Digging and Road making- No.3080 Dafadar Santokh Singh, 21st Cavalry attached 20th D.H. granted Medaille Militaire R.O. 31.5.17.	
	2.6.17		Situation Quiet- Night working parties as above.	
	3.6.17		Situation quiet - As above.	
	4.6.17		Situation Quiet- Relief of S.S.T. by S.O. commenced 9.45.p.m. completed 12.5.a.m. 5.6.17. Regiment disposed in depth one Squadron R/half of out post line. One Squadron L/half of ditto 1 Squadron in counter attack line and 1 Squadron Regimental Reserve.	
	5.6.17		Situation quiet - 3 small reconnoitring Detachments worked in no man's land during night 5/6.6.17. 2 Patrols encountered superior enemy forces Results Objective attained. Casualties No.3268 L.D. Ali Muhammad Khan 21st Cavalry attached XX Deccan Horse killed by rifle fire. Lieut Godfree slightly wounded by Grenade splinter, at Duty. Reports attached.	A/A.C.
	6.6.17		Situation Quiet- One strong patrol under Lieut Rayneau and Jemadar Bhawani Singh 29 O.R.I. was sent out with the object of capturing or destroying enemy patrols- No enemy were encountered. Desired information was obtained. Patrol returned. Jemadar Dhalip Singh I and 2 O.R.I. proceeded to Gas Course. Captain T.K. Wilson, Ressaidar Muhammed Khan, Jemadar Zaferyab Khan one O.R.B. and 2 horses proceeded to join I.C. Entrenching Battalion.	
	7.6.17		Situation Quiet- 2 strong patrols and one small reconnoitring Detachment went out at dark object destruction of enemy patrol, and recommaissance of ASCENSION WOOD. No enemy were encountered desired information was obtained.	

WAR DIARY
or
INTELLIGENCE SUMMARY

(Erase heading not required.)

Army Form C. 2118

Place	Date	Hour	Summary of Events and Information	Remarks and references to Appendices
Field	8.6.17		Situation Quiet. 2 small reconnoitring detachments each under 1.N.C.O. and 1 Troop under Lieut Rayneau reconnoitred ASCENSION Wood. Useful information obtained. No casualties. Later Lieut Barrow and 3 O.R.I. reconnoitred same locality and returned with information. 2nd Lieut A.3.Godfree awarded Military Cross. Captain Larkin evacuated sick believed to be measles.	
	9.6.17		Situation Quiet. A strong patrol under Lieut Barrow wentout at midnight. Objective, interior of ASCENSION WOOD, not attained Reports attached. No.134 Dafadar Rai Singh 20th Deccan Horse awarded Indian D.S.Medal. No.1146 Sr.Jug Lall B.Squadron killed by Grenade. Jemadar Ganga Bishen slightly wounded in the hand at duty. D.Squadron relieved by C.Squadron under Lieut Lawford.	A/A. D
	10.6.17		Situation Quiet. Patrol under Lieut Lawford penetrated ASCENSION WOOD but returned without going far in on approach of daylight. Operations were hindered by heavy storm of rain.	
	11.6.17		Situation Quiet. Small patrols reconnoitred ASCENSION WOOD at S and E sides Objective preparation for raid on night 12/13th June. Captain C.D.Gregson reported unfit for duty by Medical Board & struck off strength of Regiment from 7.6.17. Ressaidar Dalip Singh reported arrival from Back Area vice Jemadar Ganga Bishen.	
	12.6.17		Situation Quiet. Lieut Tinley reported arrival from Back Area and took over "C" Squadron in forward line. Preparation for Raid completed.	
	13.6.17		Raid commenced with Artillery and M.G.Barrage at 2.a.m. Raiding party moved at ASCENSION WOOD at 2.5.a.m. Returned to Outpost line 3.15.a.m. Report attached. Casualties as per list attached. Lieut E.E.Lawford and 4 O.R.I. missing. Situation remained quiet until evening when intermittent shelling of Outpost line by enemy was commenced. 20 O.R.I. reported arrival from Back Area to replace casualties. Lieut Glasspoole slightly wounded by Bomb evacuated. Ressaidar Dalip Singh wounded by Bomb- evacuated. Search parties for missing ranks worked all day & night 13th/14th June.	o/p. E.

Army Form C.2118

WAR DIARY
or
INTELLIGENCE SUMMARY

(Erase heading not required.)

Instructions regarding War Diaries and Intelligence Summaries are contained in F.S. Regs., Part II. and the Staff Manual respectively. Title Pages will be prepared in manuscript.

Place	Date	Hour	Summary of Events and Information	Remarks and references to Appendices
Zi.11	14.6.17		Situation Quiet, except for shelling of varying intensity of Outposts Line Retaliation by Heavy Artillery was called for at 5.30.p.m.and checked enemy's fire. This recommenced at 11.p.m. A direct hit on No.6 post at 3.30.a.m.killed 4 and wounded 3 O.R.I. At 2 p.m.1 man was killed and 3 wounded in same post by H.E.Shrapnel.List attached. During night relief of regiment was commenced at 10.p.m.by Fort Garry Horse Can.Cav. Brigade. Major O.M.Dyke,Lieut F.C.Guthrie,Jemadars Ganga Bishen,Dhalip Singh I and Syed Ahmed; 1 O.R.B. 2 O.R.I.1 Follower proceeded to join dismounted reinforcements.	APP. F.
	15.6.17		Relief completed at 3.15.a.m.Regiment returned to TREFCON at 5.30.a.m. Lieut W.S.C.Hamley,Jemadar Bowani Singh,1.O.R.B.and 99 O.R.I.proceeded to join Dismounted Reinforcements. Lt.Col.F.Adams Captain C.Jarvis M.C. Captain N.F.C.Mulloy,Captain J.R.Collins,Lieut F.B.N.Tinley M.C.Lieut W.G.Figg,Lieut W.W.Barrow Lieut L.A.Rayneau,Lieut A.S.Godfree M.C.,Ressaldar Ali Sher Khan Ressaidars Richpal Singh, Gugan Singh, Woordie Major Sher Singh,Jemadars Sheikh Mohiuddin, Nihal Singh, Dalip Singh II,Yousuf Ali Khan I,1 Sub Asst. Surgeon 10 O.R.B. and 167 O.R.I. returned from forward area. Inspection of Horses of Secunderabad Cavalry Brigade by Corps Commander General KAVANAGH.	
	16.6.17		G.O.C.Sec'bad Bde.compliments(1)the Regimental Signallers on their work during passed month. (2)All ranks during the same period.	
	17.6.17		No.13 Farrier Major Tika Ram,No.441 Dafadar Mirza Muhammad Ali Beg,No. 3080 Dafadar Santokh Singh awarded the I.D.S.Medal.	
	18.6.17		Cavalry Corps Commander General KAVANAGH visited camp TREFCON met B.Os and Indian Officers expressed his satisfaction with Regiment during time spent in Trenches.Referred in gratifying manner to leadership of Officers and fighting spirit of men "One Indian Cavalry man on foot was proved a better man than 1 German soldier"	

Army Form C. 2118

WAR DIARY or INTELLIGENCE SUMMARY

(Erase heading not required.)

Instructions regarding War Diaries and Intelligence Summaries are contained in F.S. Regs, Part II. and the Staff Manual respectively. Title Pages will be prepared in manuscript.

Place	Date	Hour	Summary of Events and Information	Remarks and references to Appendices
Lule	19.6.17		The following Officers promoted to Lieutenants, 2nd Lieut J.D.Heaton Armstrong (8th September 1915), Frederick Charles Guthrie (13th Novr.15), Leonard Alfred Glasspoole (20th Novr.15), Reginald Percy Nugent Swayne (19th March 1916), Victor William Murray (29th May 1916),	
"	20.6.17		2nd Lieut F.R.H.Robinson reported arrival from M.G.School from Musketry Course. Jemadar Bhawani Singh reported his arrival from Dismounted Reinforcements and proceeded to Gas course. Major O.M.Dyke, 1 O.R.B. 1 O.R.I. reported their arrival from Dismounted Reinforcements.	
	22.6.17		Jemadar Nihal Singh evacuated sick.	
	23.6.17		Captain E.P.Larkin, 1 O.R.B. reported arrival from Casualty clearing Station. Lieut F.C.Guthrie, Jemadar Dhalip Singh I, Jemadar Rahim Sher Khan 41 O.R.I., 1 Follower reported their arrival from Dismounted Reinforcements. Following reported their departure for duty in Trenches Major O.M.Dyke Captains C.Jarvis M.C., N.F.C.Mulloy, Lieutenants F.B.N.Tinley M.C., W.G.Figg, W.S.C.Hamley, W.W.Barrow, L.A.Rayneau, A.S.Godfree, M.C., 2nd Lieut F.R.H.Robinson, Captain R.C.P.Berryman, I.M.S. Risaldars Kurshed Muhammed Khan, Ali Sher Khan, Ressaidar Gugan Singh Woordie Major Sher Singh, Jemadars Ganga Bishen, Dalip Singh I and II, Bhowani Singh Syed Ahmed 10 O.R.B. 280 O.R.I. 1 private follower. Dismounted Regiment as above left TREFCON at 1.p.m.and arrived VADENCOURT Chteau at 3.p.m. Relief of S.U. (18th Lancers completed 4.45.p.m. reported to Brigade 2.p.m. Regiment in Brigade Reserve Subsector A.2.	
	24.6.17		Captain E.P.Larkin reported arrival at 5.30.p.m.from Back Area.	
	25.6.17		Captain N.F.C.Mulloy evacuated sick. Following reinforcements joined the Regiment Jemadar Sheikh Fayazuddin and 20 O.R.I.	
	26.6.17		Announcement of Immediate Award of following honours— Military Cross— Captain N.F.C.Mulloy, 32nd Lancers attached 20th D.H. Indian Distinguished Service Medal Ressaidar Dalip Singh, Jemadar Dalip Singh II, 226 K.Dafr Lehri 284 K.Dafr Hira Singh, 3702 Dafr Muhd.Ali Khan 1328 Sowar Mam Chand.	

App. C.

To
 The O.C.
  S.O.A.
   Dated 6.6.17

A patrol composed of 1.B.O. & I.O. two Dafadars and two Lance Dafadars under me left post 7 at 10.p.m.5th to make myself and others members of the patrol acquainted with the ground between our line and ASCENSION WOOD- in accordance with your instructions.

The patrol moved N.outside our wire to the Sunken road at G.35.b.3.3.This road was then reconnoitred to G.35.b.6.9.and found unoccupied.

The patrol then moved S.to G.35 d.5.7.and halted for 15 minutes. It then returned to G.35.b.3.9.and again entered the road. Thence moving S for some 50 yards the patrol lay up for some 20 minutes while I pointed out the features visible to the patrol. At the end of that time the patrol started to return to our lines when 3 bombs were thrown at us- apparently from the sunken road. Time 11.30.p.m.

Being at a serious disadvantage with the moon at my back and being practically on the sky line and having no knowledge of the strength of the enemy,I considered it best to retire,which I did. The bombs thrown were well aimed and landed with in a dozen yards of me. No enemy movement in ASCENSION WOOD was heard until 11 O.C The patrol returned at 12.30.

(Sd)A.S.Godfree Lieut
 S.O.

s.o. Off: C

Report by Listening Patrol.

At 10.p.m. I left No.9 Post with 3 men with a view to ascertaining what routes were being used by the enemy for his patrols.

I took my patrol to the Northern corner of ASCENSION wood, and waited there for about 45 minutes.

Not hearing any sound and thinking it would not be advisable to make for LITTLE BILL owing to the moon and having to cross the Sky line, I took my patrol to a point at the back of ASCENSION wood at about point G.26.a 59, on the East of the road between LITTLE BILL and ASCENSION Wood

I waited at this point till about 12-15 a.m., and just then I saw a party of enemy perhaps about 25 strong walking

towards ASCENSION Wood.

When these people got clear I thought it was time to return and accordingly retreated back in the direction of rockets sent up from between our Nos.8 & 9 posts.

I brought my patrol safely back to within 20 yards of

the wire of my O.P.No.2 in front of No.9 Post, when suddenly I saw a party of enemy at our wire.

I thought it advisable to lie quiet as they numbered about a dozen, and I thought they would pass.

They however made straight in my direction and I thought my only way was to effect a surprise. I waited till they came to within 10 yards of me and then charged them.

The enemy fired a volley from the hip and then ran towards ASCENSION WOOD; I saw Ali Muhammed Khan standing in front of a German and thinking him quite safe, and under the impression he had got a prisoner. I with the balance of my patrol chased what remained of the enemy right up to ASCENSION WOOD being just in time to hit one of the enemy with my stick and also in time to prevent my men from entering the wood. I brought my two men back to No.9 Post and enquired if Ali Muhammed Khan had brought back a prisoner, and was told that he had not returned.

I then returned to the scene of the conflict at G.25 d 0.5.9 and searched the ground, and found Ali Muhammed Khan lying shot through the chest, I got him carried back to the post, but he expired on the way.

(sd) L.A. Rayneau Lieut

II

Lieut Rayneau carried out my instruction to the letter up to the time he charged the enemy. I consider that in doing so he was absolutely justified and while it is to be regretted that a good man lost his life, the fact that nine or ten of the enemy ran from Lieut Rayneau and his two remaining men should not be lost sight of.

(Sd) N.F.C. Mulloy Captain

Prefix .... Code .... m.	Words	Charge	This message is on a/c of :	Recd. at .... m.
Office of Origin and Service Instructions.	Sent		.... Service.	Date ....
....	At .... m.			From ....
....	To			
....	By		(Signature of "Franking Officer.")	By ....

TO {

Sender's Number.	Day of Month.	In reply to Number.	A A A

From
Place
Time

The above may be forwarded as now corrected. (Z)

Censor. Signature of Addressor or person authorised to telegraph in his name.

* This line should be erased if not required.

750,000. W 3186—M509. H. W. & V., Ld. 6/16.

Patrol Report S.O.A & B.   Dated 9.6.17.

Strength- Lieut Barrow 1 I.O. 24 O.R.I.

Departure 12.45.a.m. Return 3.0.A.M.

Object - To ascertain whether ASCENSION WOOD was held and the nature and position of enemy's defences.

Informations The patrol left No.7 post and struck the sunken road S of ASCENSION WOOD about G.25.b.9.1, they then moved along the Southern edge of the road as far as about G.25.d.0.0. there rifle and M.G.fire was opened on the patrol from the wood, after the patrol had been lying in that position for about 20 minutes under a heavy fire, a party of at least 40 enemy came over the hill from the direction of No.6 and 7 Posts, the patrol faced round to meet them & at the same time were fired on by rifle and M.G. from the ridge at the S.W. corner of ASCENSION wood.

The enemy threw bombs at our patrol who opened fire at a close range, they then moved round our left flank towards the wood and our patrol having waited for some time without finding a chance of entering the wood in face of the superior numbers returned at 3.15.a.m.

                          (Sd)C.Jarvis Captain
                            S.O.A and B

Field
13.6.17

In accordance with Sec'bad Brigade O.O.No.43.A raid was carried out in ASCENSION WOOD, with the object of killing and capturing Germans who were holding the wood, and of destroying the posts.

I ordered a Squadron under Captain Mulloy to carry out the actual raid, sending a troop under Lieut Barrow to act as covering party, and afterwards to take over prisoners.

Covering troops were put out well to the front (i.e.East) of posts Nos.6 & 9 down the hill towards ASCENSION WOOD.

The raiding Squadron left GRAHAM'S Post at 12.30.a.m. and passed through our wire near No.9 Post about 30 minutes later- Just after they had passed through our wire a post on our left was apparently attacked by an enemy's bombing party, which necessitated, the regiment on our left opening Hotchkiss Rifle Fire and using Very lights. This somewhat delayed the arrival of the two rear troops at the position of readiness, which was some 150 yards to the NORTH of the Wood.

At Zero hour (2.a.m.) the Artillery opened fire and Captain Mulloy advanced on the wood which he entered 2 or 3 minutes later, without opposition. There appear to have been some Germans in the Wood, who left it on hearing our approach.

The raiding party destroyed some dug outs, cut wire where it existed, and having thoroughly searched the wood, left it in accordance with orders at 2.30.a.m. Troops having been ordered to return to our line as follows; 1 troop to No.9 Post,1 to No.6 post,1 to the North of the Sunken road and one to the South of the same.

On emerging from the wood the Squadron came under very heavy rifle and Machine Gun Fire from the Sunken Road, which they attacked, but owing to the intensity of the fire and the free use of ~~the~~ hand grenades it was found impossible to surround the enemy. In this conflict several

Germans were killed, but under the conditions existing at the moment, it was impracticable to carry out a systematic examination of the bodies. One of these was carried back for purposes of identification, from his shoulder straps & identity disc, he belonged to the 73 Fus.R. A shoulder strap bearing No.453 was taken from another body.

The Squadron carried out its task without casualty, but during the action on the return to our lines, I regret to report Lieut Lawford to be missing. It is said that he was seen to be wounded, but this has yet to be confirmed, Lieut Glasspoole was wounded slightly as was Ressaidar Dalip Singh, four other ranks were killed, Four other ranks are missing, and reported by individual sowars as being killed, this latter statement requires further confirmation. Twenty two other ranks are wounded, of whom 5 are slightly and at duty.

The Squadron carried out its mission, and having completed its task returned to our lines about 3.15 a.m. I consider the leading of the Squadron reflects considerable credit on Captain Mulloy, who was undoubtedly assisted by the fire of the Artillery and Machine Gun Squadron.

Lt.Colonel
Commandant S.C.

APP.E

I left GRIFFIN post at 12.30 a.m.15.6.17 Lieut Rayner
with 1 Troop leading followed by Lieut Lawford with
1 Troop followed by myself with two troops in support
followed by the covering troop under Lieut Barrow.
Lieut Barrow accompanied Lieut Rayner in order to pick
a position for his troop Lieut Glasspoole with a Lewis
Gunner accompanied me. As we left our own wire the Regt.
on our left was as I understand attacked by the enemy
as they opened fire with Hotchkiss Rifles and sent up
numerous very lights as the bullets sound to be coming
fairly close to my party they in conjunction with the
lights seriously impeded my progress. When I got to my
position of readiness about G.25.a.0.0.. I found my rear
troop and the covering troop was missing, as it was near
zero hour and the scheme had been very carefully explained
to every man. I decided not to further weaken my
party by searching for them. We got to the wood at zero
hour and went straight in. We bombed and destroyed several
Dugouts none of which were more than splinter proof and
cut the small amount of wire there was At zero - 15
the enemy were reported to be in the South East corner
of the wood. I went there to reconnoitre with three men
and found no one there but was heavily fired on by an
Automatic rifle and about 10 men who were in the Sunken
road at G.25.b.0.0.I retired to the wood at G.25.b.7.4.
and waited for the signal rocket. As I had given orders
for 1 Troop to return S of the Sunken road. I collected
two more troops as they came out and took them in a
semicircle to about G.25.b.7.2.and succeeded in gaining
the sunken road,being fired on and bombed as we came
up we returned the enemy's fire at very short range but
could not see them in the bushes in order to attack with
the bayonet. I did not see anything of the troop which

2

should have gone South of the road. While this was going on I found myself being fired on by single men lying about in the open about G.35.b.5.4.(i.e. from my rear) I took a troop back and killed seven of the enemy. We could take no prisoners as they bombed and fired until we were on to them. I here met Major Campbell Ross who told me he was wounded and that there were some of the enemy in the Sunken road about G.35.b.5.2.

I collected as many men as I could roughly a troop and a half and ordered Lieut Glasspoole to go for the enemy. I sent in two of the German bodies for identification purposes as owing to Machine Gun and Rifle fire it was too unhealthy to stand still and search them on the spot. As soon I saw I had a good many wounded men I recalled Lieut Glasspoole about zero plus 75 and gave the order for the wounded to be collected and for the party to retire as it was then getting light. I found Lieut Rayneau with his troop at G.35.b.5.5.

Lieut Lawford I had no news of from the time he entered the wood when I last saw him. The two Troops leading at the commencement went together to the place detailed for the rear troop and carried on. (bombing)

I know the enemy had one automatic rifle and I believe them to have had at least one more and a strength in my opinion of about 30-35 rifles. They used rifle fire and bombs.

I would like to add that all the men showed the greatest dash and gallantry mentioning the names of No.2230 Kote Dafadars Lehri and Hira Singh.

[signature]
Captain
2nd i/c O.

The following casualties which occurred on 13th instant are published for information.

Killed

No.3659 Sowar Neki Ram 7th H.L.attached B.Sqdn
No.3380 Sowar Rustam Khan " D.Sqdn
No.1301 " Gokul Singh 3rd D. "
No.3650 " Abdur Rahman Khan 32nd L.attached D.Sqdn.

Missing

Lieut E.E.Lawford.
No.924 A.L.D.Nand Ram B.Squadron
No.1040 " Amar Singh "
No.1033 Sowar Sada Ram "
No.790 L.D.Kishon Singh D.Squadron

Wounded

Lieut L.A.Glasspoole
No.1062 A.L.D.Punjab Singh A.Squadron
No.757 Sowar Santa Singh "
No.1258 " Mehar Singh "
No.3450 " Rur Singh 33rd L.C.attached
Ressaidar Dalip Singh B.Squadron
No.986 K.D.Lahri "
No.3190 Dafadar Nihal Singh 7th H.L.attached
No.3195 " Niadar Singh "
3624 A.L.D.Kanhaya Singh "
No.1074 Sowar Bharat Singh II B.Squadron
No.1066 " Ranpath "
3702 Dafadar Muhammad Ali Khan 7th H.L.attached
No.3421 L.D.Muhammad Umar Khan 21st Cavalry "
No.3407 Sowar Mashuq Ali Khan " "
No.1169 A.L.D.Kundan Singh D.Sqdn
No.1411 Sowar Lakshmichand D.Sqdn
No.1509 Sowar Jhannoo Singh D.Sqdn

Wounded slightly at Duty.

No.894 K.D.Hira Singh D.Squadron
No.1338 Sowar Mamchand B.Sqdn
No.1096 Sowar Chandgi Ram B.Sqdn.
No.1132 Sowar Bhagat Singh B.Sqdn
No.943 Sowar Desraj B.Squadron
No.3544 A.L.D.Jug Lall

The following Casualties occurred on 1rth June 1917

Killed

No.1271 Sowar Kishon Lal B.Squadron

No.1120 Sowar Sukh Lal   B.Squadron

No.3685 Sowar Nathu Ram 7th H.L.attached B.Sqdn

No.1141 Sowar Rupchand B.Squadron

No.1284 Sowar Hira Singh   "

Wounded

No.1050 Sowar Molar B.Squadron

No.1415   "   Munshi Ram   "

No.1336   "   Rizak Ram   "

No.1231 A.L.D.Khema   "

No.3515 Sowar Kapur Singh 7th H.L.attached A.Sqdn

No.1259   "   Mehar Singh   A.   "

Serial No: 120.

War Diary
of
XXth Decean Horse.

From 1st July 1917 to 31st July 1917.

(Vol I)

Confidential

Army Form C. 2118

WAR DIARY
or
INTELLIGENCE SUMMARY

(Erase heading not required.)

Instructions regarding War Diaries and Intelligence Summaries are contained in F.S. Regs., Part II. and the Staff Manual respectively. Title Pages will be prepared in manuscript.

Place	Date	Hour	Summary of Events and Information	Remarks and references to Appendices
Field	3.7.17		Sower No.1131 Chanan Singh 20th Deccan Horse died at Marseilles on 25.6.17. Captain Jarvis M.C. to be Major from 18.1.17. Captain Gregson to be Major from 15.2.17 Lieut Tinley to be Captain from 6.3.15.	
	4.7.17		Captain Malloy M.C. 32nd Lancers rejoined Regiment from Hospital.	
	5.7.17		The following reinforcements arrived and were taken on the strength of Regiment 10 O.R.I. reference R.O.891 Ressaidar Delip Singh rejoined from Hospital.	
	6.7.17		Lieut L.A.Glasspoole I.A. reported arrival from Hospital.	
	8.7.17		Brevet Major R.B.Worgan D.S.O. rejoined from Line Battn (9th Cheshire Regiment) The following reported arrival from Indian Cavalry Entrenching Battalion Captain T.K.Wilson, Lieut Murray Ressaidar Muhammed Khan Jemadar Zafaryab Khan 2 O.R.B. 2 horses.	
	9.7.17		Trench party under Major O.M.Dyke reported arrival at 7.30.p.m. from Forward area.	
	13.7.17		Captain E.P.Larkin reported departure to England on duty Regiment received orders to march Northwards on 14th- Captain Collins Glasgow Yeomanry Lieut Rust, Ressaidar Muhammed Khan- Jemadar Zafaryab Khan, 87 O.R.I. 2 O.R.B. remained as Dismounted Reinforcements at TREFCON. Order received from G.O.C.Brigade for No.575 Dafadar Sirdar Khan to be reduced to the ranks from 13.7.17 by order of G.O.C.Brigade for continued sickness on duty.	Reference R.O.10th July No.902
	14.7.17		Regiment left TREFCON at 1.30.p.m.and arrived at Bivouacs CARTIGNY at 5.p.m.	
	15.7.17		Regiment left CARTIGNY at 7.0.a.m. and arrived at Camp SUZANNE at 10.30.a.m.	

Army Form C. 2118

WAR DIARY
or
INTELLIGENCE SUMMARY

(Erase heading not required.)

Instructions regarding War Diaries and Intelligence Summaries are contained in F.S. Regs, Part II. and the Staff Manual respectively. Title Pages will be prepared in manuscript.

Place	Date	Hour	Summary of Events and Information	Remarks and references to Appendices
Field	16.7.17		Regiment left QUESNEL at 7.15.a.m.and arrived at Camp MORLANCOURT at 10.a.m.	
	17.7.17		Regiment left MORLANCOURT at 7.0 a.m.and arrived at THIEVRES(Billets)at 12.30.p.m.	
	18.7.17		Regiment left THIEVRES at 6.0.a.m.and arrived at TROIS-VAUX(St.Pol)at 2.15.p.m. Temporary Lieut H.F.Halifax General Last Cav lry rejoined from 20th Lancers. C.Sdn Collins Mout Rust,2 I.Os 67 O.R.I.,2 O.R.B.Dismounted party rejoined	
	19.7.17		One O.R.I.transferred from 33rd S.I.H. reported arrival	
	20.7.17		Regiment left TROISVAUX at 3.30.a.m.and arrived at MONCHY-CAYEUX(Billets)at 3.30.p.m.	
	26.7.17		Jemadir Zafaryab Khan 38nd Lancers(attached)and two O.R.I.Reported departure to ROUEN on duty.	
	29.7.17		Lieut T.W.Barrow appointed to officiate as Quarter Master vice Lieut F.H.Rust as from 14.7.17	
			[signature] Lt.Colonel	
	31.7.17		Commandant XX Deccan Horse	

Serial No: 120.

War Diary

20th Deccan Horse

From 1st August 1917
To 31st August 1917

WAR DIARY

INTELLIGENCE SUMMARY

(Erase heading not required.)

Army Form C. 2118

Instructions regarding War Diaries and Intelligence Summaries are contained in F.S. Regs., Part II. and the Staff Manual respectively. Title Pages will be prepared in manuscript.

Place	Date	Hour	Summary of Events and Information	Remarks and references to Appendices
The Field.	2.8.17.		Eight remount horses arrived.	
	5.8.17.		Sentence 1 enforced punishment 1 twenty lashes for disobeying the lawful commands of a superior officer on No.1376. Sowar LAL MUHAMMAD Khan. (Summary Court Martial) duly promulgated and carried out.	
	14.8.17.		One N.C.O. arrived from ROUEN.	
	16.8.17.		Lieut BARROW, Lieut GODFREE M.C., 2/Lieut ROBINSON, Jemadar SHER SINGH and 3 N.C.O.s attended a Course in Pioneering at TROISVAUX, on the 16th 17th and 18th. Lieut Col ADAMS was appointed "Officier de l'Ordre de la Couronne". (D.O. 1570)	
	19.8.17.		Captain LARKIN (Glasgow Yeomanry) reported from Sutton in England	
	20.8.17.		The Brigade was inspected in Marching Order by the Divisional Commander.	
	22.8.17.		Lieut RAYNEAU appointed Signalling Officer vice Lieut GLASSPOOLE on duty with the Bde.	
	23.8.17.		Lieut HALLIFAX appointed Offg. Asst. from 20.7.17 vice Capt. TINLEY relieved. (D.O. 1581) Two L.D. horses received from No. 13. M.G. Sqdn.	
	24.8.17.		One N.C.O. proceeded to ROUEN on duty. No.1053. Sowar SADA RAM reported missing on 13.6.17, now reported killed.	
	25.8.17.		No.1053 Sowar SADA RAM reported previously missing on 13.6.17 now reported killed.	

Army Form C. 2118

WAR DIARY
or
INTELLIGENCE SUMMARY
(Erase heading not required.)

Place	Date	Hour	Summary of Events and Information	Remarks and references to Appendices
The Field.	27.8.17.		Lieut. Col. ADAMS proceeded to ROUEN on duty.	
	29.8.17.		Lieut-Col ADAMS returned from ROUEN.	
	31.8.17.		Eight remount horses arrived.	
			Dated 31 August 17.	
			[signature] Lt Col.	
			Comdt 26 Reserve Horse.	

Confidential

Serial No. 120.

War Diary

20th Deccan Horse

S'bad Cavalry Bde.

From 1st to 30th Septr. 1914

Army Form C. 2118.

WAR DIARY
or
INTELLIGENCE SUMMARY.
(Erase heading not required.)

Place	Date	Hour	Summary of Events and Information	Remarks and references to Appendices
The field	8.9.17		The Regiment was inspected by Lieut. Genl. Sir H.V.Cox KCMG,CB, CSI. Military Sec'y to the Hon'ble Sec'y of State for India.	
	11.9.17		Capt. C.F. CLARKE relinquished the appointment of Adjutant with effect from 1.8.17	
	13.9.17		Jemadar SHER SINGH was removed from the appointment of Wordi Major and Jemadar SHEKH FAYAZUDDIN was appointed in his stead with effect from 11.9.17.	
	14.9.17		Twenty seven O.R.I. left to proceed to the General Indian Base Depot MARSEILLES.	
	16.9.17		Six O.R.I. left to proceed to ROUEN for a course of training as Ward Orderlies.	
			2/Lieuts A.J. SCHOFIELD, W.D. SYKES and W.J. HOPKINS reported their arrival for duty with the regiment. Lieut Genl Sir C.T. McM. KAVANAGH, Commanding Cavalry Corps, presented medal ribbons as follows:- Officier de l'Ordre de la Couronne. Lieut Col. E. ADAMS. Military ~~Distinguished Service~~ (Cross) 2 Indian Distinguished Service Medal. Ressaidar DALIP SINGH, No 441 Dafadar MIRZA MUHAMMAD ALI BEG. Indian Meritorious Service Medal. No 221 Kot Dafadar BHARAT SINGH, No 425 Kot Dafadar ABDUL RAZAK KHAN, No 528 Q'M' Dafadar SHEKH MUHAMMAD IBRAHIM, No 588 Trumpt. Major SHEKH ZAHUR MUHAMMAD, No 1192. Sowar SAWAI SINGH, No 927 A.L.D. LAHRI.	
	19.9.17		Capt. E.T. SALVESEN, Royal Glasgow Yeomanry reported his arrival for duty with the regiment.	5th Cav Div 9/4335 of 20.9.17
	27.9.17		One local L.D and Six A.L.D were promoted to L.D with effect from 10.9.17 to complete establishment. Twenty one O.R.I. were classified as First Class Signaller and one as a Second Class Signaller	

Army Form C. 2118.

WAR DIARY
INTELLIGENCE SUMMARY.
(Erase heading not required.)

Instructions regarding War Diaries and Intelligence Summaries are contained in F. S. Regs., Part II. and the Staff Manual respectively. Title pages will be prepared in manuscript.

Place	Date	Hour	Summary of Events and Information	Remarks and references to Appendices
The Field	29.9.17		Major R.B. WORGAN, D.S.O. was appointed to be a Temporary Brigadier General and to command the 173rd Infantry Brigade.	G.H.Q- A/1427. of 26.9.17.
			Two O.R.1. reports their departure on duty to ROUEN.	
	30.9.17		Six remounts arrived from the Base Remount Depot.	

K. Adams
Lieut. Col.
Commdt. 20th Bureau HOTSS

(120)

Confidential

War Diary
of
3rd Indian Corps

From 1st October 1914
to 31st October 1914

Army Form C. 2118.

WAR DIARY
INTELLIGENCE SUMMARY.
(Erase heading not required.)

Instructions regarding War Diaries and Intelligence Summaries are contained in F.S. Regs., Part II. and the Staff Manual respectively. Title pages will be prepared in manuscript.

Place	Date	Hour	Summary of Events and Information	Remarks and references to Appendices
The Field	3.10.17		Major (Tempy Brigr Sir Genl) R.B. WORGAN, D.S.O. having taken command of the 173rd Infy Bde was struck off the strength of the regiment.	
	6.10.17		The Signallers of the regiment were formed into a Separate Signal Troop.	
	7.10.17		The regiment marched (in Brigade) from MORCHY CAYEUX to WITTES, arriving 2.30 p.m. The regiment marched (in Brigade) from WITTES to WATOU (BELGIUM) arriving at 4.15 p.m. and went into bivouacs.	
	11.10.17		Lieut W.W. BARROW (2nd Ind Cav) reported his departure for MARSEILLES to join Brit. Ammunition Column R.A. ———— Lieut F.H. RUST. I.A.R.O. reported his departure for England to report himself to the India Office with a view to proceeding to India. Jemadar ZAFAR YAB KHAN (32nd Lancers) one O.R.B. and two O.R.I. reported arrival from ROUEN	
	12.10.17			
	14.10.17		Ten remounts were received from the Cavy Corps Advanced Remount Depot.	
	15.10.17		The regiment marched (in Brigade) from WATOU to WARDRECQUES arriving at 2 p.m. and went into billets and bivouacs.	
	16.10.17		The march was continued to FAUQUEMBERGUES, where the regiment arrived at 12.30 p.m. and went into billets and bivouacs.	
	17.10.17		The march was continued to the area between ROYON and LOISON, arriving at 1 p.m., and	

WAR DIARY

INTELLIGENCE SUMMARY

Army Form C. 2118.

Place	Date	Hour	Summary of Events and Information	Remarks and references to Appendices
	18.10.17		The regiment went into billets as follows. HQ., Signal Troop and Transport at OFFIN. — "A" Sqn. at LOISON. — "B" Sqn. at HESMOND — C. Sqn. at LEBIEZ. — D. Sqn. at ROYON. Capt R.C.P. BERRYMAN, I.M.S., Ressaidar GUGAN SINGH, Jemadar ZAFAR YAB KHAN, one O.R.B. and eight O.R.I. left the regiment to join the 5th Cavalry Pioneer Battalion.	
	19.10.17		Capt. I.G.M. FIRTH, R.A.M.C. arrived and took temporary medical charge of the regiment.	
	20.10.17		2/Lieut F.R.H. ROBINSON, Jemadar SAYYAD AHMAD, one O.R.B. and twenty three O.R.I. who was left at MORCHY CAYEUX on Divnl. Reinforcements on 6.10.17 rejoined, leaving the rest (Lieut L.A. RAYNEAU, fifty four O.R.I. and one follower) to form part of the 5th Cavalry Pioneer Battalion.	
	21.10.17		Capt. N.F.C. MULLOY, M.C. (32nd L.) reports his return to the regiment, having gone on leave from ROUEN on 9.10.17.	
	22.10.17		Jemadar SHER SINGH and twenty O.R.I. left to join a Working Party.	
	23.10.17		Lieut F.C. GUTHRIE, I.A.R.O. was appointed Offg Quarter Master from 12.10.17. Lieut W.W. BARROW.	
	24.10.17		2/Lieut J.F.S. WILSON, 2/Lieut H.B. HUMFREY and four O.R.I. arrived from ROUEN.	
	26.10.17		Jemadar SHER SINGH and twenty O.R.I. (who left on the 22nd) reports their return.	

Lieut Col Commanding Horse

Army Form C. 2118.

WAR DIARY
INTELLIGENCE SUMMARY

(Erase heading not required.)

To From
20th Deccan Horse

Place	Date	Hour	Summary of Events and Information	Remarks and references to Appendices
The Field			November 1917	
	2.11.17		Lieut. C.C.L. RYAN, Lieut. J.S. HALLIFAX and four O.R.I. joined the regiment from ROUEN.	
	4.11.17		Lieut. F.R.H. ROBINSON reported his departure to ROUEN on duty.	
	6.11.17		Report received of the death at ROUEN on 25.10.17 of General Tuberculosis of No.3491 L.D. MUHAMMAD UMAR KHAN, 21st Cavalry (attached)	
			No 446 Dafadar GULAM RASUL KHAN (C. Sqn.) appointed Salutri with effect from 15.10.17 vice	
			No 340 Salutri SAYYAD GULAM MAHBUB evacuated for return to INDIA	
			Capt. J.R. COLLINS, Royal Scots Greys Yeomanry (attached) returned to the regiment from the Corps Advanced Remount Depot.	
	7.11.17		Lieut. Col. F. ADAMS reported his departure on leave to England and the command of the regiment passed on Major O.M. DYKE, 21st Cavalry (attached)	
	8.11.17		Capt. E.P. LARKIN, Lieut. H.B. HUMFREY, Jem: SAYYAD AHMAD, one O.R.B. and twelve O.R.I. left for WAMIN, to join the Dismounted Reinforcements of the Brigade.	
	9.11.17		The regiment marched at 9 a.m. to BOSBERGUES, arriving there at 6 p.m. The men went into billets, whilst the horses in the open.	
			The following promotions appeared in orders:	
			Jem: SHEIKH FAYAZ UDDIN to be Resaidar with effect from 25.5.17 to complete	

WAR DIARY
INTELLIGENCE SUMMARY.
(Erase heading not required.)

Army Form C. 2118.

Instructions regarding War Diaries and Intelligence Summaries are contained in F. S. Regs., Part II. and the Staff Manual respectively. Title pages will be prepared in manuscript.

Place	Date	Hour	Summary of Events and Information	Remarks and references to Appendices
	9.11.17 (cont)		Establishment.	
			No. 221. Kot Dafr. BHARAT SINGH to be Jemadar with effect from 24.7.17 vice Jem.r YUSUF ALI KHAN, classified P.B.	
			No. 165. Kot Dafr. DALIP SINGH to be Jemadar with effect from 26.7.17 vice Jem.r NIHAL SINGH, evacuated sick.	
	10.11.17		The regiment marched from BOISBERGUES (8.30.a.m.) to CONTAY (1.30.p.m.)	
	10.11.17		The regiment marched from CONTAY (3.30.p.m.) to FROISSY (9.p.m.)	
			Major C. JARVIS. M.C. reports his departure for PARIS on duty.	
	12.11.17		The regiment marched from FROISSY (8.30.p.m.) to BEAUMETZ (9.45.p.m.)	
	13.11.17		Six O.R.I. and two followers arrived from ROUEN as reinforcements.	
			Capt. E.P. LARKIN, Lieut. A.B HUMFREY, Jem.r SAYYAD AHMAD, one O.R.B. and Twelve O.R.I. (dismounted reinforcements) rejoined the regiment.	
			Capt. R.C.P. BERRYMAN I.M.S., Lieut. L.A. RAYNEAU, Revr. G.U.S.M. SINGH, Jem.r ZAFAR YAB KHAN, Six O.R.I. and one Private follower rejoined the regiment from the 5th Cavalry Punies Battalion.	
	20.11.17		The regiment left BEAUMETZ at 1.a.m. and arrived at the Jonzac General Station	

Army Form C. 2118.

WAR DIARY
INTELLIGENCE SUMMARY.
(Erase heading not required.)

Instructions regarding War Diaries and Intelligence Summaries are contained in F. S. Regs., Part II. and the Staff Manual respectively. Title pages will be prepared in manuscript.

Place	Date	Hour	Summary of Events and Information	Remarks and references to Appendices
	21.11.17		Area (DESSART WOOD, N.E. of FINS) at 6 a.m. It moved (found as Brigade at 1.30 p.m. and halted) at MAREOING and bivouacked at 7 p.m. about two miles South of MARCOING. Lt. Col. F. ADAMS rejoined from (was recalled) at 11.30 a.m. The regiment remained in a fraction of trenches about le made and a half N.E. of VILLERS PLOUICH. One O.R.I. was accidentally wounded.	
	22.11.17		The regiment marched in Brigade to EQUANCOURT and FINS arriving about 3.30 p.m.	
	23.11.17		The regiment marched in Brigade from EQUANCOURT at 8.45 a.m. and arrived in billets at MERICOURT SUR SOMME at 2 p.m. and remained on half an hours notice to move.	
	24.11.17		Jem. GANGA BISHAN appointed Sjt. LocaI Major vice Risr. FAYAZ OBI DIN granted on promotion, with effect from 25.8.17. Major C. JARVIS M.C. rejoined his return to the regiment from duty in PARIS. Lieut H.T. POLLITT from O.R.I. and one follower arrived as reinforcements from	
ROUEN.	25.11.17			
	26.11.17		Ress. SHEKH FAYAZUDDIN and Jem. SAYYAD AHMAD reported their departure for England on leave, and No. 1329 Sowar FARZAND ALI accompanied them on duty.	

Army Form 2118.

WAR DIARY
INTELLIGENCE SUMMARY.
(Erase heading not required.)

Instructions regarding War Diaries and Intelligence Summaries are contained in F. S. Regs., Part II. and the Staff Manual respectively. Title pages will be prepared in manuscript.

Place	Date	Hour	Summary of Events and Information	Remarks and references to Appendices
	26.11.17		Report received of the death from P.U.O. at MARSEILLES on 23.11.17. of No 1459. Sowar HARNAM SINGH. (A. Sqn.)	
	27.11.17		The regiment marched from MERICOURT SUR SOMME at 8.30. a.m. and arrived at the hut encampment at TREFCON at 1.30. p.m. — Lieut V.W. MURRAY, Lieut H.B. HUMFREY, one O.R.B and 83. O.R.I. who were left at BEAUMETZ as Dismounted Reinforcements on the night of the 19/20. rejoined the regiment at TREFCON.	
	30.11.17		Fifteen minutes approval from Rev.IV. — Orders were received at 9.30 a.m. for the regiment to move forward in Brigade at once. The regiment paraded at 10.45 a.m., marched at 11.15 a.m., reached VILLERS FAUCON at 2. p.m. and moved on via EPEHY to a spot half a mile N.E. of REVELON, where it remained in readiness during the rest of the day.	

Army Form C. 2118.

20th Deccan Horse.

WAR DIARY
INTELLIGENCE SUMMARY.
(Erase heading not required.)

December 1917.

Place	Date	Hour	Summary of Events and Information	Remarks and references to Appendices
The field	1.12.17		At 10.30 a.m. the regiment moved to a point 1000 yards S.E. of HEUDECOURT and remained there in a position of readiness during the rest of the day and the night. At 6.30 p.m. the regiment moved up dismounted to take over a portion of the line, relieving detachments of the Grenadier Guards, Coldstream Guards and 9th Hodson's Horse on a line running about 1000 yards S.W. from the S.E. corner of GAUCHE WOOD. Just before the regiment left HEUDECOURT Interpreter R.E. AZEMAR was wounded by shell fire.	
	2.12.17		Capt. Two O.R.I. were killed and Capt. N.F.C. MULLOY, M.C. (32nd Lancers) and Two O.R.I. were wounded by shell fire. Between 11.15 p.m. and 11.45 p.m. the regiment was relieved by the 18th Hussars and marched back to the bivouac 1000 yds S.E. of HEUDECOURT.	
	3.12.17		At 11.30 a.m. the Bde. moved mounted to bivouac 1000 yards S.W. of SAULCOURT and there remained in readiness to move at one hours notice by night and half an hours notice by day.	
	4.12.17		Fifteen remounts arrived with the regiment which had arrived from ROUEN at TREFCON after the regiment had marched on the 30th November.	
	5.12.17		Report received that No 3525 Sowar HARDATT SINGH 21st Cav. attd (A.Sqdn.) was wounded on 1.11.17 whilst with the 5th Cav. Pioneer Battalion, and died of wounds at ROUEN on 2.11.17.	

Army Form C. 2118.

WAR DIARY
INTELLIGENCE SUMMARY.
(Erase heading not required.)

Instructions regarding War Diaries and Intelligence Summaries are contained in F. S. Regs., Part II. and the Staff Manual respectively. Title pages will be prepared in manuscript.

Place	Date	Hour	Summary of Events and Information	Remarks and references to Appendices
	6.12.17		Risaldar ALI SHER KHAN (21st Cav. att?), Jemadar ZAFARYAB KHAN (32nd Lancers att?) and one O.R.I. returned from leave in PARIS.	
	8.12.17.		The regiment marches in Brigade at 1 p.m. for the COURCELLES-BUIRE area, but on arrival at BUIRE received orders to move on to DEVISE arriving at the hut encampment there at 4.30 p.m. While at DEVISE the regiment "stood to" ready to saddle up every morning from 6.30 a.m. to 8 a.m. and in a state of readiness to move at short notice during the rest of the day. One O.R.I. returned from ROUEN and joined the Dismounts Reinforcements which were in a Rest Camp on the West of DEVISE.	
	9.12.17.		Thirty eight O.R.I. left the Dismounts Reinforcements to form a working Party at POEUILLY under orders of the 5th Cav. Div.	
	12.12.17.		Lieut W.S.C. HAMLEY rejoined the regiment for duty from ROUEN. Res? DALIP SINGH, Jem? DALIP SINGH I and two O.R.I. left on leave for PARIS.	
	13.12.17.		Six O.R.I. left the regiment to proceed to MARSEILLES for return to INDIA. The regiment marched at 11. a.m. from DEVISE and arrived at 12.30 p.m. at the hut encampment at TREFCON. Capt J.R. COLLINS, Lieut? W.D SYKES and H.T. POLLITT two O.R.B and 59 O.R.I., the Dis and Reinforcements, rejoined the regiment.	
	17.12.17.			

Army Form C. 2118.

(3)

WAR DIARY
INTELLIGENCE SUMMARY.
(Erase heading not required.)

Instructions regarding War Diaries and Intelligence Summaries are contained in F. S. Regs., Part II. and the Staff Manual respectively. Title pages will be prepared in manuscript.

Place	Date	Hour	Summary of Events and Information	Remarks and references to Appendices
The Field.	18.12.17		No 375. Sr SARDAR KHAN (B.Sqr.) was appointed Acting Lance Dafadar for gallantry in the field on the 25 December.	
			No 1095. A.I.D. SHAIKH AHMAD HUSSAIN (C. Sqr.) and No 1156. Sr SAYYAD ABDUL MAJID were awarded the Indian Distinguished Service Medal as "immediate rewards" on account of themselves on the 20 December.	Car Corps A.O./500/149 L.13.12.17.
	19.12.17		Capt. F.P. LARKIN. Royal Glasgow Yeomanry att? was seconded for service with the Indian Army in the rank of Lieutenant on probation 14th August 1917.	Left H.Q. Supplied to Lieutenant. Gazette of 27.11.17.
	20.12.17		Reg? DALIP SINGH, Jem? IDALIP SINGH, I and Two O.R.I. returned from leave in PARIS. Twenty one Riding Horses, one L.D. Horse, two Pack Horses and two Pack Mules returned as remounts from ROUEN.	
	22.12.17		Three hundred O.R.I. with Indian and British Officers under Capt. F.B.M. TINLEY M.C. left the camp at 1.45 p.m. in lorries for digging work on the Corps Switch Trench and returned at 11.15 p.m.	
	24.12.17		Three hundred O.R.I. with Indian and two British Officers under Capt. T.K. WILSON (with an equal dismounted party from the POONA HORSE) marched to VERMAND starting at 12.15 a.m. and took three by train for wiring work in the front line. Two O.R.I. were	

Army Form C. 2118.

WAR DIARY
INTELLIGENCE SUMMARY.
(Erase heading not required.)

Place	Date	Hour	Summary of Events and Information	Remarks and references to Appendices
Field	23/12/17		Escorted. The party returned to camp at about 2.30 a.m.	
	26/12/17		Reinforcements 3 ORI were received from ROUEN as reinforcements. Sowar E.P. Larkins, Jemadar Tha Singh, & 3 ORI reported their departure to ROUEN had as instructor at I.C.A.B.D.	
	26/12/17		2/Lt A.J. Schofield & 2 ORI reported their departure to YZEUX to & Poona Brigade Brains. 2/Lt J.P. Hallifax reported his departure to attend a Hotchkiss Rifle Course at LE TOUQUET. 1 Dafadar was appointed Not Dafadar, 13 Lance Dafadars were promoted Dafadars. 16 Acting Lance Dafadars were promoted Lance Dafadars.	
	28/12/17		A working party from B squadron of 40 ORI under Capt J.R. Collins proceeded to 2nd line defences near VENDELLES to clear snow from trenches roots, and returned at 7pm.	
	29/12/17		Captain E.J. Solomon, Glasgow Yeomanry, att'd reported his departure for duty with the Tank Corps and is struck off the strength of the regiment.	
	29/12/17		Lt D.J.C. Hamley reported his departure for duty at 1.B.D. MARSEILLES and is struck off the strength of the regiment. Jemadar George Bralan promoted Ressaidar from 11/10/17. Jemadar Shaikh Kohi-uddin promoted Ressaidar from 12/10/17.	

Army Form C. 2118.

WAR DIARY
or
INTELLIGENCE SUMMARY.
(Erase heading not required.)

Place	Date	Hour	Summary of Events and Information	Remarks and references to Appendices
Field	29/12/17		No 226 Not Dafadar Lahri promoted Jemadar from 11/10/17	
			No 425 Net Dafadar Mithit Rajah Khan promoted Jemadar from 12/10/17	
			No 79 Not Dafadar Sarwan Singh promoted Jemadar from 25/8/17	
			vide Divisional Order 1695 of 29/12/17	
			The Indian Meritorious Service Medal was awarded to:-	
			No 219 Lft Thander Singh, No 301 Dafadar Nahabula Singh, No 639 L/D Gopal Singh	
			No 450 A/L/D Ahmad Khan, No 375 C/L/D Immiyatoon Khan, No 73 W.O. Damodar Rao.	
			vide Divisional Order 1692 of 29/12/17	
			No 1142 Sowar RAM SARUP was tried by summary court martial sentenced to	
			two months rigorous imprisonment.	
	30/12/17		Captain E.J. Clarke + 6 O.R.s arrived as reinforcements from RODEN	
			Captain E.J. Clarke took over command of B Squadron to day	
			Jemadar Jhuj Ali Khan appointed officiating Woordie Major from 29/12/17	
	31/12/17		Lt Col Holman reported his departure to 5 Army School of Instruction at TOUTENCOURT	
			and the command of the regiment devolves on Major O.M. Dyke 2nd Bro (att)	
			The sentence of the Summary Court-Martial held on the 29-12-17 was promulgated	
			on parade. Fred. W. Van Jager	
			Commdg 12 Deccan Horse

Army Form C. 2118.

(120)

30th Decem Coy.

WAR DIARY
or
INTELLIGENCE SUMMARY.
(Erase heading not required.)

January 1918

Place	Date	Hour	Summary of Events and Information	Remarks and references to Appendices
Field	2/1/18		A/S. A.J. Schofield, 1 Briman + 2 ORs reported their arrival from town Bruge barns at YZEUX	
			2 ORB reported their departure for duty with Hour Corps	
	4/1/18		15 ORs reinforcements from 4th Can Pioneer Batt.	
	5/1/18		1 OR -do- -do- been taken on the strength	
	5/1/18		No 11142 Driver RAM SAROOP left the command for employment in Mob. Station from DIEPPE	
	6/1/18		Risaldar GUNGA BISHAN + 4 ORs reported their departure to Sanitary School	
	7/1/18		Lt Col F. ADAMS reported his return from 5th Army School of Instruction	
	9/1/18		Jemadar SHEIK FAYAZ UDDIN appointed Woodie Major vice Jemadar SHER SINGH relieved with effect from 11.9.17	
			Jemadar GUNGA BISHAN -do- -do- vice Risaldar FAYAZ UDDIN reverted on termination from 24.11.17	
			Jemadar YUSAF ALI KHAN -do- -do- vice Risaldar GUNGA BISHAN -do- -do- 29.12.17	
			No 667 Cpl. GORDAYAL Lait as Regimental Sanitary NCO	
			A/S A.J. Schofield with 1 ORB reported his departure & attend course of abnormal Apaillant School	
	10/1/18		A working party of 50 ORs under A/S #3 Humphrey proceeded to VERMAND for huttey work	
	12/1/18		2/S J. Halligan reported his return from hospital via Sher School S LE TOUQUET	
			A/S H.T. POLITT relieved A/S W.G. FIGG rank as "Sub Pioneer Battn	
	13/1/18		Marching party of 120 ORs under Lt. J.S. Halligan proceeded to BEHICOURT for training work	

WAR DIARY or INTELLIGENCE SUMMARY

Army Form C. 2118.

(Erase heading not required.)

Instructions regarding War Diaries and Intelligence Summaries are contained in F. S. Regs., Part II. and the Staff Manual respectively. Title pages will be prepared in manuscript.

Place	Date	Hour	Summary of Events and Information	Remarks and references to Appendices
Field	13/1/18		2/Lt W.J. HOPKINS, Jemadar DALIP SINGH & 10 OR & 5 OR proceeded to Scottish horse at Desert Stab	
	"		2/Lt W.G. FIGG reported his departure to England on duty, was struck off strength	
	"		13 OR, reinforcements from ROUEN arrived were taken on the strength	
	14/1/18		Risaldar GUNGA BISHAN & 4 OR reported their arrival from Scottish horse at Dismount School	
	"		Risaldar ALI SHER KHAN 3rd (invalid) was struck off the strength	
	15/1/18		Capt N.F.C. MULLOY M.C. reported his arrival from Convalescent home was taken on the strength	
	"		6 OR, reported their departure to MARTEILLES for duty with Divisional Pioneer Battalion	
	"		Jemadar AZEMAR died in hospital on 31/1/18 of wounds received will report on 1/12/17	
	16/1/18		100 OR, under 2/Lt Lythes proceeded to VENDELLES for work on the Brown Line	
	"		120 OR, under 2/Lt Watson proceeded to GEMICOURT for tunneling work	
	"		6 OR, reinforcements from 1st Cavalry Pioneer Battn, were taken on the strength	
	"		Lt. Dafadar JHANDA SINGH to be Jemadar with effect from 25/8/17 to complete establishment	
	"		Lt. Dafadar MAHFUZ ALI KHAN — — 25/8/17 — —	
	17/1/18		100 OR, under 2/Lt H.B. Humphrey proceeded to VENDELLES for work on the Brown Line	
	"		2/Lt W.D. SYKES departed for duty with Dismounted Party at POVEILLY	
	18/1/18		100 OR, under Capt MULLOY proceeded to VENDELLES for work on the Brown Line	

WAR DIARY OR INTELLIGENCE SUMMARY

Army Form C. 2118.

Place	Date	Hour	Summary of Events and Information	Remarks and references to Appendices
Field	18/1/18		25 Remounts were received on 16/1/18	
	19/1/18		100 ORs under Jemadar Ghafoor proceeded to VENDELLES for work on the Brown line	
			No 1073 L/Dfr SHAIKH AHMAD HUSAIN and No 1156 Sowar SAYYAD ABDUL HAMID were presented with the India Distinguished Service heart by corps commander	
	20/1/18		100 ORs under Capt COLLINS proceeded to VENDELLES for work on the Brown line	
	21/1/18		150 ORs under Capt T.K. WILSON	—
			2/Lt M.J. HOPKINS, Jemadar DALIP SINGH III, 1 OR & 5 ORs returned from Scouting course at Divisional Head	
	22/1/18		Jemadar ZAFARYAB KHAN (from RAVEN) + 14 ORs departed their departure for MARSEILLES en route for India	
	23/1/18		Jr Mr under 2/Lt H.B.HUMFREY proceeded to VENDELLES for work on the Brown line	
	24/1/18		Jr V.W. MURRAY — 10 ORs reported for return from cavalry School Equitation course	
			26 M.J. SCHOFIELD — 10 ORs reported his return from Lewis Signalling course	
			Lt Col A N FLEMING I.M.S was awarded the D.S.O.	
			Risaldar KHURSHED MOHD KHAN — 14 ORs were awarded the Indian Distinguished Service Medal	
			× No 670 Dafadar RAM SAROOP, No 3125 L/D NADAR SINGH, No 3461 L/D AUTAR SINGH	
			No 1108 R/D MIR RONAQ ALI	
	25/1/18		2/Lt W.D. SYKES, Jemadar DALIP SINGH III + 37 ORs rejoined arrived from 5 Cav Div Dropping Post at PODEILLY	

Army Form C. 2118.

WAR DIARY
or
INTELLIGENCE SUMMARY.
(Erase heading not required.)

Instructions regarding War Diaries and Intelligence Summaries are contained in F. S. Regs., Part II. and the Staff Manual respectively. Title pages will be prepared in manuscript.

Place	Date	Hour	Summary of Events and Information	Remarks and references to Appendices
Field	25/1/18		Joined Party as follows under Major D.M. DYKE relieved the 18th Hussars in Metier at VADENCOURT	
			Capt T.K. WILSON, Capt M.F.C. MULLOY, Lt A.S. GODFREE, 2Lt J.C. WILSON, 2Lt H.B. HUMFREY,	
			Ressaldar MONSUL SINGH, Ressaidar RACHPAL SINGH, Ressaidar DALIP SINGH, Ressaidar SHEIK FAYAZUDDIN,	
			Jemadars DALIP SINGH II, BHARAT SINGH, ABDUL RAZAK KHAN, MAHFUZ ALI KHAN, 7 ORs, & 249 OR1	
	26/1/18		2 OR1 reinforcement from Indian Cavalry Pioneer Battn were taken on to the strength	
	27/1/18		Hon. Lieut. & Qr Mr C. PINTO was taken on to the strength	
	"		1 RHA Driver, reinforcement from ROUEN was taken on to the strength	

Nevill
Lt Col.
Commdg IX Deccan Horse

Army Form C. 2118

WAR DIARY
or
INTELLIGENCE SUMMARY

(Erase heading not required.)

Instructions regarding War Diaries and Intelligence Summaries are contained in F. S. Regs., Part II. and the Staff Manual respectively. Title Pages will be prepared in manuscript.

Place	Date	Hour	Summary of Events and Information	Remarks and references to Appendices
Field	25th Jany. 1918		The Dismounted Regiment strength as under B.Os 7, I.Os 8, O.R.B. 7 O.R.I. 349, Followers 3 arrived at R.16.b.2.5.and relieved 18th Hussars in Brigade Reserve at VADENCOURT. Relief was completed at 7.40.p.m.	
"	26th		At VADENCOURT	
"	27th		At VADENCOURT	
"	28th		At VADENCOURT	
"	29th		At VADENCOURT	
"	30th		At VADENCOURT	
"	31st		At VADENCOURT	

1.2.18

M. Dyke Major

For Commandant XX Deccan Horse

Confidential

War Diary

93rd Deccan Horse

1st to 28th Feby 1915.

Army Form C. 2118.

WAR DIARY
INTELLIGENCE SUMMARY.
(Erase heading not required.)

Instructions regarding War Diaries and Intelligence Summaries are contained in F. S. Regs., Part II. and the Staff Manual respectively. Title pages will be prepared in manuscript.

Place	Date	Hour	Summary of Events and Information	Remarks and references to Appendices
Field	1/2/18		The regiment left TREFCON on 1st inst. arrived at billets - WEINCOURT & MARCELCAVE at 2.30 p	
	2/2/18		The regiment continued the march & arrived in billets at BETHECOURT, BERTEAUCOURT & ST OUEN at 4 p.	
	3/2/18		2/Lt A.J. SCHOFIELD appointed asst signalling officer.	
	9/2/18		Risaldar Major PREM SINGH Bahadur & Risaldar KHURSHED MOHD KHAN reported for duty to England to attend the opening of Parliament.	
	"		3rd class S.A.S. KRISHNASAMI PILLAI promoted to 2nd class S.A. Surgeon from 7/3/17	
	11/2/18		No 115b Sowar SAYYAD ABDUL MATID awarded the Belgian Croix de Guerre.	
	"		Capt C.F. CLARKE appointed Offg Squadron Commander from 30/12/17 vice Capt F.R.N. TINLEY M.C.	
	17/2/18		French party as follows reported their return from leave:- Major C. JARVIS M.C., Capt N.F.C. MULLOY M.C., Capt J.R. COLLINS, 2/Lt J.F.S. WILSON, 2/Lt H.B. HUMFREY, 2/Lt C.C.L. RYAN, 2/Lt J.S. HALLIFAX, Risaldar KONSAL SINGH, Risaldar RACHPAL SINGH, Risaldar DALIP SINGH, Risaldar SHEIK FAYAZUDDIN, Jemadar DALIP SINGH II, BHARAT SINGH, ABDUR RAZAK KHAN, MAHFUZ ALI KHAN, ORI.6. - ORI.249	
	23/2/18		An overseas advance party composed of following departed for TORONTO:- Capt N.F.C. MULLOY M.C., Lt A.S. GODFREE M.C., 2/Lt A.J. SCHOFIELD, Risaldar GUGAN SINGH, Jemadar DALIP SINGH I, DALIP SINGH II, DALIP SINGH III, ABDUR RAZAK KHAN, 1 ORR & 50 ORI.	
	24/2/18		An record advance party departed for TORANTO as follows:- Capt J.R. COLLINS, 2/Lt H.B. HUMFREY	

Army Form C. 2118.

WAR DIARY
INTELLIGENCE SUMMARY.
(Erase heading not required.)

Place	Date	Hour	Summary of Events and Information	Remarks and references to Appendices
Field	24/2/18		2/Lt J.S. HALLIFAX, 2/Lt W.D. SYKES, Jemadar RAHIM SHER KHAN, Jemadar SAYYAD AHMAD, 1 ORR & 10 ORS	
	"		15 RHA Indian Transport drivers attached to the regiment were returned to base & struck off strength.	
	25/2/18		Capt A.E.G. PLUMLEY R.A.M.C. joined the regiment as M.O.	
	27/2/18		10 British Rank attached to the regiment were sent back to 1st D.Ys & struck off.	
	28/2/18		The regiment left the ST OUEN area & marched to billets at SAINS-EN-AMIÉNOIS, GUYENCOURT.	
			REMIENCOURT and COTTENCHY, where it arrived about 2 p.m.	

Dated 27/3/18

[signature]
Lt Col
Comm'd'g XX Deccan Horse

Army Form C. 2118.

WAR DIARY of *2nd Bath*
INTELLIGENCE SUMMARY.
(Erase heading not required.)

Instructions regarding War Diaries and Intelligence Summaries are contained in F. S. Regs., Part II, and the Staff Manual respectively. Title pages will be prepared in manuscript.

Place	Date	Hour	Summary of Events and Information	Remarks and references to Appendices
Field	1.2.18		The Dismounted Regiment in Brigade Reserve at VADENCOURT.	
"	"		do	
"	3.2.18		The Regiment took over the outpost duties of the Left Regtl. Right Sub-Sector as follows. Front Line Lone Tree Post- Leg Post and Forward Gun Post. D.Squadron Captain T.K.Wilson Dragoon Nos 3 and 4 Posts and Forward Rifle Posts. B.Squadron Captain N.F.C.Mulloy M.C. Support A.Squadron. Reserve C.Squadron. The Relief from 8th Hodson's Horse was completed at 8.40.p.m. A Patrol of 10.O.R.I. and 1 I.O. of C.Squadron under 2nd Lieut A.F.J.S.Wilson reconnoitred SOMERVILLE Wood and ANGLE BANK from 11.30.p.m.-3.40.a.m.4th without encountering the enemy.	
"	4.2.18		Disposition same as on 3rd.	
"	5.2.18		During the evening D and B Squadrons were relieved in forward post by C and A Squadrons respectively. D and B.Squadrons going into reserve and support respectively. 2/Lieut J.S.Woolfox reported his arrival from Base Ana.	

Army Form C. 2118.

WAR DIARY of Head Qrs
INTELLIGENCE SUMMARY.
(Erase heading not required.)

Place	Date	Hour	Summary of Events and Information	Remarks and references to Appendices
Field	6/2/18		Lieut A.S.Godfree M.G. reported his departure on leave to Paris	
Field	7/2/18		D.Squadron changed their position from Red Crater to JEB post and took over 3 and 4 posts from A.Squadron.	
	8/2/18		Major C.Jarvis M.C. and Capt.J.F.Collins and 2 O.R.B. reported their arrival from back area.	
	9/2/18		Major O.M.Dyke reported his departure to Back area. The Command of the Regiment devolved on Major C.Jarvis M.C..Captain T.K.Wilson reported his departure on leave to England. Captain J.R.Collins took over command of D.Squadron in the place of Captain T.K.Wilson.	
Field	10/2/18		2nd Lieut C.C.L.Ryan reported his arrival from the Back area.	
			The regiment was relieved in the Outpost line by the 34th Poona Horse on the night of the 10/11th. The relief commenced at 7.p.m. and was completed at 9.30.p.m. Disposition as follows:- B and A Squadrons PONTRU and MOREVAL trench. D.Squadron COOKERS trench and C.Squadron in DEAN trench.	
Field	11/2/18		Lieut J.D.Heaton Armstrong reported his departure to Back Area, 2nd Lt. C.C.L.Ryan took over the duties of Adjutant, Signalling Officer and Intelligence Officer in his place. 2nd Lieut J.S.Hallifax took over the duties of Qr.Mr.	
			2nd Lieut H.B.Humfrey took over command of B.Squadron.	
	15/2/18		The Regiment was relieved on the night 15th/16th by Units of the 2nd Dragoon Guards,11th Hussars, and 19th Hussars. The relief commenced at 6.p.m. and was completed at 8.40.p.m. The Dismounted regiment then marched to Q.30.central(reference 62 C)and proceeded thence by light railway to ROISEL, arriving at 1.a.m. The regiment entrained at ROISEL at 11.a.m. and arrived at SALEUX at 5.30.p.m. whence it proceeded by Motor lorry to billets arriving at 9.30.p.m.	

27.2.18

Lt.Colonel
Commandant XX Deccan Horse.

1917-1918
5TH CAVALRY DIVISION
SECUNDERABAD CAV. BDE

34TH POONA HORSE

JAN 1917-MAR 1918

To EGYPT GHQ TROOP
7 MOUNTED BRIGADE

SERIAL NO. 124.

Confidential

War Diary

of

34th POONA HORSE.

FROM 1st January 1917 TO 31st January 1917

CONFIDENTIAL:

34th POONA-HORSE

WAR DIARY.

5 CAN DIV
Recd. Un

FROM 1ST JANUARY 1917 TO 31ST JANUARY 1917.

Army Form C. 2118.

WAR DIARY
or
INTELLIGENCE SUMMARY.
(Erase heading not required.)

Instructions regarding War Diaries and Intelligence Summaries are contained in F. S. Regs., Part II. and the Staff Manual respectively. Title pages will be prepared in manuscript.

Place	Date	Hour	Summary of Events and Information	Remarks and references to Appendices
AGNEVILLE	1st Jan. 1917.		No change in billets.	
	3rd		Captain A.A. Kirkpatrick proceeded to England on duty - honorarily.	
			The Pioneer Company reported from Leith with XIV Corps.	
			The following Officers & men awaited leave discharged hence since Reminder Depot Leigh. No 1766 Sgt Rafter Hans. 2162. Sgt Shutham Luttifar. Britt Khan. 3323 A.W.O. Brotin Khan. (Reposted to Depot of 1.1.1917)	
	5th.		Jem. Mehr Singh Jem. Sirdan Lieutenant whan & Sub. Munnawar Khan proceeded on leave to England.	
	10th.		Captain MWP Stanton proceeded on interprete Course at East Depot Unghi. Lieut E.O. Davison to take charge for duty.	
	11th.		Lecture about received of arrival of one J. Brinah Singh from (? Same) to his unit from Army Khan's Brigade - Murdered Hermit Singh.	
	14th.		Lieut J.C. Phillip & his Servt Raman proceeded to School on Bombing & General Course respectively.	
	19th.		Captain B.H. Alderson promoted Temporary Major.	

2353 Wt. W2344/1454 700,000 5/15 D. D. & L. A.D.S.S./Forms/C. 2118.

Army Form C. 2118.

WAR DIARY
or
INTELLIGENCE SUMMARY.
(Erase heading not required.)

Place	Date	Hour	Summary of Events and Information	Remarks and references to Appendices
January 1917	20th		Lieut. H.A. Greenly returned from Machine Gun Regimental School to C Squadron.	
	22nd		Captain R.L. MacGregor proceeded to Poona for ordinary leave pending return to England.	
	26th		Captain W.G. Roston on return from duty in England resumed duty and Graham transferred proceeded to B.G. Dept.	
	28th		Lieut. H.O. Weeden upon arrival from Mesopotamia assumed duty.	

Aldwell Lieut
adj. on about for
Officer Commanding
34th Poona Horse

Confidential   Serial No: 121.

WAR DIARY

OF

34th POONA-HORSE

From 1st Feb 1917 to 28th Feb 1917.

(Vol VIII)

Army Form C. 2118.

WAR DIARY
or
INTELLIGENCE SUMMARY.
(Erase heading not required.)

Instructions regarding War Diaries and Intelligence Summaries are contained in F. S. Regs., Part II. and the Staff Manual respectively. Title pages will be prepared in manuscript.

Place	Date	Hour	Summary of Events and Information	Remarks and references to Appendices
AIGNEVILLE	1st FEB.		No change in billets. Individual Training continues.	
	9th		Pioneer Company proceeded for work on Railway in Rive AUTHIE and via billets at AUTHIEULE. The following proceed with Company.	
			OC. Capt. R.H. O'D PATERSON.	
			Rifle & Bomb. Inst. T.S. APCAR. I.A.R.O.	
			Capt. W.V. HOLLAND. Yeomanry.	
			Lieut. E.E. ANSON. Yeomanry.	
			Company Officers. 3.	
			Indian Officers. 246.	
			O.R.	
	11th		Lieut. K. YATES rejoined from 13th M.G. open on 9th Feb. 1917.	
	15th		Annual Classification of Regtl. Signallers.	
	19th		Capt. H.A. HILDEBRAND proceeded to Base, MARSEILLES. 19 Riding Horses were taken in strength to-day viz 17 from Poro Halt & 2 from XX Deccan Horse.	

Army Form C. 2118.

WAR DIARY
or
INTELLIGENCE SUMMARY.
(Erase heading not required.)

Place	Date	Hour	Summary of Events and Information	Remarks and references to Appendices
AIGNEVILLE.	22 FEB.		Major T PETERS. 10th Lancers rejoined Regiment from duty at Base. MARSEILLES. Lieut. J. O. HAYWELL. 11th Lancers joined Regiment from Base. Nothing further to report. Very severe weather which had not continued until 19th Feb.	

Nelis Major.
Commanding Poona Horse.

Serial No: 121.

Confidential

War Diary
OF
34th POONA- HORSE

From 1st March 1917 to 31st March 1917

Vol IX

Army Form C. 2118.

WAR DIARY
or
INTELLIGENCE SUMMARY.
(Erase heading not required.)

Place	Date	Hour	Summary of Events and Information	Remarks and references to Appendices
AIGNEVILLE.	MARCH 1st		No change in billets.	
	2nd		Major J. PETERS 10th Lancers. proceeds to assume command Pioneer Bn.	
	3rd		Lieut Manning proceeds on special duty as M.G. Instructor to the HEDJAZ:—	22nd Cav.
			1206. A.L.D. GULAM NABI KHAN.	
			1108. ,, MUHAMMAD KHAN.	
			1127. Sr. SAJAWAL KHAN	
			1086 G. MURAD ALI KHAN	
			1135 Sr. KHAN MULAN KHAN	
			1642 S. SHER ZAMAN KHAN	
	7th		Prosecution by Divis Command (follow and unable to respond Prisoners under:—	
			Resaidar REWAT SINGH.	
			Resaidar ABDUL GAFOOR KHAN.	
			3074. hildaf. ALLAH UD DIN KHAN.	
			2743. ALD. MAHDU SINGH	
			3323. — BUDDHA KHAN.	

Army Form C. 2118.

WAR DIARY
or
INTELLIGENCE SUMMARY.
(Erase heading not required.)

Instructions regarding War Diaries and Intelligence Summaries are contained in F. S. Regs., Part II and the Staff Manual respectively. Title pages will be prepared in manuscript.

Place	Date	Hour	Summary of Events and Information	Remarks and references to Appendices
AIGNEVILLE	12th		The Division had in 48 hours which with effort from to-day.	
	14th		Pioneer Company rejoined Regiment for duty.	
	20th	9.45 AM	The Brigade marched from billets and reached FRESNEVILLE at 2.30 P.M.	
FRESNEVILLE	21st	9.15 AM	— — — — — — — — — — — — — —	
PLACHY BUYON	22nd	10 AM	— — — — — — — PLACHY BUYON at 3.30 P.M.	
	23rd		Regiment Bivouac near HAMEL at 4 P.M.	
	24th	10 AM	The Brigade marched to bivouac near BOIS DE MEREAUCOURT – FEUILLERES and arrived at 1 P.M.	
BOIS DE MEREAUCOURT	25th 26		Regiment remained in camp.	
	27th		Lieut H.H. GREEN and Lieut H.R. PILCHER proceeded on Yeomanriar duty to Hdqrs. of Regiment covering the infantry advance.	
HALLE	27th	1 P.M.	The Brigade marched to bivouac at HALLE and arrived at 3.15 P.M.	

Army Form C. 2118.

WAR DIARY
or
INTELLIGENCE SUMMARY.
(Erase heading not required.)

Instructions regarding War Diaries and Intelligence Summaries are contained in F. S. Regs., Part II and the Staff Manual respectively. Title pages will be prepared in manuscript.

Place	Date	Hour	Summary of Events and Information	Remarks and references to Appendices
HALLE.	28th	3 P.M.	The Brigade marched 4 kilometres to a bivouac near CLERY - sur - SOMME.	
	29th	3.30 P.M.	" " " 3 " " " HEM.	
	30th	11.30 P.M.	" " " marched to billets at BAYONVILLERS; a distance of	
GUYONVILLERS	31.5 P.M.	12 miles and arrived at 3.15 P.M. The weather during the last 3 days has been very inclement.	
			Since 2nd March the Fifteenth Aus. Cav. Bde. has been in reserve, the Australia and Canadian Cav. Bdes. operating in conjunction with 2 Infantry Divisions and successfully driving back the enemy in the front EQUANCOURT — LONGAVESNES — ROISEL — BEAUVOIS. During these operations the cavalry captured villages by mounted attack.	

GP Cooper Lieut Colonel
Cmdg. Poona Horse.

Vol 10
Confidential
Serial No: 121.

War Diary

34th POONA-HORSE

From 1st April 1917 to 30th April 1917.

(Vol I)

Army Form C. 2118.

WAR DIARY
or
INTELLIGENCE SUMMARY.
(Erase heading not required.)

Place	Date	Hour	Summary of Events and Information	Remarks and references to Appendices
BAYONVILLERS.	April 1st – 5th		Nothing to Report.	
	6th		Orders received that Bde. would march on 8th April to a bivouac near BOIS D'AULNAIES, East of PERONNE.	
	14th	9 A.M.	The Bde. marched to a bivouac at TREFCON (9 miles from ST QUENTIN) and arrived at 3.30 P.M. The Regiment bivouac'd on the left bank of the L'OMIGNON river, South of CAULAINCOURT. The vicinity of camp was shelled at night.	
	15th & 16th		Standings and stables to an hour were begun to be built out of debris of neighbouring villages. Squn training was continued in a large open area.	
	17th			
	29th		The vicinity of camp was shelled at night.	

L. G. Cooper Lieut Colonel.
Cmdg Royal N. Dr.

CONFIDENTIAL

Serial No: 124

From 1st May to 30th June 1917.

WAR DIARY

OF

34th POONA-HORSE

From 15th May 1917 to 30th May 1917

Vol II

Army Form C. 2118.

WAR DIARY
or
INTELLIGENCE SUMMARY.

(Erase heading not required.)

Instructions regarding War Diaries and Intelligence Summaries are contained in F. S. Regs., Part II, and the Staff Manual respectively. Title pages will be prepared in manuscript.

Hour, Date, Place.	Summary of Events and Information.	Remarks and references to Appendices.
15.5.17. CAULAINCOURT	Dismounted Regiment about 250 strong under Major B.H. Atkinson left billets at 8 pm to take over front line North of LE VERGUIER from 2/4 Leicester Regt. They dismounted at JEANCOURT, & the relieve was taken over without a hitch. The night was calm & the weather fine but threatening.	
16.5.17.	Situation Normal; weather wet & misty. Little activity on enemy's part. Night spent in improving the outpost positions, which were small isolated posts about 100 yds from enemy front line. A few shots fired, but no actual encounter took place.	
17.5.17	Situation Normal. Weather slightly improved, but still damp. One post shelled with shrapnel at 1 pm. About 4 pm Sowadar Ranjit Singh & six men were wounded, none of them seriously, by shell fire. Previous to this Sowadar Urat Singh had R?ft gone on a German working party & wounded two.	

Gulab Singh & Sons, Calcutta—No. 22 Army C.—5-8-14—1,07,000.

Army Form C. 2118.

WAR DIARY
or
INTELLIGENCE SUMMARY.
(*Erase heading not required.*)

Instructions regarding War Diaries and Intelligence Summaries are contained in F. S. Regs., Part II, and the Staff Manual respectively. Title pages will be prepared in manuscript.

Hour, Date, Place.	Summary of Events and Information.	Remarks and references to Appendices.
18.5.17	At 3.15 a.m. an enemy patrol nearly thirty in apparent strength attacked our No 2 post commanded by Jemindar Balwant Singh. A musketry battle developed with rifle fire & bombs, three other posts & some of the 7th D.G. all joining in. The return of ammunition expenditure was abnormally large. No casualties were suffered & it is not known if any were inflicted on the enemy. The small Lieut Sullivan took a patrol out to "cut down" "trees", & encountered a hostile patrol, which he attempted to entice into a prepared ambush, but unfortunately they were too wary.	

Army Form C. 2118.

WAR DIARY
or
INTELLIGENCE SUMMARY.
(Erase heading not required.)

Instructions regarding War Diaries and Intelligence Summaries are contained in F. S. Regs., Part II, and the Staff Manual respectively. Title pages will be prepared in manuscript.

Hour, Date, Place.	Summary of Events and Information.	Remarks and references to Appendices.
19.5.17	In early hours of morning a German patrol twenty to thirty strong attacked our left post, held by Jemadar Taj Mohd Khan, but was driven off. Great credit is due to the men of 2 saw concerned in this affair. Shelling was light during the day.	
20.5.17	Situation normal. Enemy artillery gave little trouble. During night 20th-21st Regiment was relieved by XX D.K.	
21st 5.17	Situation Normal. Regiment remained in Support. Working parties furnished to assist	
22nd 5.17	Situation Normal	
23-d.5.17	XX DH by night. Situation normal. Work as above	
24.5.17	" "	
25.5.17	"	
26.5.17	HQRS was shelled during the afternoon, slightly. 4 No. of 48 men relieved	
27.5.17	Ground near support line was shelled with 5.9 HE. One shell unfortunately landed in a dug out killing three men & wounding four. J & S Squadron, Regiment relieved the Reg't in the front line the night without incident but were lucky in having no casualties from shells which fell during the

WAR DIARY
or
INTELLIGENCE SUMMARY.
(Erase heading not required.)

Army Form C. 2118.

Hour, Date, Place.	Summary of Events and Information.	Remarks and references to Appendices.
27.5.17. (cont)	Just after relief was completed it was found that a party of the enemy had made their way through our outer wire & had occupied the old abandoned no 8 post, when a they bombed the wire Commander on his round. Dafadar from Trench report Khan & two men was were an observation them employed while supports were being fetched, & on arrival of Lt Sullivan two troops the Germans were expelled without casualty.	
28.5.17	Situation normal. A few short range 77 mm H.E. shells fell near Runng M.G.Ps. Enemy fired a few rifle grenades & threw a few bombs at our posts during the night. This night we shifted our one tent to one new front-line became rather shorter, we now held from ARTILLERY TREE to ASCENSION FARM. A, B & C SQDNs were up in front line. D. returning in support	
29.5.17	Shelling was light in our area. Two patrols were sent out. One under Lt ANSON went to ASCENSION wood with a view to taking any German patrols in rear. It nearly succeeded, but owing to a man firing his rifle, the	

Army Form C. 2118.

WAR DIARY
or
INTELLIGENCE SUMMARY.
(Erase heading not required.)

Instructions regarding War Diaries and Intelligence Summaries are contained in F. S. Regs., Part II, and the Staff Manual respectively. Title pages will be prepared in manuscript.

Hour, Date, Place.	Summary of Events and Information.	Remarks and references to Appendices.
29.5.17	enemy patrol escaped. We had one man killed & three wounded by bombs from another party which came in on a flank, flung their grenades & ran away.	
30.5.17	Dafadar Lachman Singh & another man went to the S.E. corner of ASCENSION WOOD where they saw four Germans in a trench, & a small cart visits the front line. Shelling was light during the day, situation unchanged. A patrol of 15 men under Lt ANSON went to Little Bill but saw nothing. They were shot at & bombed from long range. Dafdr Lachman Sing again went out to S. of ASCENSION WOOD but saw thirty Germans going in the direction of ng. in our right.	

B.E.Cooper Lt. Col.
Lanne Horse

Army Form C. 2118.

WAR DIARY
or
INTELLIGENCE SUMMARY.
(Erase heading not required.)

Instructions regarding War Diaries and Intelligence Summaries are contained in F.S. Regs., Part II, and the Staff Manual respectively. Title pages will be prepared in manuscript.

Hour, Date, Place.	Summary of Events and Information.	Remarks and references to Appendices.
31.5.17	Situation Normal. Lt.Col. W.G. Cooper came up from back area to assume command of dismounted regiment. One of our posts was slightly shelled in the evening but no casualties were inflicted. Lieut Sullivan took a patrol out to Little Bir but encountered no enemy. An NCO & three men went to SE corner of Asensorn wood.	

C.F. Dickson Lt.
Adj: for Lt.Col.
Comdg Poona Horse

Gulab Singh & Sons, Calcutta—No. 22 Army C.—5-8-14—1,07,000.

CONFIDENTIAL

WAR DIARY

OF

34th POONA-HORSE

From 1st June to 30 June 1917

(Vol I)

Army Form C. 2118.

WAR DIARY

or

INTELLIGENCE SUMMARY.

(Erase heading not required.)

Instructions regarding War Diaries and Intelligence Summaries are contained in F. S. Regs., Part II, and the Staff Manual respectively. Title pages will be prepared in manuscript.

Hour, Date, Place.	Summary of Events and Information.	Remarks and references to Appendices.

Gulab Singh & Sons, Calcutta—No. 22 Army C.—5-8-14—1,07,000.

Army Form C. 2118.

WAR DIARY
or
INTELLIGENCE SUMMARY.
(Erase heading not required.)

Instructions regarding War Diaries and Intelligence Summaries are contained in F. S. Regs., Part II, and the Staff Manual respectively. Title pages will be prepared in manuscript.

Hour, Date, Place.	Summary of Events and Information.	Remarks and references to Appendices.
1.6.17.	Situation Normal. Col W.G. Cooper assumed command vice Major B.H. Alderson, who returned to Back Area. Following Arrivals.— Major G.W.C. Lucas. Departures. Major B.H. Alderson Capt. R.G. McGregor Lts J.G. J.H.B. Sullivan 2 patrols went out. No special incident occurred.	
2.6.17	Situation Normal. No special incidents during night patrols.	
3.6.17	At 7:30 pm. Enemy was seen to be shelling ASCENSION & LITTLE BILL WOODS. Patrols were sent out under D:r FATTEH MOHDSHAH, C son, & D:r AMIR KHAN, D son, to find out if enemy were occupying these woods. Valuable information was obtained by these patrols which stayed out from 2 pm — 10 pm whose work under continuous artillery & M.G. fire, only returning on approach of enemy in greatly superior numbers, after all information required had been obtained. Jem. AMIR KHAN also volunteered & was permitted to go out and ascertain the situation & remained in Charge of the party in Ascension wood. D:r Fatteh Mohd Shah	

WAR DIARY or INTELLIGENCE SUMMARY

Army Form C. 2118.

Place	Date	Hour	Summary of Events and Information	Remarks and references to Appendices
	3.6.17		made an attempt to take 3 men to enter LITTLE BILL, but was driven back by shell fire. Although himself wounded in this attempt he later made a second attempt with one man to enter the wood, but again failed this time owing to M.G. fire from the wood itself. These work done & information obtained reflects greatest credit on all concerned, as the whole affair took place in broad daylight in full view & within easy range of the enemy.) A patrol commanded by Lt MAXWELL went out at 11.45 p.m. & perceived a party of 40 germans about 30 m returning towards BIG BILL, & followed them until they were observed to enter it.	
	4.6.17		The following were gazetted in the "TIMES" of 2.6.17 the following as "mentioned in despatches" in Gazette of 1.6.17. Lieut. Col. W. G. Cooper Major G.W.C. Lucas. Regiment was relieved in front line by XV Deccan Horse, & came into Brigade Reserve.	
	5.6.17		Situation Normal. 3.D Sheitan Singh & two men killed, & 1 man wounded while on guard in LE VERGUIER. Act A/Sgn	
	6.6.17		Situation Normal.	
	7.6.17		Extract from Regimental orders of 7.6.17. Following appointment wants: Lieut H.M. GREEN to be acting adjutant vice Lieut G.O. SIMPSON	

Army Form C. 2118.

WAR DIARY
or
INTELLIGENCE SUMMARY.
(Erase heading not required.)

Place	Date	Hour	Summary of Events and Information	Remarks and references to Appendices
	7.6.17		To be acting Staff Captain See "BAD" SEE "BAD" CAV. BDE. order 3rd CAV. Div order of 22.5.17	
	8.6.17		Extract from R.O. of 8.6.17 — The commanding Officer has much pleasure in notifying the following awards (Times Wednesday 6 June 1917) INDIAN DISTINGUISHED SERVICE MEDAL Risaldar SATTAR SHAH 2146 H. Sowar ABDULAA KHAN 3079 Dfr. SYER BAZ KHAN	
	9.6.17		Situation normal	
	10.6.17		Extract from R.O. No 2 — The C.O. has much pleasure in notifying the following awards — INDIAN DISTINGUISHED SERVICE MEDAL 37854 Dfr. SOHAN SINGH 3584 Sr. RASIM NAI KHAN Authority Cav Corps No AMS 300/21	
	11.6.17		Situation normal	

Army Form C. 2118.

WAR DIARY
or
INTELLIGENCE SUMMARY.
(Erase heading not required.)

Instructions regarding War Diaries and Intelligence Summaries are contained in F. S. Regs., Part II. and the Staff Manual respectively. Title pages will be prepared in manuscript.

Place	Date	Hour	Summary of Events and Information	Remarks and references to Appendices
	12.6.17		Extract from R.O. No 2. APPOINTMENTS.— Following appointments are made with effect from 25 May 1917:— Major G.W.C. LUCAS to be 2nd in Command 1st Squadron, vice Major G.M. MOLLOY (seconded) and A.G. G.H.Q. A/25081 dated 25.5.17 Capt. H.A. HILDEBRAND to be 4th Squadron Commander	
	13.6.17		Two men wounded by machine gun fire while D Sqdn was engaged in supporting XX Division Horse	
	14.6.17		Regiment was relieved by Lord Strathcona's Horse & returned to CAULINCOURT.	
	23.6.17		Regiment went into the front line on A.2. sz[t]h E. of LE VERGUIER, relieving the 9th Hodson's Horse. Under Command of Lieut. Col. W.S. Cooper. One patrol under 15 iLES/2. troops searched SOMERVILLE WOOD and vicinity. A second small patrol under Lieut. MUIR	
			no incident occurred. Two patrols went out that night to troops under Lieut. RILEY situation normal. Two patrols went out. First of 10 troops under Lieut. RILEY after searching SOMERVILLE WOOD and vicinity without incident proceeded N.E. of	
	24.6.17		reconnoitre cross roads near enemy's SWITCH LINE. On nearing objective they came under considerable rifle fire from enemy line. They opened fire and after killing 3 & taking rifle fire from enemy line. They opened fire and after killing 3 & taking men who had been wounded walking. A.L.B. MANCO KHAN one of the wounded died on the way home. The second patrol had no incident	

2353 Wt. W2541/1454 700,000 5/15 D. D. & L. A.D.S.S./Forms/C. 2118.

Army Form C. 2118.

Instructions regarding War Diaries and Intelligence Summaries are contained in F. S. Regs., Part II. and the Staff Manual respectively. Title pages will be prepared in manuscript.

WAR DIARY
or
INTELLIGENCE SUMMARY.
(Erase heading not required.)

Place	Date	Hour	Summary of Events and Information	Remarks and references to Appendices
	25.6.17		Situation normal. Two troops B Sqdn under Lt LEIGH CLARE reconnoitred SOMERVILLE	
		10 pm to 3 am	WOOD then NE towards cross road. A second patrol 1 O. + 10 men C Sqdn searched banks to the North. Neither met with any incident. Daff. LACHMAN SINGH returned at 10 PM after being missed from patrol of previous night. A second patrol of [illegible] men searched [illegible]	
	26.6.17		Situation normal. One patrol went out at 11 pm under Lt LEIGH CLARE, strength 1 O. 35 O.R. to ELEVEN TREES. Enemy were heard near XI TREES in force, no encounter took place. A second patrol of 1 O. + 10 O.Rs searched banks to North without incident.	
	27.6.17		Situation normal. A patrol of 2 B.O.s 1 I.O. 40 O.Rs under Lt LEIGH CLARE went out at 10 pm to clear up situation at ELEVEN TREES. At ANGLE FARM, 400 yds from objective, support party (Lt ANSON + 10 men) were left in position. Attacking party took up position parallel to XI TREES and advanced [illegible] to within 20 yds of objective. They were then challenged, whereupon order to charge was given + the [illegible] position with the bayonet. The garrison which appeared to number 20 men in 3 parties fled towards their line 150 yds distant. According to plan pursuit was not carried beyond the road, but rapid fire with rifle + Hotchkiss gun [illegible] in front of retreating enemy. [illegible] estimated at [illegible] [illegible] SINGH pursued a small party alone, [illegible] one man through the [illegible], but in attempting to bring the wounded man back as prisoner he was [illegible] on the head by the German from behind + forced to relinquish his hold. Ten mins later, seeing no more of the enemy in the vicinity of ELEVEN TREES [illegible] been examined, the patrol withdrew + returned about 1.30 am. [illegible] up from the enemy [illegible] the patrol in describing an accurate [illegible]	

2353 Wt. W2544/1454 700,000 5/15 D. D. & L. A.D.S.S./Forms/C. 2118.

Instructions regarding War Diaries and Intelligence Summaries are contained in F. S. Regs., Part II. and the Staff Manual respectively. Title pages will be prepared in manuscript.

WAR DIARY
or
INTELLIGENCE SUMMARY.
(Erase heading not required.)

Army Form C. 2118.

Place	Date	Hour	Summary of Events and Information	Remarks and references to Appendices
			The only casualty sustained was one man killed. The body was [illegible]	
	28.6.17		Situation normal. No operations took place.	
	29.6.17		Situation normal.	
			3177 Daffadar FATEH MAHOMED SHAH was awarded with the I.D.S.M. (the award was notified on 21st) by the Cavalry Corps Commander.	
			At 10 P.M. a patrol of 2 B.O., 1 I.O. + 32 O.R. under LT ANSON moved out [illegible] corner of SOMERVILLE WOOD to reconnoitre cross roads on WATLING STREET 400 yds W. of enemy line. After an advance of some 700 yds a party of 5 enemy were met with + seen to make off towards other [illegible]. As the patrol advanced [illegible] were heard in broken [illegible] reaching [illegible] within 60 yards of cross roads at 1.55 a.m. when heavy rifle fire from about 25 rifles + some [illegible] [illegible] from the left front. At the same time a party of 20 enemy [illegible] at [illegible] + [illegible] our [illegible]. The [illegible] patrol opened fire on the 20 men + 5 were [illegible]	
			The rest of the patrol [illegible] on enemy [illegible] its left [illegible]. Enemy [illegible] 17 [illegible] were then seen to [illegible] from [illegible] REDOUBT, they were [illegible] and [illegible] seen to [illegible]. At this moment [illegible] came [illegible] M.G. [illegible] the direction of ELEVEN TREES to avoid which LT ANSON withdrew [illegible] Enemy then fired [illegible] which [illegible] [illegible] + [illegible] outnumbered + some enemy were working round the patrol's left flank [illegible] also [illegible] getting light, LT ANSON decided to withdraw [illegible] at 2.10 A.M. [illegible] successfully accomplished.	

2353 Wt. W2544/1454 700,000 5/15 D. D. & L. A.D.S.S./Forms/C. 2118.

Army Form C. 2118.

WAR DIARY
or
INTELLIGENCE SUMMARY.
(*Erase heading not required.*)

Instructions regarding War Diaries and Intelligence Summaries are contained in F. S. Regs., Part II, and the Staff Manual respectively. Title pages will be prepared in manuscript.

Hour, Date, Place.	Summary of Events and Information.	Remarks and references to Appendices.
30.8.17	Situation normal - O Patrol of 1.00, 1.10, 1.30 O.R.'s under Lieut Denton reconnoitred "inads" close TRENCH returning at dawn having found no enemy. A second Patrol of 1/10 + 11 O.R's reconnoitred SOMERVILLE WOOD + recently intact trenches. W.E. Cooper Lt Col Comm Hove	

Serial No: 121.

See /5

WAR DIARY
OF
34th POONA — HORSE

from 1st July 1917 to 31st July 1917

(Vol I)

Army Form C. 2118.

WAR DIARY

or

INTELLIGENCE SUMMARY.

(*Erase heading not required.*)

Instructions regarding War Diaries and Intelligence Summaries are contained in F. S. Regs., Part II, and the Staff Manual respectively. Title pages will be prepared in manuscript.

Hour, Date, Place.	Summary of Events and Information.	Remarks and references to Appendices

Gulab Singh & Sons, Calcutta—No. 22 Army C.—5-8-14—1,07,000.

Army Form C. 2118

WAR DIARY
or
INTELLIGENCE SUMMARY.
(Erase heading not required.)

Instructions regarding War Diaries and Intelligence Summaries are contained in F. S. Regs., Part II, and the Staff Manual respectively. Title pages will be prepared in manuscript.

Hour, Date, Place.	Summary of Events and Information.	Remarks and references to Appendices
1st July 1917	Situation normal. At 10 p.m. a patrol of 2 B.Os, 1 N.O. & 32 O.Rs under Lieut Sullivan went out to reconnoitre vicinity of Cross Roads at G.33.a.39. Patrol reached a point about 350 yds W. of ROSE TRENCH whence it moved in a southerly direction parallel to enemy line searching vicinity of cross roads & the road as far as ELEVEN TREES. Rifle fire was directed on patrol & flares sent up at two points, but enemy listening post were found unoccupied. Patrol reentered DRAGON POST at 3 a.m. after obtaining some useful information.	
2.7.17	Situation normal. A small patrol searched SOMERVILLE WOOD & vicinity without incident.	
3.7.17	Situation normal. At 2.10 a.m. a listening post of 1 N.C.O. & 2 O.Rs at N. corner of SOMERVILLE WOOD were approached by a party of 15 enemy. At 30 yds distance post challenged, received the reply "Kamerad". The N.C.O. at once threw a bomb & one of the enemy was wounded & assisted away by his companions. Enemy then retired out of sight followed by rifle fire from the post.	

Army Form C. 2118.

WAR DIARY
or
INTELLIGENCE SUMMARY.

(Erase heading not required.)

Instructions regarding War Diaries and Intelligence Summaries are contained in F. S. Regs., Part II, and the Staff Manual respectively. Title pages will be prepared in manuscript.

Hour, Date, Place.	Summary of Events and Information.	Remarks and references to Appendices
13/7/19	A Patrol of 6 under Lieut Anson reconnoitred approaches to cross roads at 6.33.c.3.9 after reaching a point 50 yds S.W. of x roads. They were discovered by an enemy party & fired on. The enemy were in superior strength & Patrol was gradually withdrawn.	
4.7.19	Situation normal. Lieut Vates with 2.1.0s 29 O.Rs went out to form a flanking party to the 4/5 D.G.s who were to carry out a raid on FISHER REDOUBT. They reached a point at 6.33.a.1.9 where position was taken up. Owing to torpedo party being discovered the raid was [?] & 4/5 Vates returned with his party. Left a hour after zero on the way back they encountered a party of 15- enemy & endeavoured to close with them. Enemy slipped away in the dark after an exchange of rifle shots. Situation normal.	
5.7.19	A Patrol of 1 I.O. & 29 O.Rs under Lieut Sullivan cooperated as left flank guard to a party of 4/5 D.G.s who reconnoitred vicinity of KITTREES. No incident of note took place	

Army Form C. 2118

WAR DIARY
or
INTELLIGENCE SUMMARY.

(Erase heading not required.)

Instructions regarding War Diaries and Intelligence Summaries are contained in F. S. Regs., Part II, and the Staff Manual respectively. Title pages will be prepared in manuscript.

Hour, Date, Place.	Summary of Events and Information.	Remarks and references to Appendices
6.7.19	Situation Normal.	
7.7.19	Situation Normal. 4th D.G. raided KITTREES. A patrol of 10 O.Rs. under Capt. Macgregor took up a position in front of DOGSLEG during raid returning after the raiding party had withdrawn.	
8.7.19	Situation Normal. Canadian Bde. raided the enemy line. A patrol of 10 O.Rs under Lt. Leigh Clare patrolled SOMERVILLE WOOD & vicinity without incident. Two officers of the 16th Royal Scots accompanied patrol to see the ground.	
9.7.19	Situation Normal. The regiment was relieved by the 16th Bn. Royal Scots., the relief being completed by midnight.	

Army Form C. 2118.

WAR DIARY
or
INTELLIGENCE SUMMARY.
(Erase heading not required.)

Instructions regarding War Diaries and Intelligence Summaries are contained in F.S. Regs., Part II. and the Staff Manual respectively. Title pages will be prepared in manuscript.

Place	Date	Hour	Summary of Events and Information	Remarks and references to Appendices
CAULAINCOURT	10-7-17		5th Cavalry Division wires that Lieut. H.J.L. LEIGH-CLARE I.A.R. and JEMADAR JATTAY SINGH 32nd LANCERS are awarded Military Cross and Indian Distinguished Service Medal respectively.	
	11-7-17 TO 13-7-17		NOTHING TO REPORT.	
CARTIGNY	14-7-17		Brigade Marched at 2.15 pm from CAULAINCOURT AREA to CARTIGNY AREA arriving at 4.10 pm. Regiment Billeted in HUTS.	
SUZANNE	15-7-17		Brigade Marched at 5.45 AM from CARTIGNY and arrived at SUZANNE at 10 AM. Regiment Billeted in HUTS.	
MORLANCOURT	16-7-17		Brigade Marched at 7.30 am from SUZANNE and arrived in TREUX AREA at 10 am Regiment Billeted in MORLANCOURT.	
AUTHIE	17-7-17		Brigade Marched at 6 am from MORLANCOURT and arrived in AUTHIE AREA at 11.30 AM. Regiment Billeted in AUTHIE.	

2353 Wt. W2544/1454 700,000 5/15 D.D.&L. A.D.S.S./Forms/C. 2118.

Army Form C. 2118.

WAR DIARY
or
INTELLIGENCE SUMMARY.
(Erase heading not required.)

Instructions regarding War Diaries and Intelligence Summaries are contained in F. S. Regs., Part II and the Staff Manual respectively. Title pages will be prepared in manuscript.

Place	Date	Hour	Summary of Events and Information	Remarks and references to Appendices
BELVAL	18-7-17		Brigade marched from ANTHIE area at 6am and arrived in ST. POL area at 1pm. Regiment Billeted at BELVAL	
"	19-7-17		Nothing to Report.	
EPS	20-7-17		Brigade marched to MONCHY-CAYEUX area. Regiment marched at 3.30 pm and arrived at Eps. at 5pm. & is Billeted the following have been awarded the Indian Meritorious Service Medal. 1319. 2nd. Class. Sub-Asst Surgeon. MURAR RAO NAORE 2215 Dafadar HUKAM SINGH 2072 L/Daf. FEROZE KHAN 2289 Trumpet Major NARAYAN SINGH 2382 Sowar GHULAM HAIDER KHAN 2480 " GHULAM ALI 1967 " UGAM SINGH.	
"	21-7-17		Nothing to Report.	
"	22-7-17			

Army Form C. 2118.

WAR DIARY
or
INTELLIGENCE SUMMARY.
(Erase heading not required.)

Place	Date	Hour	Summary of Events and Information	Remarks and references to Appendices
EPS.	23-7-17 to 27-7-17		Nothing to Report.	
"	28-7-17		Nothing to Report	
"	29-7-17		Major H.A. Hildebrand rejoined the Regiment from Base Rouen.	
"	30-7-17		Nothing to Report	
"	31-7-17		" " "	

B.V. Cooper Lt-Col
Commdg 34th Pooma Horse

Serial No: 121.

Confidential

War Diary

of

34th Poona Horse

From 1st August 1917 to 31st August 1917

Army Form C. 2118.

WAR DIARY
or,
INTELLIGENCE SUMMARY.

(Erase heading not required.)

Instructions regarding War Diaries and Intelligence Summaries are contained in F. S. Regs., Part II, and the Staff Manual respectively. Title pages will be prepared in manuscript.

Hour, Date, Place.		Summary of Events and Information.	Remarks and references to Appendices.
1-8-17	EPS.	Nothing to Report.	
2-8-17	"	2 . O.R's arrived from Base MARSEILLES.	
3-8-17 TO 13-8-17	"	Nothing to Report.	
14-8-17	"	14 . O.R's arrived from Base ROUEN.	
15-8-17	"	2 . O.R's arrived from Base ROUEN	
16-8-17 TO 31-8-17	"	Nothing to Report.	

Amedeo
Cmdg
34TH POONA HORSE.

Serial No. 121.

Confidential

WAR DIARY

of

34th POONA HORSE

FROM 1st SEPTEMBER to 30th SEPTEMBER 1917.

Army Form C. 2118.

WAR DIARY
or
INTELLIGENCE SUMMARY.
(Erase heading not required.)

Instructions regarding War Diaries and Intelligence Summaries are contained in F. S. Regs., Part II. and the Staff Manual respectively. Title pages will be prepared in manuscript.

Place	Date	Hour	Summary of Events and Information	Remarks and references to Appendices
EPS.	1.9.17.		Nothing to report.	
	2.9.17.		MAJ. B.H. ALDERSON died in No. 12 Stationary Hospital, received as a result of a riding accident.	of injuries
	3.9.17.		A course on HOTCHKISS GUNNERS was started under R.A.Q. 1425, 16 O.R.I. attached to the course.	
	4.9.17.		Nothing to report.	
	5.9.17		Capt. G.O. SIMSON appointed Staff Captain Seconded to Cav. Brigade with effect from 1/22.8.1917 and was struck off the strength of the regiment.	
	6.9.17.		Nothing to report.	
	7.9.17.			
	8.9.17.		Lt. GEN. SIR H.V. COX K.C.M.G, C.B, C.S.I, Military Secretary India Office inspected the 4 Indian Cavalry regiments of the 5th Cav. Division.	
	9.9.17		MAJ. R.H. O'D PATERSON, and British O.R. & 30 O.R.I. arrived from New Brea.	
	10.9.17		Nothing to report.	
	11.9.17.		Lt. H.H. GREEN I.V.O. appointed Adjutant vice Capt. G.O. SIMSON, Staff Captain, with effect from 23.8.1917.	
			MAJ. H.A. HILDEBRAND appointed 4th Squadron Commander vice MAJ B.H. ALDERSON deceased with effect from 8.9.17.	
	12.9.17.		Nothing to report.	

Army Form C. 2118.

WAR DIARY
or
INTELLIGENCE SUMMARY.
(Erase heading not required.)

Place	Date	Hour	Summary of Events and Information	Remarks and references to Appendices
EPS.			I.A.R.	
	13.9.17		2/L T. G.H.B. SULLIVAN promoted Lieutenant with effect from 18.6.1917.	
	14.9.17		A party of 36 O.R. proceeded to BASE, MARSEILLES on duty, under 2/Lt G. DEACON (conducting officer)	
	15.9.17		6. O.R. proceeded on duty to BASE, ROUEN.	
	16.9.17		2/Lts T.H. LUNHAM, D.S.E. McNEILL & J.P. ACKWORTH arrived from BASE ROUEN	
			2/Lt A.G. ILES & 1 I.O. & 1 B.O.R & 11 O.R. proceeded to join 4th FIELD SQUADRON	
	17.9.17 to 23.9.17		Nothing to report.	
	24.9.17		2/Lt C.G. DEACON arrived from MARSEILLES.	
	25.9.17 to 28.9.17		Nothing to report	
	29.9.17		Lt. J.O. HANWELL 11th Hrs. proceeded to join School of HOTCHKISS RIFLE Instruction.	
	30.9.17		Capt. R.G. MacGREGOR, 2 I.Os, 1 A. I.O.R. proceeded to Bao ROUEN on duty.	

G Cooper Lt. Col.
Commanding 34th (A Poona Horse)

121

Confidential

WAR DIARY

OF

34th POONA HORSE

FROM 1st OCTOBER to 31st OCTOBER 1917.

Army Form C. 2118.

WAR DIARY
or
INTELLIGENCE SUMMARY.
(Erase heading not required.)

Instructions regarding War Diaries and Intelligence Summaries are contained in F. S. Regs., Part II. and the Staff Manual respectively. Title pages will be prepared in manuscript.

Place	Date	Hour	Summary of Events and Information	Remarks and references to Appendices
EPS.	1-10-17 to 5-10-17		Nothing to Report	
EPS	6-10-17		Regiment marched from Billets at 9.30 AM to Brigade Rendezvous. Brigade arrived at BOESEGHEM area about 2 PM. Regiment was billeted at LES-CISEAUX.	
LES. CISEAUX	7-10-17		Regiment marched from Billets to Brigade Rendezvous at 11AM. D Squadron formed advanced Guard to the Brigade. Brigade moved to WATOU area about 4 PM. The Regiment was billeted in ARTILLERY (area) Camp. S.E exit of WATOU. Part of the Regiment accommodation in huts remainder in Tents & under Covers.	
	8-10-17 to 9-10-17		2/Lt W.S.H. HEARN I.A rejoined his unit & was posted to C. Sqd Nothing to report	
WATOU	10-10-17		Belgian Interpreter Robert du LEENER rejoined his unit	
"	11-10-17		Nothing to report	
"	12-10-17		Jemadar SULEMAN KHAN & ZORAWAR SINGH also 15.O.R.T arrived from Base ROUEN.	

Army Form C. 2118.

WAR DIARY
or
INTELLIGENCE SUMMARY.

(Erase heading not required.)

Instructions regarding War Diaries and Intelligence Summaries are contained in F. S. Regs., Part II. and the Staff Manual respectively. Title pages will be prepared in manuscript.

Place	Date	Hour	Summary of Events and Information	Remarks and references to Appendices
MATOU	12/10/17		Lieut R. YATES and Lieut C.S. DEACON I.A.R.O. report to their office. Lieut ILES departure on duty to U.K. As Lieut T.S. APCAR with 1.O.R.B. infantry apparently attached the O.C. Dismounted Reinforcements is proceeding to MARSEILLES to form D.A Column Regiment supplied eight horse transport to Base MARSEILLES for dispatch to INDIA	
"	13/10/17		2. O. R.I. & 1st Lancers provided eight horse transport to Base MARSEILLES for dispatch to INDIA willing to Return.	
"	14/10/17			
"	15/10/17		Regiment marched from Billets to Brigade Rendezvous. Brigade reached RENESCURE over about 3 P.M. the Regiment was billeted at HEURINGHEM.	
HEURINGHEM	16/10/17		Regiment marched from Billets to Brigade Rendezvous at 9:30 A.M. C.Sqt fast Rear Guard. Brigade reached FAUQUEMBERGUES over about 2 P.M. Regiment was billeted in MERCK - ST. LIEVIN.	
MERCK ST LIEVIN	17/10/17		Regiment marched at 8:10 A.M. from Billets to Brigade Rendezvous. D Sqn formed advance guard to Bde. Brigade reached FRUGES over at 1 P.M. Regiment to billets in CREQUY & TORCY all under RILLET 2/3 of horses under cover.	

A5834 Wt. W4973/M687 750,000 8/16 D. D. & L. Ltd. Forms/C.2118/13.

WAR DIARY
or
INTELLIGENCE SUMMARY.
(Erase heading not required.)

Army Form C. 2118.

Place	Date	Hour	Summary of Events and Information	Remarks and references to Appendices
CRÉPUY	18/10/17		Owing to Regiment being very cramped for space, the village of SAINS LEZ FRESSIN is allotted to the Regt. for billeting. Regt. billets as follows. H.Q. Personnel, 2 Troops 1/B Sqdn & C Sqdn in CRÉPUY. D Sqdn & 2 Troops in TRPCL A Sqn & Signal Troop in SAINS LEZ FRESSIN.	
"	19/10/17		Mr J.R. ACKWORTH, I.A. & Jmdr SHER BAHADUR KHAN with 1 U.R.B + 4 O.R.I. proceeded to BAILLEUL to join Cavalry Pioneer Battalion formed from Dismounted Reinforcements. 2 O.R.I. joined the Regt. from ROUEN.	
"	20/10/17		Mr J.T. DUPACK, I.A.R., reports his intention to join the Field Survey Company at imminently probation. Mr J.O. HANWELL, 11th Lancashire Hutchins Riffle came on GHQ school at LA TOUQUET. awaiting report.	
"	21/10/17			
"	22/10/17		Mr G.K. MITCHELL I.A.R. reports his arrival from Signal Cav. Corps returns to Report.	

WAR DIARY or INTELLIGENCE SUMMARY.

Army Form C. 2118.

Place	Date	Hour	Summary of Events and Information	Remarks and references to Appendices
CRÉGNY	23.10.17		Lt. C.K. Nicholl Tar Master Quarter Master vice Lt. A.F. Dickson TAR reverts to squadron officer with effect from date	

"	24.10.17		The following officers returned this command from the Base ROUEN 2/Lt G.C. HOWLAND IA posted to A squadron
			  " " W.R. BEER IA " " D "
			  " " C.C. SPENCER IA " " B "
			  " " H.D. WHITTICK IA " " D "
			
			23. O.R.I. arrived from Base ROUEN	

"	25.10.17		2. O.R.I. proceeded to Base MARSEILLES to join D.A. Column Lieut J.O. HANWELL 11th LANCERS proceeded to Base ROUEN for duty as Hotchkiss Rifle instructor. Belgian interpreter Adrien Van LOGNOR proceeded to H.Q. 2nd ARMY	
"	26.10.17		nothing to report.	
"	27.10.17			
"	28.10.17		1. O.R.I. proceeded to Base Marseilles to join D.A. Column nothing to report.	

Army Form C. 2118.

WAR DIARY
or
INTELLIGENCE SUMMARY.
(Erase heading not required.)

Place	Date	Hour	Summary of Events and Information	Remarks and references to Appendices
CREPUY	24-10-17 to 31-10-17		Nothing to Return	

E.G. Cooper Lt Col
Commanding 34th Poona Horse

(121)

WAR DIARY

of

34th POONA HORSE

FROM 1st NOVEMBER 1917 TO 30 NOVEMBER

Army Form C. 2118.

WAR DIARY
or
INTELLIGENCE SUMMARY.
(Erase heading not required.)

Instructions regarding War Diaries and Intelligence Summaries are contained in F.S. Regs., Part II. and the Staff Manual respectively. Title pages will be prepared in manuscript.

Place	Date	Hour	Summary of Events and Information	Remarks and references to Appendices
CREQUY	1-11-17		2.O.R.I. joined the Regiment from Base Rouen.	
"	2-11-17		nothing to report	
"	3-11-17		" " "	
"	4-11-17		" " "	
"	5-11-17		The following promotions were made with effect from 25th August 1917 to complete establishment.	
			Jemadar. Ganpat Singh } to be Ressaidar	
			" Amir Khan.	
			2947 Dfr. Sher Bahadar Khan	
			2872 K.Dfr. Pem Singh	
			2899 " Kali Khan } to be Jemadars	
			3172 " Rawat Singh	
			Vide D.O. 1148 d/3-11-17 and D.O. 1654 d/5-11-17	

Army Form C. 2118.

WAR DIARY
or
INTELLIGENCE SUMMARY.

(Erase heading not required.)

Instructions regarding War Diaries and Intelligence Summaries are contained in F.S. Regs., Part II. and the Staff Manual respectively. Title pages will be prepared in manuscript.

Place	Date	Hour	Summary of Events and Information	Remarks and references to Appendices
CREPUY	5/11/17		Honorary Rank of JEMADAR was conferred on No 2146 Drift Head Sadular ABDULLAH KHAN for meritorious service with effect from 14th September 1917. Authority Gazette of India notification No 1547 d/14-9-17.	
"	6/11/17		awaiting transport	
"	7/11/17		" "	
"	8/11/17		" "	
"	9/11/17		The Brigade marched to OUTREBOIS area. The Regt left billets at 8:30am, Regt found Rearguard to Brigade. Regiment arrived at 6pm & was billeted in HEUZECOURT - ST ACHEUL and GRIMOND	
HEUZECOURT ST ACHEUL	10-11-17		The Brigade marched to CONTAY area. Regiment marched from billets at 8:30 AM arriving at BEAUCOURT at 3 pm where Regt. was billeted	
BEAUCOURT	11-11-17		Major T. Peters reconnoitred Rout to MERICOURT-SUR-SOMME The Brigade marched to BRAY and at 3 pm Regiment left billets arriving at MERICOURT-SUR-SOMME at 8 pm & was billeted there. D Coy formed advance guard to the Brigade.	

A 5834 Wt.W4973/M687 750,000 8/16 D. D. & L. Ltd. Forms/C.2118/13.

Army Form C. 2118.

WAR DIARY
or
INTELLIGENCE SUMMARY.
(Erase heading not required.)

Instructions regarding War Diaries and Intelligence Summaries are contained in F. S. Regs., Part II. and the Staff Manual respectively. Title pages will be prepared in manuscript.

Place	Date	Hour	Summary of Events and Information	Remarks and references to Appendices
MERRICOURT SUR SOMME.	12.11.17		Brigade marched to VRAIGNES aux Regt. left Billets at 4.15 pm arriving at HANCOURT at 10 pm leaving Billets in Hutments of the Horse under cover.	
HANCOURT	13.11.17		Jemadar GHULAM MOHD KHAN 21. L.C. Rejoined Regiment with 1. O.R.I. from Base ROUEN.	
"	14.11.17		Mr B.G. SPENCER reported sick - to join the 4th FIELD SPD for duty with Ammunition Lorries	
"	15.11.17		Lieut. A.S. ILES reported his arrival from duty with 4th FIELD SPD.	
"	16.11.17		nothing to report	
"	17.11.17		The following reinforcement draft arrived from Cavalry Remount Battalion Mr J.P.ACWORTH and 10.I.O.R.B. 56 O.R.I. 2 followers Jemr. SHER BAHADUR KHAN.	
"	18.11.17		Lieut. J.H.B. SULLIVAN proceed to LA TOUQUET. 1.O.R.I. joint to Regt. from return HRifle Course at- S.H.Q. at Base ROUEN	
"	19.11.17		nothing to report.	

A 5834 Wt. W4973/M687 750,000 8/16 D. D. & L. Ltd. Forms/C.2118/13.

WAR DIARY or INTELLIGENCE SUMMARY

Place	Date	Hour	Summary of Events and Information	Remarks and references to Appendices
HANCOURT	20/11/17		The Regiment left billets at 1 AM & marched with Brigade to concentration area at DESSART WOOD H.E. of FINS arriving at 6 AM. Horses were off saddled & watered. Orders were received to be ready to move off at 8.30 AM. 3 officers Patrols were sent off to find for infantry objectives & the news of cavalry breaking through Enemy's line. Orders were received at 12.15 PM. the Infantry having secured the Bridge Heads at MARCOING & MASNIERES. The Regiment moved forward with 7th Dragoon Guards as advanced guard towards the Premy Hotel & Deanns Hover Heights. On reaching MARCOING & getting well into the village at 2.15 PM the Regiment was ordered to withdraw to a position 500 yds S of the village, the advance front of Bde having proved impossible to advance further owing to uncut wire in front of Enemy's third line of Resistance which was successfully held & strongly held. At 6.30 PM a further withdrawal was ordered to a position in field about S of MARCOING where the Brigade Bivouacked for the night.	
Near X Roads Hurley M.C. of LA VACQUERIE Which is N of VILLERS PLOUICH	21/11/17		At 6 AM orders were received to saddle up & the Regiment moved to leave ground near VILLERS PLOUICH for W. of VILLERS PLOUICH – MARCOING ROAD 2 E of 12 railway. The Horses were off saddled and breakfast was again served by 11 AM.	

Army Form C. 2118.

WAR DIARY
or
INTELLIGENCE SUMMARY.

(Erase heading not required.)

Instructions regarding War Diaries and Intelligence Summaries are contained in F. S. Regs. Part II. and the Staff Manual respectively. Title pages will be prepared in manuscript.

Place	Date	Hour	Summary of Events and Information	Remarks and references to Appendices
"	21-11-17		2/Lieut J.D. ACWORTH proceeded at 11.45 am on liaison with 88th Infantry Bde at MASNIERES & remained at Bde H.Qrs until 4.30 pm from the Brigade marched at 6.30 pm to Bivouacked for the night from N.E. of Villers Ploiuch Rept. Halted.	
BIVOUAC N.E. of Villers Ploiuch	22-11-17		Entry arrived to water at 6 am. A, B & C Sqd watered. Regt. moved onwards to stables at 1.30 am & moved off again at 7.30 pm Brigade moved at 8 am via MARCOING - RIBECOURT to FINS, arriving there at 3 pm. Men were Billeted in huts.	
FINS	23-11-17		Brigade marched to BRAY over Regt. left Billets at 5.30 am reaching CHUIGNOLLES at 3 pm where the Regt. were Billeted. All Horses under cover.	
CHUIGNOLLES	24-11-17		T/Lt J.A.H. GREEN and 34th HORSE took ADJUTANT 14th H.O. R.I.G. and the A/CAPT with Army Allowances as Light, whilst is employed via Capt. G.O. SIMCOX appointed Staff Captain SEC-BDE - CAV-BDE 2/22 B-17. Authority (extract from list of officers of appointments) to commence 7/11/17. 4th & 5th CAV DIV A/5021 2/24-11-17. Regt. on to horse watering to move from 8 am	
"	25-11-17		Bde "A" short notice to move" cancelled	
"	26-11-17		antrine training	
"	27-11-17		Regiment marched to TREFCON over Regt. marched at 8.30 am A fog being abroad Great difficulty Regt. arrived at Bivouac TREFCON at 2 pm. Men in huts horses under cover.	

A 5834 Wt.W.4973/M687 750,000 8/16 D. D. & L. Ltd. Forms/C.2118/13.

Army Form C. 2118.

WAR DIARY
INTELLIGENCE SUMMARY
(Erase heading not required.)

Instructions regarding War Diaries and Intelligence Summaries are contained in F. S. Regs., Part II. and the Staff Manual respectively. Title pages will be prepared in manuscript.

Place	Date	Hour	Summary of Events and Information	Remarks and references to Appendices
TRÉFCON	28/11/17		Nothing to report. Holding to Refuse	
"	29/11/17			
"	30/11/17		Received orders to move at once at 9:15 AM. Brigade marched via VILLERS FAUCON ME 11:30 AM arriving in valley S.W. of GONZEAUCOURT at about 3:15 PM. 1 OR killed 1 OR wounded on edge of REVELON by shell fire. Regiment several times twice midnight [illegible] advanced twice shifted twice shells near HQ [illegible] 2nd shift Regt [illegible] started 11:30 Position [illegible] [illegible] move back to Camp of Bde HQc

Valley [illegible]
W of GONZEAUCOURT

[Signature] Lt Col
Commdg 34th Poona Horse
30/11/17

121.

WAR DIARY

OF

34" POONA HORSE

FROM 1ST DECEMBER 1917 TO 31ST DECEMBER 1917.

CONFIDENTIAL.

Army Form C. 2118.

WAR DIARY
or
INTELLIGENCE SUMMARY.
(Erase heading not required.)

Instructions regarding War Diaries and Intelligence Summaries are contained in F.S. Regs., Part II. and the Staff Manual respectively. Title pages will be prepared in manuscript.

Place	Date	Hour	Summary of Events and Information	Remarks and references to Appendices
VALLEY ½ mile S. of SUGAR FACTORY HEADICOURT.	1/12/17	1.A.M	Received orders from Brigade that Battn. suddenly & anxious notify Stand to at 5.30 A.M. Regiment Stood to until 1 P.M. when Horse went back to walls at VILLERS FAUCON, maintaining complete observation at Bivouac at 2.30 P.M.	
		4 P.M	Received orders to be prepared to move downwards into trenches.	
		7 P.M	Regiment fell in dismounted strength 262 all ranks & marched at 7.30 P.M. via REVELON arriving at BOIS GAUCHE (about 500x W. of (VILLERS GUISLAIN) at 10 P.M. The Regiment relieved the 18th LANCERS by 11.55 P.M. dispositions A.B. & C. sqdns in front line Regt. & D Sqdn in reserve near Regimental H.Qrs. Continued sniping & heavy bursts of Machine Gun fire throughout the night.	
BOIS GAUCHE	7/12/17	2-45 A.M	Received warning from O.C. 3rd Bn. R.S.O.F regarding enemy that an attack was expected from GONNELIEU just before dawn. This information was obtained from a prisoner. Enemy aeroplanes passed over Regimental H.Qrs flying very low for over ½ hour from 4.9 A.M. with a view to obtain latest information by observation. No H.Qrs.	
		6.A.M.		
		12.30 P.M	Enemy warned through Brigade that enemy was reported to be massing E. of VILLERS GUISLAIN & that an attack might be expected at dusk. Sgd. Country was again subjected to severe enemy shell fire. Trenches had been greatly interfered with during the night & day	

Army Form C. 2118.

WAR DIARY
or
INTELLIGENCE SUMMARY.
(Erase heading not required.)

Instructions regarding War Diaries and Intelligence Summaries are contained in F. S. Regs., Part II. and the Staff Manual respectively. Title pages will be prepared in manuscript.

Place	Date	Hour	Summary of Events and Information	Remarks and references to Appendices
BOIS GAUCHE	2.12.17		and by very slow along the E edge of GAUCHE WOOD. Sniping was maintained.	
		4.50 pm	Right flank of Regiment (A Sqd) was attacked by enemy estimated at 600. 2 troops of D Sqd. were immediately sent to counter attack & enemy driven off by rifle & machine gun fire. Enemy suffered heavy casualties. We had only (2 O.R.s wounded).	
			Situation remained quiet until about 6 pm when enemy shelled GAUCHE WOOD very heavily, continued sniping & M.G. fire throughout evening.	
		8.10 pm	An officer of the 4th Dragoon Guards arrived to reconnoitre the Regiment. Relief was completed by 10.30 pm. The enemy shelling heavily at intervals of 15 minutes about 9.15 pm. M.G. fire was particularly heavy at 9.15 pm.	
		10.30 pm	Regt. marched back to cantonments. Further casualties being 1 O.R. killed & O.R.s wounded. Regt. was billeted for the night in huts. Weather was very cold though fine at night.	

A5834 Wt. W4973/M687 750,000 8/16 D. D. & L. Ltd. Forms/C.2118/13.

Army Form C. 2118.

WAR DIARY
or
INTELLIGENCE SUMMARY.
(Erase heading not required.)

Instructions regarding War Diaries and Intelligence Summaries are contained in F. S. Regs., Part II. and the Staff Manual respectively. Title pages will be prepared in manuscript.

Place	Date	Hour	Summary of Events and Information	Remarks and references to Appendices
Nr SUGAR FACTORY HENDICOURT	3-12-17	11:30 am	Brigade marched at 11:30 am to Bivouac ½ mile south of SAULCOURT arriving there at 2 pm. Regiment was bivouaced in Enclosure Road running SW/NE of SAULCOURT. Tents were issued afterwards. Hard frost.	
½ mile S.W. of SAULCOURT on SPENISH ROAD	4-12-17	2 pm	Received orders that tents were only to be in brigade notice by day & 1 hour by night to proceed dismounted into trenches.	
"	5-12-17		Nothing to report.	
"	6-12-17		" " "	
"	7-12-17		" " "	
DÉVISE	8-12-17	1:15 pm	Brigade marched across country to BUIRE Regiment marched via MONS EN CHAUSSEE to DÉVISE occupying JODHPUR LANCERS Camp arriving there at 4.30 pm.	
"	9-12-17		First Piquet reconnoitred 2 m line running N from JEANCOURT	
"	10-12-17		Regiment put on short notice from 6 pm. 1 troop NCO & daily from 6:30 am to 8 am. Sqd Leaders reconnoitred 2nd line running N from JEANCOURT	
"	11-12-17		Awaiting Orders.	

Army Form C. 2118.

WAR DIARY
or
INTELLIGENCE SUMMARY.
(Erase heading not required.)

Instructions regarding War Diaries and Intelligence Summaries are contained in F. S. Regs., Part II. and the Staff Manual respectively. Title pages will be prepared in manuscript.

Place	Date	Hour	Summary of Events and Information	Remarks and references to Appendices
DEVISES	12-12-17	—	Nothing to report	
"	13-12-17	—	"	
"	14-12-17	—	Ressaidar BALWANT SINGH 27 L Cav attd 34th POONA HORSE awarded the Indian order of merit 2nd class	
"			3212 L/Dafdar JAIT SINGH 34th Poona Horse awarded Indian Distinguished service medal	
"	15-12-17	—	Nothing to report	
"	16-12-17	—	"	
"	17-12-17	—	50 O.R.s proceed from MARSEILLES to TREFCON AREA at 11 AM arriving at camp at 11.30 PM. Regiment marched independently. Lt Col WG Cowie Arrived to MARSEILLES on duty	
TREFCON	18-12-17	—	Nothing to report	
"	19-12-17	—	"	
"	20-12-17	—	Wiring party of 5 N.C.O. & IO.R & 300 O.R.s went by lorry to TEMPLEUX LE GUERARD horses left at 1 pm & returned at 10:30 pm State of rainess. 1st more orderlies was moved from 1.pm	
"	21-12-17	—	Ressaidar Sattar Shah & Ressaidar MCA Karim Khan Avvrived GBase Rouen for duty	
"	22-12-17	—	Nothing to Report	

Army Form C. 2118.

WAR DIARY
or
INTELLIGENCE SUMMARY.
(Erase heading not required.)

Instructions regarding War Diaries and Intelligence
Summaries are contained in F. S. Regs., Part II.
and the Staff Manual respectively. Title pages
will be prepared in manuscript.

Place	Date	Hour	Summary of Events and Information	Remarks and references to Appendices
TRGFCOM	23/12/17		1. O.R.I proceeded to Base MARSEILLES for outpost Div. ammunition Column	
"	24/12/17		Party of 5 B.Os, & I.Os, & 300 O.R.I. proceeded by train from VERMAND to winter quarters (COLOGNE FARM PARIS) left at 12 noon returned at 12 midnight.	
	25/12/17		Major J. Petrie proceeded to Rouen for duty. 2. O.R.I. at Base Marseilles for duty with Div. ammunition column. Indian Cavalry advanced Base Depot.	
	26/12/17		Regiment put on 1 hours notice. The following proceeded to duty at Indian Cavalry advanced Base Depot. 2/Lt D.S.G. McNeil & 2 O.R.I. from PARBUZIER course at Base MARSEILLES for return to India. 3 O.R.I., 1 follower proceeded to Base MARSEILLES for return to India. 2 Jattan Singh & 3. O.R.I. & 1. O.R.B.	
	27/12/17		" " " "	
	28/12/17		Nothing to report.	
	29/12/17		1 hours notice removed. Regt now in state of Readiness to move at one the following were awarded Indian Meritorious Service Medal (without annuity). 1129 K.Daf To Singh. 29/L Cay also 34/P Horse 2531 L/Daf Devi Singh 2099 R- BAHAWAL Bux KHAN- 34/P Horse 2547 N/D ALIH ALI KHAN 3353 Farrier Major Abdul Jabba 740 Dr SHEIKH CHAND 21.L Cay	
	30/12/17		Risaldar Major HAMIR SINGH and 30 O.R.I. joined from Base RUEN.	

Army Form C. 2118.

WAR DIARY
or
INTELLIGENCE SUMMARY.

(Erase heading not required.)

Instructions regarding War Diaries and Intelligence Summaries are contained in F. S. Regs., Part II. and the Staff Manual respectively. Title pages will be prepared in manuscript.

Place	Date	Hour	Summary of Events and Information	Remarks and references to Appendices
TREFCON	31/1/17		Nothing to report	

Anders Junjor
Comdg. 34th POONA HORSE

Army Form C. 2118.

3rd "B" Poona Horse

(121)

WAR DIARY or INTELLIGENCE SUMMARY

January 1918

Place	Date	Hour	Summary of Events and Information	Remarks and references to Appendices
TREFCON	1-1-18		2/Lieut. E.C. SPENCER. I.A., RESSAIDAR GANPAT SINGH with 1.0.R.I. and 1.0.R.B. rejoined Regt. from 4th Field Squadron. Regiment on 1 hour notice.	
"	2-1-18		2/Lieut. J.P. ACWORTH I.A. JEMDR. PEM SINGH with 1.0.R.I. & 1.0.R.B. proceeded to join 47th CAV. PIONEER BATTALION.	
"	3-1-18		2/Lieut. D.S.E. McNEILL with 2.0.R.I. rejoined Regt. from "Power Buzzer" Course at 1/2 Bde.	
"	4-1-18		Nothing to Report.	
"	5-1-18		Major's R.H. O'D. PATTESON and H.A. HILDEBRAND attended 5th Cav. Divisional Gas Course at MONCHY LA SACHÉ.	
"	6-1-18		Majors R.H. O'D. PATTESON and H.A. HILDEBRAND Gas School. (Complete course)	
"	7-1-18		Nothing to Report.	
"	8-1-18		Regt. removed from 1 hour notice to furnish working parties for our Division. Lieut's A. STILES and A.F. DICKSON attended 5th Cav. Div. Gas School MONCHY LA SACHÉ	
"	9-1-18		do. " " " " "	
"	10-1-18		Lt.Col. W.G. COOPER rejoined the Regiment from leave MARSEILLES. RISALDAR HAMIR SINGH BAHADAR to be Tirsformming RISALDAR MAJOR with effect from 14-10-17 Vice Risaldar Major HUSSAIN BUX KHAN sailed for INDIA on return. (D.O. 170+/35-1-18	

Army Form C. 2118.

WAR DIARY
or
INTELLIGENCE SUMMARY.

(Erase heading not required.)

Instructions regarding War Diaries and Intelligence Summaries are contained in F. S. Regs., Part II. and the Staff Manual respectively. Title pages will be prepared in manuscript.

Place	Date	Hour	Summary of Events and Information	Remarks and references to Appendices
TREFCON	11/1/18		Nothing to Report.	
"	12/1/18		2/Lieut. J.P. Acworth proceeds to U.K. under orders to report to INDIA OFFICE. Captain. R.S. MacGREGOR, Ressaidar SULTAN SINGH, Ressaidar ANNU KHAN, I.O.R.B. and 28. O.R.I. arrived from Base ROUEN.	
"	13/1/18		2/Lieut. E.C. SPENCER proceeded to La Touquet on HOTCHKISS RIFLE COURSE. 2/Lieut C.C. HOWLAND, JEMDR JAS. MOHD KHAN & 2 N.C.O., rejoined from 5th CAV. DIV. SCHOOL on completion of scouting course. JEMDR SHER BAHADAR KHAN & 2 N.C.O. proceed on scouting course. Du Schut. Burry 15/70 U.R.B	
"	14/1/18		Major. G.W.C. LUCAS proceeded to Army Infantry School. LT. J.H.B. Sullivan proceeded to join 4 Cav Reserve Battalion. (also I.O.R.B)	
"	15/1/18		1.O.R.I. proceeded Urban MARSEILLES for employment with D.A. COLUMNS.	
"	16/1/18		Nothing to report.	
"	17/1/18		3329 Dfr UMED SINGH promoted JEMADAR with effect from 11/1/17 vice JEMADAR Kalyan Singh P.B. (D.O. 1711E/15/1/18) Lt Col W.G.C. cope evacuated to C.C. Station (sick). Major G.W. Innes assumes command.	
"	18/1/18		Jemdr Salim Singh, Jemdr Annu Khan and 3 N.C.O's attended 5th Cav Div Sgt School at Monchy- La-Sache.	

WAR DIARY or INTELLIGENCE SUMMARY

Army Form C. 2118.

Place	Date	Hour	Summary of Events and Information	Remarks and references to Appendices
TROFCON	19-1-18		Jemadar Sher Mahadur Khan & 2 N.C.O.'s returned from Scouting course at 5th Cav. Div. school at Busny Les Doves.	
"	20-1-18		Nothing to report.	
"	21-1-18		Major W.J.E. Lucas reported from 5th Army Infantry School. Captain R.S. MacGregor attached 5th Cav. Div. G.w behind at MONCHY LAGACHE.	
"	22-1-18		Do " " " "	
"	23-1-18		SSRI mounted orderly Marseilles for draft with to INDIA. Nothing to Report	
"	24-1-18		The following were awarded "Indian Distinguished Service Medal." RESSAIDAR BALWANT 27.L.C. atd 34? P.H. Jemadar JAJ MOHD KHAN " ANNU KHAN " SHER BAHADAR KHAN " — (D.O. 1720 d/13-1-18) Ressaidar Sultan Singh evacuated sick to C.F.A.	
"	25-1-18		Dismounted Regiment strength as follows Arrived nd Commenced Mnpr R.H.U.D. Patterson into trench line (in Reserve at VADENCOURT)	

Army Form C. 2118.

WAR DIARY
or
INTELLIGENCE SUMMARY.
(Erase heading not required.)

Instructions regarding War Diaries and Intelligence Summaries are contained in F.S. Regs., Part II. and the Staff Manual respectively. Title pages will be prepared in manuscript.

Place	Date	Hour	Summary of Events and Information	Remarks and references to Appendices
TREFCON	26-1-18		Relieving D.M. Regt of 4th Dragoon Guards. Strength of D.M. Regt. 7.B.Os. 8.I.Os, 245 O.R.s + 7.O.R.B. horses marched from camp at 4.30 pm. Relief was completed without incident at 7 pm.	
TREFCON	26-1-18		4.O.R.s were moved from Base ROUEN.	
VADENCOURT	27-1-18		D.M. Regt. practised morning alarm positions from L.34.d.50.2 to R.4.b.5.7 D.M. Regt. furnished 2 working parties of 40 men each to dig a w.c. attached infantry to work digging at R.6.c.9.4 + L.13.d.5.4.	
"	28-1-18		D.M. Regt. was Duty Regt of Bde.	
TREFCON	29-1-18		2 Lt. E.C. Spencer rejoined Regt from Hotchkiss Rifle school (also 1 O.R.B.) D.M. Regt. furnished 2 working parties of 60 men each as on 27th morning at R.6.C.9.9.	
VADENCOURT	"			
TREFCON	30-1-18		Jemr KALI KHAN proceeded to join 4th Cav-Pioneer Battn- for duty. Rsldr SINGH arrived from duty with 4" Cav. Pioneer Battn.	
VADENCOURT	30-1-18		D.M. Regt was Duty Regiment of Bde.	
"	31-1-18		D.M. Regt furnished working parties as on 29 Jan at R.6.C.9-9 mining	

Major
Cmdg 34th POONA HORSE

Confidential.
Original

WAR DIARY
of
34th POONA HORSE

For the month of February 1918.
(From 1st to 28th February 18).

WAR DIARY or INTELLIGENCE SUMMARY

Army Form C. 2118.

Place	Date	Hour	Summary of Events and Information	Remarks and references to Appendices
TREFCON	1-2-18		See Cov. Brigade less Dismounted Regiment marched from TREFCON to Guillaucourt area. The Regiment furnished Rear Guard & struck Billets allotted to the Regiment - LAMOTTE - WARFUSÉE - ABANCOURT which were reached at 3PM.	
VADENCOURT LAMOTTE	2-2-18		Dismounted Regiment at VADENCOURT in Reserve, relating to report. Regiment left Billets at 8.40 AM joining up with Brigade at 9AM & marching to BELLOY - SUR - SOMME area. Regiment was allotted the village of HAVERNAS - WARGNIES - NAOURS for Billets & arrived there at 3.30PM. Distribution of billets as follows :- MG's & Transport in HAVERNAS, Bsqdn in WARGNIES, AC & D Sqdn in NAOURS, Q.M.RS. 2nd from Base Rouen Dismounted Regiment suffered (2) working parties of 60 men under 2/Lt C Hamilton & Lt T M Lunham, parties worked on Wire on NAB POST & mending W/ TUMULUS. 1.ORE arrived from Rgn (Back area) to replace 1.ORE evacuated to CEA. Nothing to Report. Rest in Bath area.	
HAVERNAS {3¾ mls NE of VADENCOURT}	3-2-18		Dismounted Regiment Relieved 18th Lancers in Red Line (support-line) A Sqdn in PUNTRU & MORGVAL Trenches, B Sqdn in COKERS TRENCH, C Sqdn in DEAN TRENCH, D Sqdn in DEAN QUARRY. Patrol of 1/2 20.O.R.I. Regt under Capt. W G MacGregor with the WR Beer for instruction visited Vicinity of ETINEHEM	

WAR DIARY or INTELLIGENCE SUMMARY

Army Form C. 2118.

(Erase heading not required.)

Instructions regarding War Diaries and Intelligence Summaries are contained in F.S. Regs., Part II. and the Staff Manual respectively. Title pages will be prepared in manuscript.

Place	Date	Hour	Summary of Events and Information	Remarks and references to Appendices
¾ mile E of VADENCOURT	3.2.18		MAXWOOD, FISHER CRATER, no contact with enemy. Patrol left LONETREE POST at 8 pm returning by DRAGOON POST at 10.30 pm. Quiet night.	
HAVERNAS	4.2.18		Nothing to report. With Regt in Back area.	
¾ mile E of VADENCOURT			Dismounted Regiment. Day very quiet. Patrol left LONETREE POST at 8 pm under Lieut O.S.T. Lee, consisting of I.S.O. & 20 ORs & proceeded by DOGS LEG MAXWOOD & trees to angle. Enemy wire located from 50 x S of southern trees to ONE TREE TRENCH. Patrol returned via DRAGOON POST at 10.10 pm having encountered no enemy.	
HAVERNAS	5.2.18		Captain M.H. GREEN under orders from Bde proceeded to join 13th H.Q. (D.M. Bde) to act as staff officer. Capt. W.S. ELPHINSTON rejoined the Regiment on completion of duty with IO, in U.K. 2/Lt S D'G Wheeler proceeded to join D.M. Regiment. Dismounted Regiment. Enemy Patrol consisting of I.S.O. 20 OR under 2/Lt H.B. PILCHER 1st Lt S.C. HOWLAND left LONETREE POST at 9.30 pm bombing Dog's Leg	
¾ mile E of VADENCOURT			MAXWOOD, FISHER CRATER returning by BARRIER POST at midnight. No enemy seen.	

Army Form C. 2118.

WAR DIARY
or
INTELLIGENCE SUMMARY.
(Erase heading not required.)

Instructions regarding War Diaries and Intelligence Summaries are contained in F.S. Regs., Part II. and the Staff Manual respectively. Title pages will be prepared in manuscript.

Place	Date	Hour	Summary of Events and Information	Remarks and references to Appendices
HAVERNAS (roughly 3½ miles E of VADENCOURT)	6.2.18		Nothing to Report with Regt. at Behaven. Dismounted Regt. (Strength 7 B.Os, 8 I.Os, 7 O.Rs, 246 O.Rs) Patrol, strength 1 I.O. 2 n.c.o.Rs under 2/Lt W.R. BEER left DRAGOON POST at 6pm searched SOMERVILLE WOOD then advanced to VICTORIA X Roads. No enemy being encountered, Patrol returned to ANGLE BANKS & lay up there for about 2½ hours, after which Patrol returned via SOMERVILLE WOOD entering our line through DRAGOON POST. No enemy seen. Quiet all along front. 2/Lt T.M. LUNHAM reported his return to Behaven.	
HAVERNAS (roughly 3½ miles E of VADENCOURT)	7.2.18		Nothing to Report with Regt. Behaven. Enemy shelled POPLAR TRENCH with WHIZBANGS. No damage or casualties. Report on LE VERGUIER twenty 4.2" at 3pm. Patrol. Strength 1 I.O. 10 O.Rs under 2/Lt C.G. YES, with the whole of machine gun section left DRAGOON POST at 11pm searched SOMERVILLE, DOG LEG & MAX WOODS returning by LONETREE POST. No enemy having been seen. Day & night very quiet. Little or no firing. 2/Lt T.M. LUNHAM reported Regt. Behaven.	
HAVERNAS	8.2.18		from Dismounted Regt.	

Army Form C. 2118.

WAR DIARY
or
INTELLIGENCE SUMMARY.
(Erase heading not required.)

Place	Date	Hour	Summary of Events and Information	Remarks and references to Appendices
Trenches 2½ mile E of VADENCOURT	8-2-18		Dismounted Regt. Relieved of 20 GR1 into Reserve. Rewat Singh left Lunetrez Post at 10 pm & visited other Posts returning by Dragoon Post having seen nothing of the enemy at 1 am.	
WAVERNAS	9-2-18		The following Bro: R.O. proceeded to U.K. on duty. Captain Aty (showing of Poynciana). Major G.W.C. Lucas. Risaldar Major HAMIR SINGH & Rusaidar FEROZE KHAN.	
Trenches 2 miles E of VADENCOURT			Dismounted Regiment. Risaldar Rewat Singh & 2 ORS patrolled MAX WOOD & vicinity nothing seen (Enemy Groups) ventured our own returning at 11.30 pm. Meeting together with Regt south area.	
WAVERNAS	10-2-18			
Trenches 2½ miles E of VADENCOURT			Dismounted Regiment. The Regiment Relieved the 20 Deccan Horse in front line at 5 pm. Distribution as follows: LUNETREF Post A sqdn. Hodson Post Mr 2. B. sqdn. JEB post. C sqdn. Dragoon Post. D sqdn. Hodson Post M.P1 - H.P2. Major R.W.O'D Patterson reported the defense Scheme over on SMG. Post Strength 20 GRI weak to MP Pickle out at S.DE White furniture. Patrolled MAX WOOD & vicinity no contact with enemy. Patrol left at 8 pm returning at 11.30 pm. Captain R.S. Musgrave assumed command of Dismounted Regt as Major Patterson Instructor.	

Army Form C. 2118.

WAR DIARY
or
INTELLIGENCE SUMMARY.
(Erase heading not required.)

Instructions regarding War Diaries and Intelligence Summaries are contained in F.S. Regs., Part II. and the Staff Manual respectively. Title pages will be prepared in manuscript.

Place	Date	Hour	Summary of Events and Information	Remarks and references to Appendices
HAVERNAS	11-2-18		The following were awarded Croix de Guerre (Belgian) 3050 Dafadar NAZAR MOHD Dvgds - 3216 Dafadar NADIR ALI KHAN Central Dismounted Regiment. Parade of 10.0.R.I. much abt WR BEER Estfz. Dragoon Putt at 10pm. 3 days at men were Back f/m 14 hours internment at 12.30am leaving seen nothing of enemy.	
HAVERNAS	12-2-18		Major R.H.O.D. Paterson reported Regt. Bands arr from Dismounted Regt. Capt W. Seyfidine relinquishes adjutantcy to join Brummer Regt. Dismounted Regt. Parade with Jemt Ghulam Mohd Regt. consisting of 10 ORs proceeded at 10am to large Buddy Hay up date for 2 hours returning at 1am having had no contact with enemy.	
HAVERNAS	13-2-18		6 ORs joined the Regt from Base Rouen. Fr A F Dickson reported his departure to join Dismounted Regt. all animals were mediculed by V.O. Office. Dismounted Regt. Patrol Maj C.Syd. Reeves Dvgds, Jemt Belin Singh 10th, a NCO of (I 20 ORs (Dvgds) days abt in SE corner of SOMERVILLE WOOD noting of enemy. Patrol left at 10pm Returning at 1am. Capturing reflinate animal removed command	
Trenches 14 Miles E ¢ VADENCOURT				

2353   Wt. W5344/1454 700,000 5/15 D.D.&L.   A.D.S.S./Forms/C. 2118.

Army Form C. 2118.

WAR DIARY
or
INTELLIGENCE SUMMARY.
(Erase heading not required.)

Instructions regarding War Diaries and Intelligence Summaries are contained in F.S. Regs., Part II. and the Staff Manual respectively. Title pages will be prepared in manuscript.

Place	Date	Hour	Summary of Events and Information	Remarks and references to Appendices
HAVERNAS Trenches 1¾ mile E of Vaudencourt	14.2.18		S.O.S. uneventful, all animals exercised. Dismounted Regt. Patrol of 20 O.R. under 2/Lt E.C. Howland lay up in S.E. corner of Somerville Wood. Enemy Patrol was driven off from N.W. corner of Somerville Wood from Dragoon Post at about 11.30pm. Patrol did not encounter any enemy in relief. After laying out 3 hours. Nothing to report from Regt. in reserve area.	
HAVERNAS	15.2.18		Dismounted Regt. unrelieved. Relief commenced 4pm. 11th Hussars relieving A.r.S except 19th Hussars relieving C.Sqdn. Relief was completed by 10.30pm. H.Q.S. 11th not 30 O.R. of 19 Hussars + 2nd Hodsons Horse patrolled High ground immediately E of Somerville Wood to watch approaches from Victoria Cross Roads + XI Cross	
Trenches 1¾ mile E of Vaudencourt			Patrol went out at 9pm & returned at 9pm nothing unusual any enemy. night was bright moon light. On Regt. reached G. VERNAND & bivouacked for Roisel where bivouacs for the night, arriving there at 11.30 pm.	
HAVERRIN(?)	16.2.18		Major G.W.C. Lucas, Risaldar Major Hannee Singh & Risaldar Fazl Khan reconnd from M.R. Dismounted Regt. rejoined the regt. after having concentrated at Sateux as he here from Sateux by way to Roisel. Meeting to report. (arriving HAVERNAS 10 pm)	
"	17.2.18		Lieut J.O. Hammell rejoined Regt. from Cav. Corps Equitation School.	
"	18.2.18		Nothing to report.	
"	19.2.18			

WAR DIARY or INTELLIGENCE SUMMARY

Army Form C. 2118.

Place	Date	Hour	Summary of Events and Information	Remarks and references to Appendices
HAVERNAS	20.2.18		Nothing to report	
"	21.2.18		Rissaldar Sultan Singh, Jmdr. Shumsher Ali Khan Jmdr. Mandi Singh proceed to Base Rouen. also 3.D.R.I.	
"	22.2.18		Nothing to report	
"	23.2.18		F/Major H.A. Hitchhand to our Sirkian 2/Lt D.I.G. Merritt from Baluchistan Subadar Khan 5 Cav Jmdr Eby Baluch from Pindigh from Rawalpindi 1.D.R.B & 50.P.R.I. proceeded to Egypt via Taranto	
"	24.2.18		Fwd 230 Havers to Lahore 2/Lt W.J.H. Heaven 2/Lt Tm Tuckers, Jmdrs Ghulam Mohd 9 L.C. Jmdr Jeq Mohd Khan from Bromal Singh 1.D.R.B & 6.D.R.I. proceeded to Egypt via TARANTO 15.D.R.I (R.A. Personnel) arrived to ROUEN. (B.H.E.)	
"	25.2.18		Nothing to report	
"	26.2.18		Jmdr Ghulam Mohd C. Soi (W.I.C.) Honorary Recommend with effect from 29.12.17 vice Rissaldar Pana Singh committed. No 2904 Pte. Daffadar Ghulam Shah Copl to be Jmdr meritorious accompli cultivation - district I.A.O. No 1405 of 24.11.17 with effect from 3rd Dec. 1917.	

Army Form C. 2118.

WAR DIARY
or
INTELLIGENCE SUMMARY.
(Erase heading not required.)

Instructions regarding War Diaries and Intelligence Summaries are contained in F.S. Regs., Part II. and the Staff Manual respectively. Title pages will be prepared in manuscript.

Place	Date	Hour	Summary of Events and Information	Remarks and references to Appendices
HAVERNAS	27.7.16		Nothing to report.	
HAVERNAS	28.7.16		Regiment marched independently at 8.30 pm to entraining area. Arrived at the Regiment to follows Pissy - Seux - Revelles S.W. of AMIENS. Billets were reached at 12 noon troops distributed as below. HQrs & B Sqdn in Pissy — D Sqdn in Seux C.A. Sqdn in Revelles.	

Major
Comdg. 34th POONA HORSE

35(X)

Confidential. Original Copy

WAR DIARY

of

34 POONA HORSE

From 1st March 1918 to 31st March 1918.

Army Form C. 2118.

WAR DIARY
or
INTELLIGENCE SUMMARY.
(Erase heading not required.)

Instructions regarding War Diaries and Intelligence Summaries are contained in F. S. Regs., Part II. and the Staff Manual respectively. Title pages will be prepared in manuscript.

Place	Date	Hour	Summary of Events and Information	Remarks and references to Appendices
P/55/.	1-3-18		Following personnel proceeded to Egypt. B.Os. 2. 107.4. 10R. 109. Followers. 9.	
-do-	2/3/18		Major G.W.C. Lucas promoted acting Lieut. Colonel whilst commanding the regiment with effect from 1.2.18 (Authority G.H.Q. Lit 176. (Addis.))	
-do-	3/3/18		Re above Major Hanis Knight evacuated to C.F.A. Nothing to report.	
-do-	4/3/18		-do-	
-do-	5/3/18		Major R.H.O.D. Lairson reported his detachine on duty to U.K. to report to INDIA OFFICE for orders.	
			B.I.O.R. proceeded to BASE, MARSEILLES for employment with Divisional Ammunition Columns.	
-do-	6/3/18		Nothing to report.	
-do-	7/3/18		4. B.Os. + 10s. + 6 I.O.R. arrived TARANTO for transit to Egypt.	
-do-	8/3/18		The undermentioned party proceeded to Base MARSEILLES en route for EGYPT under command of Capt. W. G. EDMONDSTON. Followers 4. Animals 195. B.Os. 4. 107.4. 9.A.I. 195. Followers H. Animals 395. Transport vehicles 13.	

A 5834 Wt W4973/M687 750,000 8/16 D.D. & L. Ltd. Forms/C.2118/13.

Army Form C. 2118.

WAR DIARY
or
INTELLIGENCE SUMMARY.
(Erase heading not required.)

Instructions regarding War Diaries and Intelligence Summaries are contained in F. S. Regs., Part II. and the Staff Manual respectively. Title pages will be prepared in manuscript.

Place	Date	Hour	Summary of Events and Information	Remarks and references to Appendices
Assy.	9.3.18		Seventh Train came into Forêt - Clocks put back one hour.	
	10.3.18		Party of 4 Bos 4 10R 6.10R sailed from TARANTO in H.T. MALWA for EGYPT.	
	11.3.18		Nothing to report.	
	12.3.18		Capt. N.F. Elphinston and Party arrived at MARSEILLES and proceeded to Camp La VALENTINE.	
Assy	13.3.18		Nothing to report.	
	14.3.18		Party proceeded for H.T. MALWA arrived KANTARA disembarked & entrained for TEL EL KEBIR.	
	15.3.18		Above party arrived TEL EL KEBIR 1 am.	
Assy	16.3.18		Nothing to report.	
-do-	17.3.18		-do-	
	18.3.18	1.30 2.10 118 10R. embarked at MARSEILLES in H.T. "KINGSTONIAN" 1.30 1.10 78 10R 307 horses embarked at MARSEILLES in H.T. "NOLUMNIA"		
	19.3.18		Above party sailed. Hd. Qrs and C & D Sqdn. entrained at SALEUX for MARSEILLES en route to EGYPT.	

Army Form C. 2118.

WAR DIARY
or
INTELLIGENCE SUMMARY.
(Erase heading not required.)

Instructions regarding War Diaries and Intelligence Summaries are contained in F. S. Regs., Part II. and the Staff Manual respectively. Title pages will be prepared in manuscript.

Place	Date	Hour	Summary of Events and Information	Remarks and references to Appendices
MISSY	19.3.18		Strength as usual. B. Os. 9. ORs. 5. 108. 197. Followers 10. Animals 364.	
	20.3.18		Train left at 8.45 a.m. On the train - nothing to report.	
	21.3.18		Advance party arrive MARSEILLES at 9 p.m. Detained & the rest to CAMP LA VALENTINE reaching there 2.30 a.m. 22.3.18.	
MARSEILLES	22.3.18		at CAMP LA VALENTINE. The following Officers reported. Lieuts. H.R. PICHER and A.G. IVES. nothing to report.	
—	23.3.18		H.T. KINGSTONIAN } units respective Katia arrived MALTA. H.T. VOLUMNIA }	
MARSEILLES	24.3.18		Regiment strength as usual nineteen from LA VALENTINE to CAMP No 19. MONT FURON - B.Os. 10. ORs. 10.5. OR.1. 205. Followers 9. Animals 361. Orders to embark on 4 hours notice received.	
	25.3.18		H.T. KINGSTONIAN left MALTA with reminder of Unit, on board for EGYPT. H.T. VOLUMNIA	

A.5834 Wt.W4973/M687 750,000 8/16 D. D. & L. Ltd. Forms/C.2113/13.

Army Form C. 2118.

WAR DIARY
or
INTELLIGENCE SUMMARY.
(Erase heading not required.)

Instructions regarding War Diaries and Intelligence Summaries are contained in F.S. Regs., Part II. and the Staff Manual respectively. Title pages will be prepared in manuscript.

Place	Date	Hour	Summary of Events and Information	Remarks and references to Appendices
MARSEILLES	25.3.18		The following appointments were made:—	
			A/Lieut. Col. G.W.C. LUCAS to be O/9. Commandant 16.1.18 vice Lieut. Col. W.S. COOPER evacuation sick.	
			Major J. PETERS Hussars to be 2nd in Command 16.1.18 vice Major acting Lieut. Col. G.W.C. LUCAS appointed O/9. Commandant.	
			Major R.H. O'D. PATERSON to be O/9. 2nd in Command vice Major J. PETERS evacuated sick 26.1.1918.	
			Capt. W.G. ELPHINSTON to be O/9. 4th Squadron Commander 16.1.18 vice A/Lieut. Col. Askewin O/9. Commandant.	
			Capt. R.C. MACGREGOR to be 4th Squadron Commander vice Major J. PETERS evacuated sick 26.1.1918.	
" "	26.3.18		Nothing to report.	
" "	27.3.18		— " —	
" "	28.3.18		Capt. Elphinston and party for Mt. KINGSTONIAN and YOKOHAMA arrived Cairo	

Place	Date	Hour	Summary of Events and Information	Remarks and references to Appendices
	28.3.18		Shore party entrained for TEN-ES-KEBIR. Carriages during voyage. NIL.	
	29.3.18		Shore party arrived and encamped at TEN-ES-KEBIR. Orders received for H.Qrs. C & D Sqdns. to embark for E.G.Y/107 for H.T. "MENOMINEE".	
	30.3.18		Lieut. Col. G.W.C. LUCAS and 9 B.Os., 2 B.O.R., 180 S.I., 10 Rs., 199 Prisoners 9 Animals 361 embarked per H.T. MENOMINEE. Left Camp MONTFURON 5.30 a.m. Embarkation commenced 7 a.m. finished 2 p.m. Steamer left MHAAF at 3 p.m. and anchored in the BAY.	
	31.3.18		Remained at anchor. The following alterations were made for the voyage:- O.C. Troop. H.T. Menominee Lieut. Col. G.W.C. LUCAS Ship's Agent Lieut. C.K. NICHOLL 9th M.R. Trooper - Qr. Mr. Trooper 9th M.R. Trooper.— SHUAIAM SHAM.	

1917-1918
5TH CAVALRY DIVISION
SECUNDERABAD CAV. BDE

SIGNAL TROOP

JAN 1917 - APL 1918

SERIAL NO. 24 C.

Confidential

War Diary

of

SIGNAL TROOP, SECUNDERABAD CAVALRY BRIGADE.

FROM 1st January 1917 TO 31st January 1917

Vol VII
Signal Troop

Army Form C. 2118.

WAR DIARY
or
INTELLIGENCE SUMMARY
(Erase heading not required.)

Place	Date	Hour	Summary of Events and Information	Remarks and references to Appendices
FEUQUIERES	Jany 1st To 31st		Billets & enquiries. The month spent in training and instruction of new R.E. men from base, in equitation + signalling & gun fire. Weather conditions interminable. January 22nd commenced a course of instruction for 6 men attached from Machine Gun Squadron. Nothing further to report. W.R.Campbell Captain OC Signal Troop Secular Cav Bde.	

Serial No. 247.

Signal Troop,

Secunderabad Cavalry Brigade.

From 1st to 28th February 1917.

Daily list of

in Adjutant

Issued to Section

From whom.	No. and date of letter received.

Army Form C. 2118.

WAR DIARY
or
INTELLIGENCE SUMMARY
(Erase heading not required.)

Instructions regarding War Diaries and Intelligence Summaries are contained in F. S. Regs., Part II. and the Staff Manual respectively. Title Pages will be prepared in manuscript.

Place	Date	Hour	Summary of Events and Information	Remarks and references to Appendices
FEUVIERES	Feb. 1917 1st		Brigade in winter billets. Training of all signallers of the brigade continues daily.	
	-19th		Nothing special to report.	
	20th		Inspection of all signallers of Signal troop and regiments by O.C. 5th Cav. Signal Squadron. Result of inspection and tests communicated to Bde Major and units concerned.	
	21st-28th		Nothing to report.	
			During this month classification tests of all signallers for 1917 were carried out, as matters & opportunities permitted. Map reading despatch riding tests still to be taken in return of "Pioneer battn"	

W. Hampshire Captain Signal Troop
5th Cavalry [illegible]

Serial No: 244

Confidential

War Diary

for March 1914

Signal Troop Vol IX

Staaf Cavy Bde

Army Form C. 2118.

WAR DIARY
or
INTELLIGENCE SUMMARY

(Erase heading not required.)

Instructions regarding War Diaries and Intelligence Summaries are contained in F. S. Regs., Part II. and the Staff Manual respectively. Title Pages will be prepared in manuscript.

Place	Date	Hour	Summary of Events and Information	Remarks and references to Appendices
FLEURVIERE'S	19th March		Billets - Nothing to report.	
	20th			
	21st		Brigade mounted Fleurvieres - burnt Boiron - Communications normal.	
			March continued burnt Boiron - Proingel - do.	
	22nd		March continued Proingel - Hamel. Stream, divisional troops came under command if Div. descended Mole and all matters for Hinderscomed no delaying. Heavy snow the motor Divs owing to long distance separating units of Div. and myself state of winds. Communication to units of Div. Hqrs arrived and horse D.R.	
	23rd		Boiron Hamel. Communications on above Divs Hqrs morning to Fleurvieres. Multer Divs Turning to and Snow to Mule no enemy trucks, communication was slow or transmission when for an hour + Found troops were uncovered. Motor Drs not all night delivering to Divs Trucks + to Div Hq at Fleurvieres.	
	24th		March continued Hamel - Bois de Meusenient. Communication normal. Except for bad roads. Relay point of travel cyclists established at CLERY to save motor-bikes. Three D.R's found Great in spite in motor bikes or track better.	
	25th		Bivouac - Communication do	
	26th		do	
	27th		Marched from to bivouac HALLE - Communication normal by D.R.	

Army Form C. 2118.

WAR DIARY
or
INTELLIGENCE SUMMARY
(Erase heading not required.)

Place	Date	Hour.	Summary of Events and Information	Remarks and references to Appendices
	28th	-	Marched Kimmel CLER-SUR-SOMNE. Communication on above state front made have de that quicker means.	
	29th	-	Brigade marched 3.30 to Kimmel via HEM, Belin, what entire mission - all communication by lines DR. Runners.	
	30th	-	Brigade marched 11.30 am to BAYONVILLERS - with DEECANTHORPE details to FRAMERVILLE. LUF us HQ must deVILLERS - BRETONNEUX. Communication to brigade by DR. Telephone communication of Bn. out certain sign Thurl 50 certain Aidny - MERICOURT.	
	31st	-	Telephone lines est'd independently from Bgde to Lynne lines. Men a movement + transport that in line. Mine was only chance by moving in link to. Bn getting own wire signal 10.20 - This mine 25 day shelling	

W. Capbell Capt
Signal Section Lev Bde.

Serial No. 1247.

Confidential

Signal Troop.

Sec'bad Cavalry Bde

From 1st April to 30th April

Army Form C. 2118.

WAR DIARY
or
INTELLIGENCE SUMMARY.
(Erase heading not required.)

Instructions regarding War Diaries and Intelligence Summaries are contained in F. S. Regs., Part II. and the Staff Manual respectively. Title pages will be prepared in manuscript.

Place	Date	Hour	Summary of Events and Information	Remarks and references to Appendices
BAYONVILLERS	1st April		Brigade in billets in and around BAYONVILLERS - Nothing special to report.	
	13th April		Brigade marches to bivouac between TREFCON and CAULAINCOURT.	
	13th April		Bivouac in above area. Nothing special to report. Despatch riders & training of signallers carried out daily.	
	30th April			

M Lamphill
Captain
R. Signal Troop
2nd Cav Bde
30.4.17

A6945 Wt. W11422/M1160 350,000 12/16 D. D. & L. Forms/C./2118/14.

Confidential

Serial No: 242

From 1st May to 30th June 1917.

War Diary for month of

May 1917

From 1st — 31st May 1917

Signal Troop

VOL. XI

Army Form C. 2118.

WAR DIARY
or
INTELLIGENCE SUMMARY.
(Erase heading not required.)

Place	Date	Hour	Summary of Events and Information	Remarks and references to Appendices
TREFCON	May 14th to 15th		BIVOUAC TREFCON. Nothing to report.	
	15th	9 a.m.	One Corporal and 3 men despatched to take over Advance Signal Office of 17th Inf Bde at JEANCOURT preparatory to relief of 82nd Inf Bde by Serbian Bde.	
	15th	8 p.m.	Remainder of Signal Troop arrived MONTIGNY FARM to take over Signal Office and communications of Sector to be held by Serbian Bde.	
	16th	9 a.m.	Relief complete, all lines & communications taken over and operators of 17th Bde relieved. Testing over complicated by wrong labelling of lines in with advance & main Signal offices. A relay post of 6 men with 2 DR5 established under L/Cpl Payne at JEANCOURT.	
	17th	midnight.	Adv Signal Office JEANCOURT converted into an advance exchange, all testing of lines, faults, maintenance done from there.	
	17th		Improvement in working of lines owing to above arrangement, less interference and induction.	
	19th		Communication normal. Lines tested & improved. Reports received from	

Army Form C. 2118.

WAR DIARY
or
INTELLIGENCE SUMMARY.
(Erase heading not required.)

Instructions regarding War Diaries and Intelligence Summaries are contained in F. S. Regs., Part II. and the Staff Manual respectively. Title pages will be prepared in manuscript.

Place	Date	Hour	Summary of Events and Information	Remarks and references to Appendices
Montagny Ferme.	19th		Regimental Signally Ofrs visits Insgrs. Diagram of circuits completed (started).	
	20th		Patrolling working besties out on lines testing & insulating. Spelling circuit all good. Direct line to regt on right cut by shell fire. Arranged a shunt and testing arrangement into night support regt.	
	20th	9.30pm	Relief by support regt of regts in front line.	
	21st	2.30pm	Relief complete. All lines taken over & tested are speaking & buzzing.	
	22nd		Visual line to left regt right support regt tested by public trunks. Realigned and tested by night. All O.C. telephone circuits working well. Power Buzzer established at Wd HQ right regt with amplifier at right regt HQ.	
	23rd		Normal, not all Signally Ofr of Regts at Jeancourt Office and discussed improvements & pointed out various faults. Ordered amplifier to change posn from HQ Right Regt to HQ left regt.	
	24th		Normal. Pole wireless pai installed at Montagny Ferme.	

WAR DIARY
or
INTELLIGENCE SUMMARY.

Army Form C. 2118.

(Erase heading not required.)

Place	Date	Hour	Summary of Events and Information	Remarks and references to Appendices
Montigny Farm	25th		Normal. Amplifier established at Left Regt HQ and posts for trench wireless set chosen	
	26th		Trench set installed at Left Regt HQ. Signals exchanged with Para Set	
	27th		Normal. Arranged with 198th Signals officers as to change of circuits necessary to following reorganization of front.	
	28th	2.30 p.m.	Local reliefs of front line by Support buried wire all OK.	
		9.30 p.m.	4th Div & Canadian Div took over portion of our front. Changes in circuits (see Diagram B) took place without hitch. Relief complete & all lines tested OK by 2 am 29th	
	29th		Normal. All lines patrolled & improved.	
	30th		New visual scheme (Diagram C) tried out & tested by helio flags all OK. Went round front line communications by night.	
	31st		Normal. All circuits OK. New air line built from VT to ___ Signals Echo Rte	

W. Cranfield Capt.
OC Signals

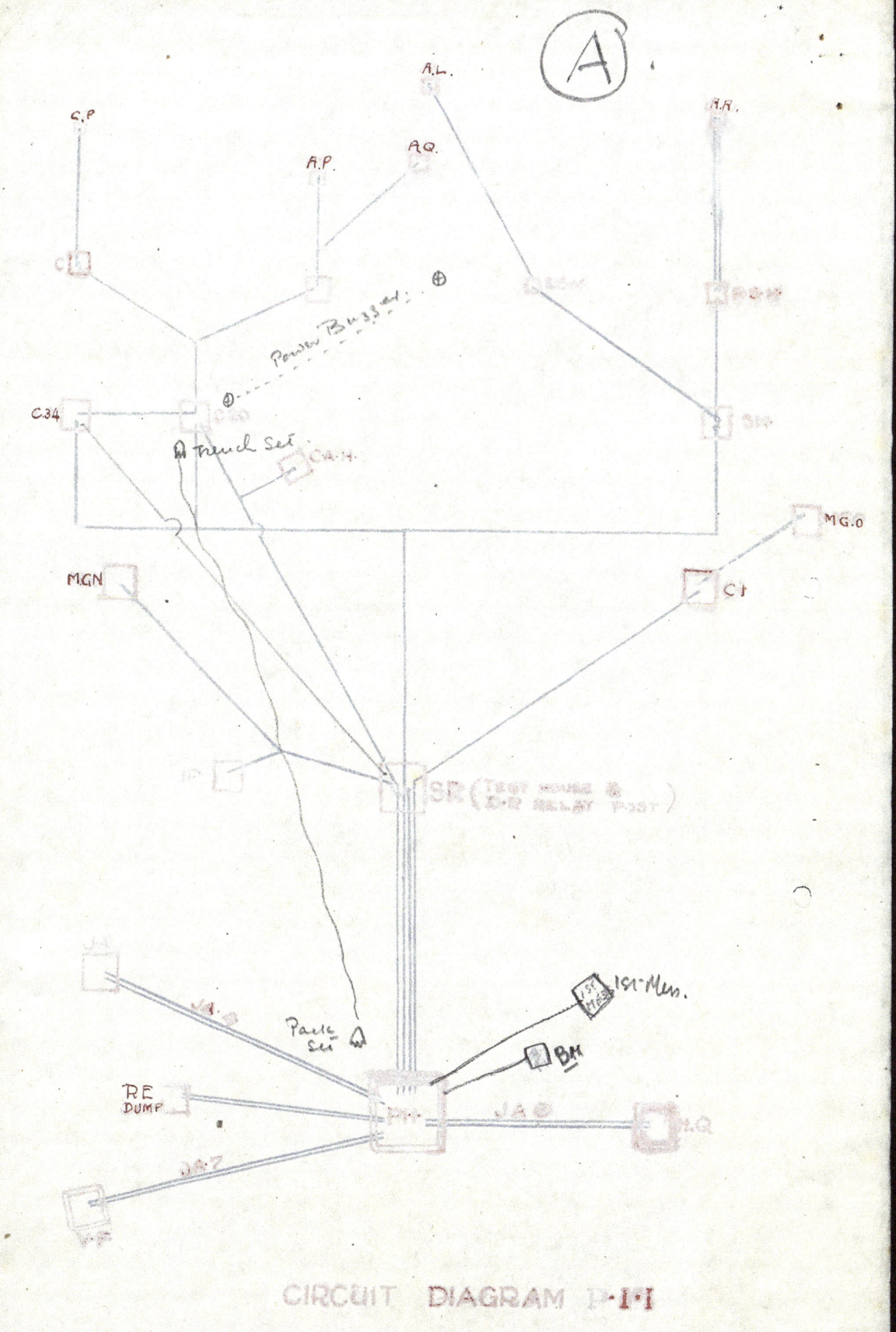

KEY TO DIAGRAM A

	Code Call	Signal Call	Map Reference	Remarks
		P11	K 35 d 9.9.	
	SR	PR	L 26 d 3.1.	
	IP	—	L 26 c 7.5	
	SS	—	L 26 d 5.4	
	SST	C.34	L 22 c 5.2.	
	SO	G 20	L 28 a 5.5.	
	UT	CAH	L 28 a 5.5.	
	SM	T 7	R 5.b.3.2	
	UO	C 1	L 33 d. 2.3.	
	US	MGO	R 5. a 2. 5.	
(Right Wing SM)	RSM	RSM	R 6. a 4.2.	
(Right Adv. Post)	AR	AR	G 32 c 2.8.	
	AL	AL	G 31. b. 3.8.	
(Left Wing SM)	LSM	LSM	L 36 c 8.6.	
(Right Wing SST)	A	A	L 29. d 8.8.	
(Left " ")	C	C	L 23 d. 5.6.	
(Right Adv. Post. 1)	AP	AP	L 24 c 6.4	
(" " 2)	AQ	AQ	G 25 b. 8. 9.	
(Left Adv. post 1)	CP	CP	L 24 a. 4.8.	
(" " 2)	No Phone available yet.			

B

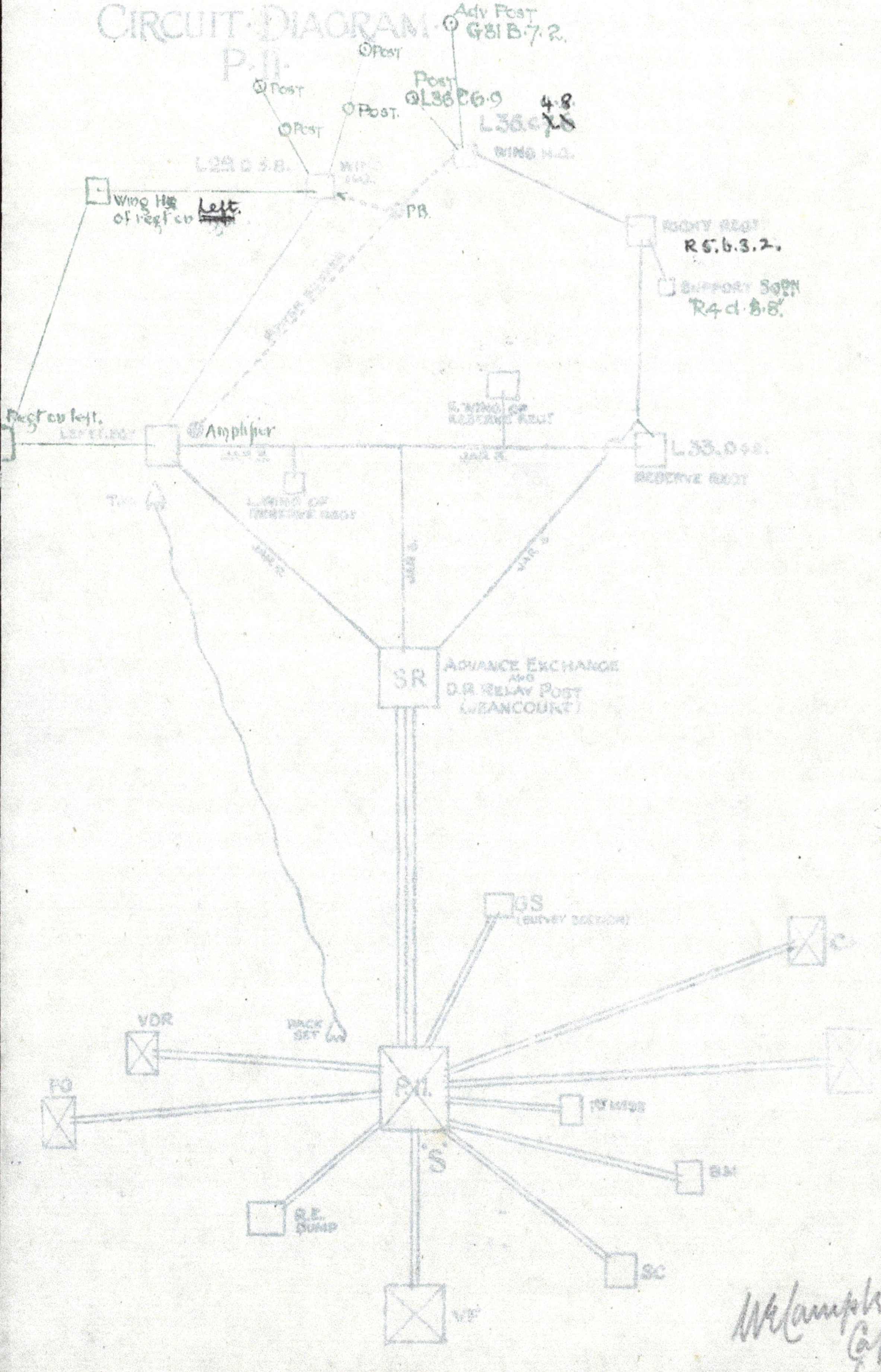

CIRCUIT DIAGRAM P.II.
Adv Post G81 B.7.2.
Post
Post
Post.
Post
Post L36 C6.9
L36.c 4.8.
WING H.Q.
L29 D 5.8.
Wing HQ of regt on Left.
PB.
RIGHT REGT
R5.b.3.2.
SUPPORT SQDN
R4 d. 8.8.
Regt on left.
LEFT REGT
Amplifier
L33.D 4.2.
RESERVE REGT
SR
ADVANCE EXCHANGE AND D.R. RELAY POST (JEANCOURT)
GS (SURVEY SECTION)
VDR
PACK SET
FO
P.II.
"S"
R.E. DUMP
SC

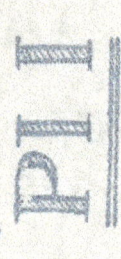

Diagram of Visual Circuits
P II

Left Regt H.Q.
L.28.a.5.5.

Phone &
Relayers

Transmitting
Post

Left Regt'
Wing Comdrs Post
L.29.d.2.8.

Red House
L.30.c.4.2.

Right Regt
R.5.b.4.2.

Mochigny Farm

Reserve Regt
L.33.d.4.5.

Kite Balloon
R.15.b.3.8.

War Diary

Signal Troop

Sec'nd Cavalry Bde.

1st June to 30th June 1917

WAR DIARY
or
INTELLIGENCE SUMMARY

Army Form C. 2118.

Place	Date	Hour	Summary of Events and Information	Remarks and references to Appendices
MONTIGNY FARM	June 1st to 11th		Nothing to report. Brigade front all quiet. Communications normal. Visual circuits as per diagram with N.O. front trenches were tested in the night 10th/11th and worked satisfactorily except for the fact that visual stations were undermanned owing to scarcity of Sappers specially in the telephones and the causes were in tampering trunk and station. Work was done every day in converting all circuits in the subsector from earth to metallic and the metallic circuits were complete and working on morning of 11th. During night 11th/12th a "Raid" was carried out by Devonshire against Ascension Wood. For the communication of the raid fruits to or Deccan (HdQrs) and for the use of aeroplanes were established. Tested at "Aerodrome" (S.34.C.4.6) and wires to me are stretched attached with the raiding party sympathy with "Fan Buzzer". This worked satisfactory the N.T.D. established and letting him report the first objective had been reached in	

Army Form C. 2118.

WAR DIARY
or
INTELLIGENCE SUMMARY.
(Erase heading not required.)

Instructions regarding War Diaries and Intelligence Summaries are contained in F. S. Regs., Part II. and the Staff Manual respectively. Title pages will be prepared in manuscript.

Place	Date	Hour	Summary of Events and Information	Remarks and references to Appendices
Hentity	11/12	2.30pm	5 minutes from time of reaching point xx Glenpark signalled to Deccan Force who went while and after signallers were slightly wounded.	
Monligny PPPCM	13th		Night 12/13 = visual scheme was carried out from front line visible to Div. HQ & Corps Balloon. Slight delay in transmission of message owing to undermanning of stations.	
	14th		Night 13/14 15th Bde men relieved by the Canadian Cav Bde. Wireless cars complete by 3 am 15th and men signal office at TREFCON	
	15th		Burma TREFCON, overhaul of equipment etc	
	16th		"	
	17th		O.T. Signal troops left on wireless course to 1st HQ. O.T. Sigs taken over by Canny Bde	
			Burma TREFCON nothing to report	
	23rd			

WAR DIARY
or
INTELLIGENCE SUMMARY.

(Erase heading not required.)

Army Form C. 2118.

Instructions regarding War Diaries and Intelligence Summaries are contained in F. S. Regs., Part II. and the Staff Manual respectively. Title pages will be prepared in manuscript.

Place	Date	Hour	Summary of Events and Information	Remarks and references to Appendices
	23rd		Brigade relieves Ambulla Bde in A) subsector. Relief complete 2am All quiet. Relief passed off smoothly.	
	24th 25 26		All quiet nothing to report. Diagram of communication established.	
	27		Of Signal troop returned for course. & close returner to rept. indg	
	28		Nil to return.	
	29		A Power Buzzer Amplifier & amp circuit established. Lamp working back for SALT TRENCH (junction with WATLING STREET) to VAUXCOURT X roads. Power Buzzer working forward to lamp via Amplifier	
	30		Nil	

M. Campbell
Captain

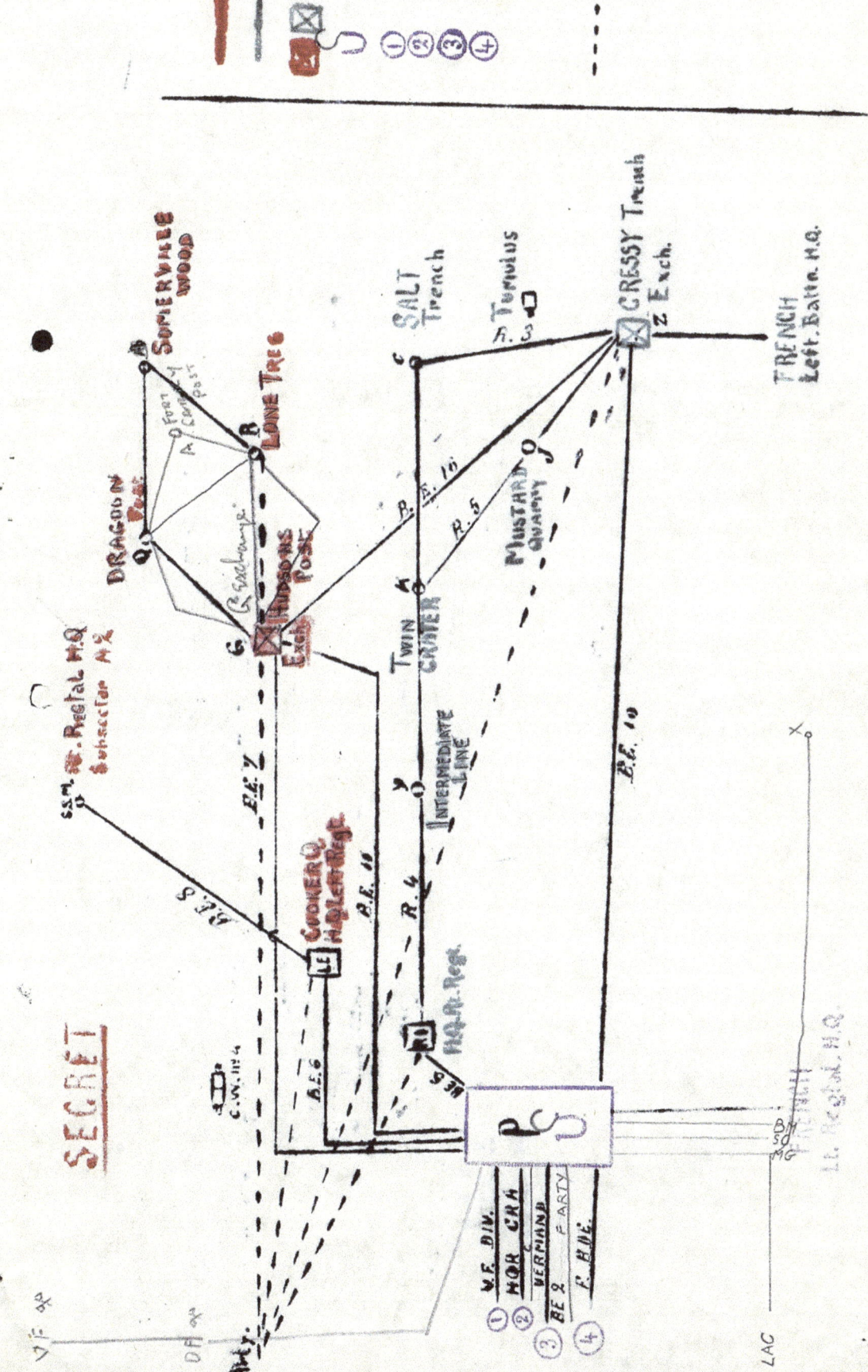

Serial No: 24 Y.

War Diary

Signal Troop, Secunderabad Cav. Bde.

From 1st July 1917 to 21st July 1917

(Vol. I)

Army Form C. 2118.

WAR DIARY
or
INTELLIGENCE SUMMARY.

Signal Troop.
Sec bad Cav Bde.

(Erase heading not required.)

Instructions regarding War Diaries and Intelligence Summaries are contained in F. S. Regs., Part II. and the Staff Manual respectively. Title pages will be prepared in manuscript.

Place	Date	Hour	Summary of Events and Information	Remarks and references to Appendices
Itapp VADENCOURT	1.7.17		Brigade remained in subsector A1 — Communications as shown in diagram attached W.D. for June	
	2nd to 4th		Nothing to report. Communications normal. Visual and extra regimental circuits tested daily	
	5th		At night of 4th/5th 7th Dragoon Guards attempted a raid against FIELD REDOUBT. Raid was unsuccessful owing to inaccuracy of enemy barrage. L/Cpl Briggs in charge of an NCO & two men of Signal Troop were sent into the raiding party to communicate to the amplifier in SALT TRENCH where a forward telephone exchange was established. Unfortunately owing to the new dry power buzzer did not get through owing to the lines of our earth "V" in the buzzer.	

Army Form C. 2118.

WAR DIARY
or
INTELLIGENCE SUMMARY.

(Erase heading not required.)

Signal Troop
Section 4 cyclists

Instructions regarding War Diaries and Intelligence Summaries are contained in F.S. Regs., Part II. and the Staff Manual respectively. Title pages will be prepared in manuscript.

Place	Date	Hour	Summary of Events and Information	Remarks and references to Appendices
VADENCOURT	4.7.17		Situation normal nothing to report.	
	6.7.			
	7.7.			
	7.7.		On night of 7th/8th 7th L Dragoon Guards carried out a raid against X1 Trench. Ts communicate with OC raid a metallic circuit was laid from CRESSY TRENCH to ANGLE SAPS by Sigs Sergt 7th Dn. This line was maintained throughout well throughout the raid. It was subsequently reeled in.	maintained wire from HQ r Div in sig lines upstairs by 1pm. in left communication.
	8.7.		Nothing to report.	
	9.7.		Enemy artillery shelled VADENCOURT rather severely since hour 10 Div + Bde in left communication.	
	9.7.		Brigade was relieved by a battalion of the 101st Infantry Brigade.	
	9/10.7		Relief complete without incident by 3 am 10th inst	

Army Form C. 2118.

WAR DIARY
or
INTELLIGENCE SUMMARY.
(Erase heading not required.)

Instructions regarding War Diaries and Intelligence Summaries are contained in F. S. Regs., Part II. and the Staff Manual respectively. Title pages will be prepared in manuscript.

Place	Date	Hour	Summary of Events and Information	Remarks and references to Appendices
Bivouac TREFCON	10th 7.17		Brigade in bivouac TREFCON. All equipment overhauled + prepares for march.	
	13th			
	14th		Brigade marches TREFCON – CARTIGNY, BUIRE, COURCELLES. Report centre BUIRE. Nothing to report.	
	15th		Brigade marches above area to SUZANNE. Report centre SUZANNE. Nothing to report.	
	16th		Brigade marches SUZANNE to TREUX. Report centre TREUX. Nothing to report.	
	17th		Brigade marches TREUX – AUTHIE. Nothing to report.	
	19th		Brigade marches AUTHIE to RAMECOURT – ST POL area. Bde HQ. Ch. steam RAMECOURT	
	20th		Brigade marches RAMECOURT – NONCHY CAYEUX. NONCHY CAYEUX area. Bde HQ chateau NONCHY CAYEUX.	

A 5834 Wt. W 4973/M687 750,000 8/16 D. D. & L. Ltd. Forms/C.2118/13.

Army Form C. 2118.

WAR DIARY
or
INTELLIGENCE SUMMARY.
(Erase heading not required.)

Place	Date	Hour	Summary of Events and Information	Remarks and references to Appendices
CHATEAU NORCHY-CAYEUX	20th – 31st		Brigade billets in MONCHY-CAYEUX area. Nothing to report. Final training of all signallers carried out daily.	

M Campbell
Captain.
O.C. Signal Troop
Secund Cav Bde.

Serial No. 244

War Diary

Signal Troop

5th Ind Cav Bd.

From 1st August 1917
To 31st August 1917

Army Form 2118.

WAR DIARY
or
INTELLIGENCE SUMMARY.
(Erase heading not required.)

Instructions regarding War Diaries and Intelligence Summaries are contained in F. S. Regs., Part II. and the Staff Manual respectively. Title pages will be prepared in manuscript.

Place	Date	Hour	Summary of Events and Information	Remarks and references to Appendices

Serial No. 24 Y.

Confidential

War Diary

Sialkot Cavalry Brigade

Signal Troop

From 1st to 30th Sept. 1917

WAR DIARY
or
INTELLIGENCE SUMMARY.
(Erase heading not required.)

Army Form C. 2118.

Place	Date	Hour	Summary of Events and Information	Remarks and references to Appendices
MONCHY-CAYEUX	15th		Nothing to report. Brigade remained in Bivouac billets.	
	30th Sept.		Training of Signallers carried on and identification of signallers of 34th & 22nd Divns completed. Weather favourable for visual Signalling.	

M Campbell
Captain
O.C. Signal Troop
Lucknow Cav Bde

Confidential

(247)

War Diary
——
Star Bde. Signal Troop
——

From 1st October 1917
to
31st October 1917
——

Army Form C. 2118.

WAR DIARY
or
INTELLIGENCE SUMMARY.
(Erase heading not required.)

Instructions regarding War Diaries and Intelligence Summaries are contained in F. S. Regs., Part II. and the Staff Manual respectively. Title pages will be prepared in manuscript.

Place	Date	Hour	Summary of Events and Information	Remarks and references to Appendices
Hinchy-Cayeux	1st		Notg to return	
	to			
	6th		Brigade marched to BOESEGHEM area	
	7th		Brigade moved to WATOU	
	?			
	16th		Brigade moved to billets in BRUGES area	
	17th			
	18th			
	18		Nothing to report	
	-			
	31st			

W Humphreys
Captain
O Signal Troop
Guards Cav Bde.

Army Form C. 2118.

Signal Troop
Cumberland Cav. Bde.

WAR DIARY
or
INTELLIGENCE SUMMARY.
(Erase heading not required.)

January 1918

Place	Date	Hour	Summary of Events and Information	Remarks and references to Appendices
TREFCON	1/1/18		Brigade in TREFCON area. All units in "johns". Very little training of any kind do.	
	2/1/18		Some six Signallers on account of men working on fatigues	
	23/1/18		Joint H.L. CHASE. Applied for appointment to England on leave of 2/Lieut L.A. GLASSPOOLE (30th DIVISION NOTICE) took over command of Signal Troop	
	24/1/18		Nothing to report	
VADENCOURT	29/1/18	6.30pm	Bde. took over communications from 3rd Brigade. 1st Devonshire in support at VADENCOURT CHAD. Relief completed by 7pm. Posts there and Brunehaut at VADENCOURT, note on "Johns". 7th Dragoon Guards and 13th MGC Sqdn. at LE VERGUIER. 7th D.G. on FULLERPHONE.	
	30/1/18		Very quiet. Link for A.A. Ltd. All lines good and more out. Arrangements made for getting posts in LE VERGUIER not find to be occupied in case of an attack. But enemy armoured cable from division. Various small improvements carried out.	
	31/1/18			

Ian Anderson Reid
OC Signal Troop
5" Cav. Bde.

WAR DIARY or INTELLIGENCE SUMMARY

Army Form C. 2118.

Place	Date	Hour	Summary of Events and Information	Remarks and references to Appendices
AT SEA.	Apr.e. 1st		H.T. MENOMINEE and PANCRAS sailed from MARSEILLES.	
	5 to 6		Arrived MALTA. Owing to engine trouble the "MENOMINEE" was delayed and aircraft were consequently transferred to CAMP RICASOLI. H.T. PANCRAS sailed on 6th for ALEXANDRIA.	
	10th		H.T. PANCRAS arrived ALEXANDRIA.	
	11th		H.T. MENOMINEE arrived from MALTA and arrived ALEXANDRIA on 15th inst.	
TEL EL KEBIR.	11-16th		Unit arrived at TEL EL KEBIR and camped at N.N.W. corner of the camp.	
EGYPT.	20th		Orders received for the POONA HORSE and xx Deccan Horse to proceed to join the 7th Mounted Brigade at BELAH. (PALESTINE).	
	22nd		POONA HORSE and xx Deccan Horse marched to KANTARA, leaving at QASSASSIN on night 22/23rd, ISMAILIAN on night 23/24, EL FERDAN on night 24/25 and on night 24/25.	
	26th		Arrived KANTARA on 25th inst. Jerboa C.T.A and M.V.Jeluni arrived TEL EL KEBIR. POONA HORSE entrained for BELAH, and arrived on 26th inst. xx Deccan Horse ---- 27th inst.	
	28 & 29		Jerboa C.T.A and M.V.Jeluni marched to KANTARA.	
	30		The break up of the Jerboads. (Cav. Bde. was completed.	

1917-1918
5TH CAVALRY DIVISION
SECUNDERABAD CAV. BDE

MACHINE GUN SQUADRON
JAN 1917- FEB 1918.

SERIAL NO. B17.

Confidential
War Diary
of

MACHINE GUN SQUADRON, SECUNDERABAD CAVALRY BRIGADE.

FROM 1st January 1917 **TO** 31st January 1917

Machine Gun Squadron
Secunderabad Cav. Bde. Vol

Army Form C. 2118.

WAR DIARY
or
INTELLIGENCE SUMMARY.
(Erase heading not required.)

from Jan 1st to 31st 1917.

Instructions regarding War Diaries and Intelligence Summaries are contained in F. S. Regs., Part II, and the Staff Manual respectively. Title pages will be prepared in manuscript.

Hour, Date, Place.	Summary of Events and Information.	Remarks and references to Appendices.
BUGNY 1-1-17	Machine Gun firing	Ref Map ADDEVILLE 14 Scale 100000
2-1-17	}	
3-1-17	Squadron training.	
4-1-17		
5-1-17		
6-1-17		
8-1-17.	Squadron Route March.	
9-1-17.	Machine Gun firing.	
10-1-17.	Brigade field day.	
11-1-17.	Squadron training.	
12-1-17.	Machine Gun firing.	
13-1-17.	Squadron training.	
15-1-17.	Machine Gun firing.	
16-1-17.	Squadron Route March.	
17-1-17.	Brigade field day.	
18-1-17.		
19-1-17.	Machine Gun firing.	
20-1-17.	Squadron training.	

Army Form C. 2118

WAR DIARY
or
INTELLIGENCE SUMMARY.

(Erase heading not required.)

Instructions regarding War Diaries and Intelligence Summaries are contained in F. S. Regs., Part II, and the Staff Manual respectively. Title pages will be prepared in manuscript.

Hour, Date, Place.	Summary of Events and Information.	Remarks and references to Appendices.
22-1-17.	Lachine Gun firing.	
23-1-17.	Squadron Route Larch.	
24-1-17.	Brigade field day.	
25-1-17.	Lachine Gun firing.	
26-1-17.		
27-1-17.	Squadron training.	
29-1-17.	Lachine Gun firing.	
30-1-17.	Squadron Route March.	
31-1-17.	Brigade field day.	

Ebrahim Khan
O.C. M.G. Sqdn.
Sec. Cav. Bde.

Gulab Singh & Sons, Calcutta.—No. 22 Army C.—5-8-14—1,07,000.

Serial No: 317

13th Squadron, Machine Gun Corps, (Cavalry).
(Secunderabad Cavalry Brigade).

From 1st to 28th February 1917.

Daily list of

in Adjutant

Issued to Section _____

From whom.	No. and date of letter received.

Army Form C. 2118.

WAR DIARY
or
INTELLIGENCE SUMMARY.
(Erase heading not required.)

From February 1st to 28/2/17

Instructions regarding War Diaries and Intelligence Summaries are contained in F. S. Regs., Part II, and the Staff Manual respectively. Title pages will be prepared in manuscript.

Place	Date	Hour	Summary of Events and Information	Remarks and references to Appendices.
BUIGNY				Refce map ABBEVILLE. 14. Scale 1/100,000
	1—2—17		Squadron training	
	2—2—17		Tactical Exercise	
	3—2—17			
	5—2—17			
	6—2—17		Squadron training	
	7—2—17			
	8—2—17			
	9—2—17		Tactical Exercise	
	10—2—17			
	12—2—17			
	13—2—17			
	14—2—17		Squadron training	
	15—2—17			
	16—2—17			
	17—2—17		Tactical Exercise	
	19—2—17			
	20—2—17			
	21—2—17		Squadron training	
	22—2—17			
	23—2—17			
	24—2—17		Tactical Exercise	

Army Form C. 2118.

WAR DIARY
or
INTELLIGENCE SUMMARY.

(Erase heading not required.)

Instructions regarding War Diaries and Intelligence Summaries are contained in F. S. Regs., Part II, and the Staff Manual respectively. Title pages will be prepared in manuscript.

Hour, Date, Place.	Summary of Events and Information.	Remarks and references to Appendices.
26.2.17 27.2.17 28.2.17	} Squadron Training	

Elborton, Major
Comdg. 13th Squadron
M.G.C. Cavalry,
Secunderabad Brigade

Serial No. 317.

Confidential

War Diary

for March 1914

13th M.G. Sqdn - Cavalry Vol IX

Sbad Cav. Bde

From March 1st to 31st 1917.

WAR DIARY
INTELLIGENCE SUMMARY.
(Erase heading not required.)

of 13th Squadron Machine Gun Corps Cavalry.
Corps Cavalry.
See Cav. Bde.

Army Form C. 2118.

Place	Date	Hour	Summary of Events and Information	Remarks and references to Appendices
BUIGNY	1-3-17		Squadron Training –	ABBEVILLE
	2-3-17			2l xx Sc /10000
	3-3-17		Church Parade.	
	4-3-17		Squadron Parade.	
	5-3-17		1st 2 Troops admitted to Hospital.	
	6-3-17		Squadron Inspection & Lecture Relations by Col. Lowgate M.G.C. Advance to Gun Corps.	
	7-3-17		Instructed parade in storming an portable formation of attack to the Bde.	
	8-3-17		Squadron Training –	
	9-3-17			
	10-3-17			
	11-3-17		Sunday.	
	12-3-17		Squadron Training – Rode on 48 hour in Tpes –	
	13-3-17			
	14-3-17		G.O.C. Bde inspected the Squadron in Reading Order.	
	15-3-17			
	16-3-17		Squadron Training –	
	17-3-17			

Army Form C. 2118.

WAR DIARY
or
INTELLIGENCE SUMMARY.
(Erase heading not required.)

Instructions regarding War Diaries and Intelligence Summaries are contained in F.S. Regs., Part II. and the Staff Manual respectively. Title pages will be prepared in manuscript.

Place	Date	Hour	Summary of Events and Information	Remarks and references to Appendices
	18-3-17		Sunday -	
	19-3-17		Orders to prepare to move -	
LE MAZIS	20-3-17		Left BUIGNY at 8-30am joined the Bde at St MAXIENT + marched via OISEMONT to LE MAZIS. Some of the horses in the open -	Maps. AMIENS 17.
RUMAISNIL	21-3-17		Bde continued the march - left LE MAZIS at 8-30am + marched via LE QUESNE - LIOMER - HORNOY. THIEULLOY L'ABBAYE - FRICAMPS - COURCELLES - NAMPS-AU-VAL - NAMPS	
HAMEL	22-3-17		Bde continued the march - Left RUMAISNIL at 9-0am marched via TAISNIL - NAMPTY RUMIGNY - BOVES - VILLERS - BRETONNEUX - HAMEL - Horses all in the open, men in huts -	
	23-3-17		No move -	
	24-3-17		Bde continued to march - Left HAMEL at 8-0am + marched via CERISY - MERICOURT - CAPPY HERBÉCOURT - FLANCOURT + bivouac at the Bois de MOREAUCOURT -	
Bois du {MOREAUCOURT	25-3-17 26-3-17 }		No move -	
HALLE	27-3-17		Bde continued the march - Left the Bois du MOREAUCOURT at 11am + marched via HERBECOURT BIACHES to HALLE - Bivouacs at HALLE	

Army Form C. 2118.

WAR DIARY
or
INTELLIGENCE SUMMARY.
(Erase heading not required.)

Instructions regarding War Diaries and Intelligence Summaries are contained in F. S. Regs., Part II and the Staff Manual respectively. Title pages will be prepared in manuscript.

Place	Date	Hour	Summary of Events and Information	Remarks and references to Appendices
CLERY	28.3.17		Bde moved this morning from HALLE at 2.30 to CLERY.	
HEM	29.3.17		" " " " - CLERY to HEM.	
BAYONVILLERS	30.3.17		Bde moved from HEM & marched via FRISE-CAPPY-PROYART & went into billets at BAYONVILLERS.	
"	31-3-17		Squadron drawing up -	

Wheaton Major
P.C. 13th Sqd M.G.C. Cav.
Sec. Cav. Bde.

Confidential

Vol 10
Serial No. 317.

War Diary

13th Sqdn. M. G. Corps (Cavalry)

from 1st April to 30th April

13th Sqd. Machine Gun Corps
5th Cav. Bde.

from April 1st to 30th 1917

Army Form C. 2118.

WAR DIARY
or
INTELLIGENCE SUMMARY.
(Erase heading not required.)

Instructions regarding War Diaries and Intelligence
Summaries are contained in F. S. Regs., Part II.
and the Staff Manual respectively. Title pages
will be prepared in manuscript.

Place	Date	Hour	Summary of Events and Information	Remarks and references to Appendices
BAYONVILLERS	1-4-17		Squadron training.	Ref Maps AMIENS 17. 32 & S./10000
	2-4-17			
RAINCOURT	3-4-17		Squadron left BAYONVILLERS & went into billets at RAINCOURT.	
	4-4-17		Settling down into billets.	
	5-4-17		Skin parade cancelled.	
	6-4-17		Inspection of Remounts by G.O.C. 2nd Lieut Pinkus & Aylett joined the Squadron.	
	7-4-17		Horse Exercise. Rain & snow.	
	8-4-17		Church parade.	
	9-4-17			
	10-4-17		Section at the disposal of Section Commander.	
	11-4-17			
	12-4-17		2nd Lt Grant joined the Squadron & posted to No. 4 dismounted	
	13-4-17			
TREFCON	14-4-17		Bde marched via LIHONS - CHAULNES - St CHRIST - ENNEMAIN - FOURQUES to camp in and about TREFCON	Ref Map ST QUENTIN 13 S.E. / 10000
	15-4-17		Settling down into camp.	

Army Form C. 2118.

WAR DIARY
or
INTELLIGENCE SUMMARY.
(Erase heading not required.)

Instructions regarding War Diaries and Intelligence Summaries are contained in F.S. Regs., Part II. and the Staff Manual respectively. Title pages will be prepared in manuscript.

Place	Date	Hour	Summary of Events and Information	Remarks and references to Appendices.
ST MARTIN du PRES	16-4-17		Squadron had to move camp to St MARTIN des PRES.	R/ Map ST QUENTIN Sect 57B30
	17-4-17		Seeking shelter & stabling for horses.	
	18-4-17			
	19-4-17		Squadron training.	
	20-4-17			
	21-4-17			
	22-4-17		Church Parade.	
	23-4-17		Squadron training	
	24-4-17			
	25-4-17		Bde Field day.	
	26-4-17		Horse Exercise.	
	27-4-17		Section training & long range firing	
	28-4-17			
	29-4-17		Sunday	
	30-4-17		Section training & long range firing.	

Wheaton Major M.G.C.
O.C. 13

Serial No. 314.
From 1st May to 30th June 1917.

Confidential

War Diary for month of May 1917

From 1st – 31st May 1917

13th Sqdn M Gun Sqdn (Cavalry)

Vol XI

Army Form C. 2118.

WAR DIARY
or
INTELLIGENCE SUMMARY.

13th Squadron Machine Gun Corps Cav.

From May 1st — 31st 1917.

(Erase heading not required.)

Place	Date	Hour	Summary of Events and Information	Remarks and references to Appendices
ST. MARTIN-des-PRES.	1-5-17		Squadron training – G.O.C. inspected east lines –	Ref. Map. Sheet 62c 1/40000
Near TREFCON	2-5-17		Squadron training –	
	3-5-17		Transport parade for G.O.C. stn – 13 Reinforcements joined the Squadron from the base.	
	4-5-17		Squadron training	
	5-5-17			
	6-5-17		Church parade.	
	7-5-17		Squadron training – 20th decease Horse Shoots –	
	8-5-17			
	9-5-17		Squadron training	
	10-5-17			
	11-5-17		Bde. parade for inspection by H.E. Army Commander	
	12-5-17		Squadron training	
	13-5-17		CO's company – CO's went round Front line east of JEANCOURT.	
	14-5-17		B.C. Sections went into the Front line to take over from the 17th Bde.	
JEANCOURT.	15-5-17		Squadron relieve the 17th Bde. in the trenches	Ref. Map. Sheet 62c NE 1/20000
	16-5-17		Improving & siting new gun position.	

Army Form C. 2118.

WAR DIARY
or
INTELLIGENCE SUMMARY.
(Erase heading not required.)

Instructions regarding War Diaries and Intelligence Summaries are contained in F. S. Regs., Part II and the Staff Manual respectively. Title pages will be prepared in manuscript.

Place	Date	Hour	Summary of Events and Information	Remarks and references to Appendices
JEANCOURT	17-5-17			
	18-5-17			
	19-5-17			
	20-5-17		Improving + making new position	
	21-5-17			
	22-5-17			
	23-5-17			
	24-5-17			
	25-5-17			
	26-5-17		Canadians made a raid captured 10.	
	27-5-17		No 12 position hit one burst gun burried, but dug out at night.	
	28-5-17		Position 12, 13, 14 & 15 handed over to Belts on our left.	
	29-5-17			
	30-5-17		Improving + making new position	
	31-5-17			

J. Hamilton Roger. C. Can.
4th Sept M.G.C.
O.C. 13" Sqn. M.G.C. Cav.

2353 Wt. W2544/1454 700,000 5/15 D. D. & L. A.D.S.S./Forms/C. 2118.

War Diary

13th Sqdn. M. Gun Corps (Cav)

1st June to 30th June 1917.

Army Form C. 2118.

WAR DIARY
or
INTELLIGENCE SUMMARY of 13th Squadron Machine Gun Corps

From June 1st 1917 to June 30th 1917.

(Erase heading not required.)

Place	Date	Hour	Summary of Events and Information	Remarks and references to Appendices
TRESCAULT	1-6-17		Squadron still in the line – G.O.C. inspected position	
	2-6-17			
	3-6-17		Squadron in the line	
	4-6-17			
	5-6-17			
	6-6-17		Col. Codding Jr. inspected M.G. position	
	7-6-17			
	8-6-17			
	9-6-17			
	10-6-17			
	11-6-17		Col. Codding Jr. came round the line	
	12-6-17		Bosche raid – 6 M.G. employed – 10000 rounds fired – No casualties	
	13-6-17		Squadron in the line	
PRES ST MARTIN Lez	14-6-17		Canadian relieved the Squadron but kept 2 machine guns & duty 1 Section in the line & their own	
	15-6-17		Cleaning up & refitting the guns	
	16-6-17		Cav. Corps Commander inspected the horses	

Army Form C. 2118.

WAR DIARY
or
INTELLIGENCE SUMMARY.
(Erase heading not required.)

Instructions regarding War Diaries and Intelligence Summaries are contained in F. S. Regs., Part II. and the Staff Manual respectively. Title pages will be prepared in manuscript.

Place	Date	Hour	Summary of Events and Information	Remarks and references to Appendices
ST MARTIN Le PRES.	17-6-17		Horse Exercise.	
	18-6-17			
	19-6-17		G.O.C. inspected transport. Horse Exercise.	
	20-6-17			
	21-6-17		1 Section went up to relieve no Section Ambala Squadron - Sergt & Horses remained.	
	22-6-17			Rifles
	23-6-17	2-2.30ᵖ	All Sections in the lines. 2 Sections with Canadian Bde & 1 Sect with Squadron - Horse exercise in back area -	

E. Whorton Major
O.C. 13ᵗʰ Sqd. M.G.C.C.

Serial No: 317.

War Diary

13th Squadron (M.G.C) Cavalry.

from 1st July 1917 to 31st July 1917.

(Vol. I)

13th Squadron Machine Gun Corps Cav
Sqdn Capt Beth

Army Form C. 2118

WAR DIARY or INTELLIGENCE SUMMARY.

From July 1st to July 31st 1917

(Erase heading not required.)

Place	Date	Hour	Summary of Events and Information	Remarks and references to Appendices
ST. MARTIN aux Pres.	1-7-17 to 5-7-17		Squadron in the Trenches 8 guns with the Canadian Sqdn, 4 guns with the 4th Bgd.	ST QUENTIN Sh. 2 Sc. 1/100000 Sh. 2. Sc. 1/10000
	6-7-17		Lce Cpl Hunter slightly wounded	
	7-7-17		Squadron in the Trenches	
	8-7-17			
	9-7-17		Squadron returned from the Trenches	
	10-7-17		Squadron training	
	13-7-17			
BUIRE sur ANCRE BUIRE SUZANNE	14-7-17		Marched via Crouy heads ESTRÉES-en-CHAUSSÉE - CARTIGNY through Ford west of BUIRE	
	15-7-17		Marched via COURCELLES - PERONNE - MARICOURT - SUZANNE and on 2 kilo East of SUZANNE hut	AMIENS
MORLANCOURT	16-7-17		Marched to BRAY & billets at MORLANCOURT	Sh.P. Sc. 1/100000
SARTON	17-7-17		Marched via VILLE-SOUS-CORBIE - TREUX - BUIRE-sur-L'ancre - LAVIEVILLE - HENECOURT - SENLIS LENS Sh 44
			HÉDAUVILLE - FARUVILLE - ACHEAUX - VAUCHELLES-la-AUTHIE - MARIEUX & west in Billets at SARTON	
CROSSART	18-7-17		Marched via ORVILLE - HALLOY - LUCHEUX - IVERGNY - OPPY - ESTRÉE-WARNIN - HOUVIN	

Army Form C. 2118

N°. 13th Squadron Machine Gun Corps Cav.

WAR DIARY
or
INTELLIGENCE SUMMARY.

18-7-17 to 31-7-17

(Erase heading not required.)

Instructions regarding War Diaries and Intelligence Summaries are contained in F. S. Regs., Part II. and the Staff Manual respectively. Title pages will be prepared in manuscript.

Place	Date	Hour	Summary of Events and Information	Remarks and references to Appendices
CROSSART	18-7-17		HOUVRIGNEUL – MONCHEAUX – TANEVILLE – MAISNIL St POL – ROELLECOURT – OSTREVILLE BRIAS to billets at CROSSART. G. net.	
	19-7-17			
MONCHY CAYEUX	20-7-17		Moved from CROSSART via TROISVAUX – HERMICOURT – WAVRANS to hut Camp at MONCHY CAYEUX.	
	21-7-17 to 31-7-17		Training under Section Commanders, Sun only 30 during training.	

E. Monkton Major
O.C. 13th Sqdn M.G.C. Cav.

Serial No. 314

Secunderabad Cavalry Bde.

13th Sqn. M. G. Corps

War Diary

From 1st August 1917.
To 31st August 1917.

Vol I

13th Squadron Machine Gun Corps Cav

WAR DIARY
or
INTELLIGENCE SUMMARY.

Army Form C. 2118.

1-7-17 to 31-7-17

Place	Date	Hour	Summary of Events and Information	Remarks and references to Appendices
HONCOURT-	1-7-17			
CAYEUX	2-7-17		Section training & gun drill	
	3-7-17		" " " "	
	4-7-17		" " Lt. Anson posted on 27th C to the 10th Sqd	
	5-7-17		" "	
FLEURY	6-7-17		Church Parade. Moved billets to FLEURY.	
	7-7-17			
	8-7-17		Section training & gun drill	
	9-7-17		" " " "	
	10-7-17		Lexington Sports	
	11-7-17		Sunday	
	12-7-17		Running Affiliated Horse Show	
	13-7-17		Preparing for Divisional Horse Show. All dismounted men to take part. Horse Shows.	
	16-7-17		Polo. Schools	

Army Form C. 2118.

WAR DIARY
or
INTELLIGENCE SUMMARY.
(Erase heading not required.)

Instructions regarding War Diaries and Intelligence Summaries are contained in F. S. Regs., Part II. and the Staff Manual respectively. Title pages will be prepared in manuscript.

Place	Date	Hour	Summary of Events and Information	Remarks and references to Appendices
FLEURY	17-7-17		Col. Cooking Tor inspected to Squadron.	
	18-7-17		G.O.C. Brigade inspected the Bde Squadron in marching order.	
	19-7-17		Church Parade.	
	20-7-17		G.O.C. instructed the Squadron Pdr in marking order.	
	21-7-17		Section Training & Gun drill.	
	22-7-17	S.		
	23-7-17		Section Training inspected by G.O.C. Brigade.	
	24-7-17		Section Training	
	26-7-17		Church Parade	
	25-7-17		Section Training	
	26-7-17		Tactical Exercise	
	27-7-17		Section Training	
	28-7-17		Section Training.	
	29-7-17		Section Training.	
	30-7-17		Section Training.	
	31-7-17		Tactical Exercise with Troops.	

Whitehead Major
13th M. G. Sqdn.

2353 Wt. W2544/1454 700,000 5/15 D.D.&L. A.D.S.S./Forms/C.2118.

Confidential.

Serial No. 314.

War Diary

Sialkot Cavalry Brigade

13th Sqn. M.G. Corps.

From 1st to 30th Sept. 1917

13th Squadron Machine Gun Corps Cav. WAR DIARY from 1st Sept 1917 to 30 Sept 1917

Army Form C. 2118.

WAR DIARY or INTELLIGENCE SUMMARY.
(Erase heading not required.)

Place	Date	Hour	Summary of Events and Information	Remarks and references to Appendices
FLEURY	1-9-17		Squadron Training – Box Respirator inspection.	LENS 11. Sc. 10000
	2-9-17		Church Parade.	
	3-9-17		Squadron Firing – Gun drill.	
	4-9-17		Tactical Exercise with troops.	
	5-9-17			
	6-9-17		Squadron training	
	7-9-17			
	8-9-17			
	9-9-17		Tactical Exercise with Regt.	
	10-9-17		Sunday. Bde. Field day.	
	11-9-17			
	12-9-17		Tactical Exercise with Regt.	
	13-9-17			
	14-9-17			
	15-9-17		Squadron Training – Box Respirator inspection.	
	16-9-17		Sunday.	

Army Form C. 2118.

WAR DIARY
or
INTELLIGENCE SUMMARY.
(Erase heading not required.)

Instructions regarding War Diaries and Intelligence Summaries are contained in F. S. Regs., Part II. and the Staff Manual respectively. Title pages will be prepared in manuscript.

Place	Date	Hour	Summary of Events and Information	Remarks and references to Appendices
FLEURY	17.9.17		Tactical Exercise with Regt.	LENS, 11. Sel. 70000
	18.9.17		" " " "	
	19.9.17		" " " "	
	20.9.17		Rest, half day.	
	21.9.17		Tactical Exercise with Regt.	
	22.9.17		Squadron training.	
	23.9.17		Church Parade.	
	24.9.17		Squadron Book Sample.	
	25.9.17		Tactical Exercise with Regt.	
	26.9.17		" " " "	
	27.9.17		Squadron training, 5 am until	
	28.9.17		" " " "	
	29.9.17		Sunday.	

Wharton Major
O.C. 13th Sqd. M.G.C.C.

Confidential

(314)

War Diary

13th N.G. Squadron

From 1st October 1917
To 31st October 1917

Army Form C. 2118.

WAR DIARY of the 13th Squadron Machine Gun Corps
or
INTELLIGENCE SUMMARY.   from Oct 1st to Oct 31st 1917.

(Erase heading not required.)

Instructions regarding War Diaries and Intelligence Summaries are contained in F. S. Regs., Part II, and the Staff Manual respectively. Title pages will be prepared in manuscript.

Hour, Date, Place.	Summary of Events and Information.	Remarks and references to Appendices.
1-10-17.	The Squadron left FLEURY & went into billets at TENEUR.	LENS 11. Scale 1/100,000.
2-10-17.	East horse lines at Bde H.Q.	
3-10-17.	G.O.C. Bde inspected Billets & horse lines.	HAZEBROUCK S.A. Scale 1/100,000
4-10-17.	Bde Field day.	
5-10-17.	Squadron drill.	
6-10-17.	Bde marched — Squadron left TENEUR at 9-45am & marched HAZEBROUCK — via HEUCHIN — St HILAIRE — AIRE & went into billets at PECQUEUR.	
7-10-17.	Bde continued the march. Squadron left PECQUEUR at 12 noon & marched via HAZEBROUCK — STEENWORE to WATOU — the Bde in camp.	
8-10-17. }	Remained at WATOU.	
14-10-17. }		
15-10-17.	Bde marched back via STEENVOORDE — CASSEL — BAVINGHOVE. The Squadron went into billets at CAMPAGNE.	
16-10-17.	Bde continued the march — Squadron left CAMPAGNE at 8-0am & marched via ARQUES — WIZERNES — CLETY — AVROULT — FAUQUEMBERGUES & billets at LE LOQUIN.	
17-10-17.	Bde continued the march. Squadron left LELOQUIN at 8-45am & marched via FAUQUEMBERGUES to billets at FRUGES.	

Army Form C. 2118.

WAR DIARY
or
INTELLIGENCE SUMMARY.
(Erase heading not required.)

Instructions regarding War Diaries and Intelligence Summaries are contained in F. S. Regs., Part II and the Staff Manual respectively. Title pages will be prepared in manuscript.

Place	Date	Hour	Summary of Events and Information	Remarks and references to Appendices
	18-10-17		Squadron moved billets from FRUGES to A & B Section & HQ to COUPELLE-NEUVE	LENS
	19-10-17		"C" Section to AVONDANGE	3.6
	20-10-17		Cleaning up	
	21-10-17			
	22-10-17		Section Parade	
	23-10-17			
	24-10-17		Weekly Pistol Parade	
	25-10-17			
	26-10-17		Section training & firing	
	27-10-17			
	28-10-17		Sunday	
	29-10-17		Section training & firing	
	30-10-17		L. G. firing 8 gun w/k 7 dys a Lestrel trainer	
	31-10-17		Section training	

1 13th Squadron Machine Gun Corps WAR DIARY or INTELLIGENCE SUMMARY

From Nov 1st to Nov 30th 1917.
Cavalry

Army Form C. 2118.
314

Place	Date	Hour	Summary of Events and Information	Remarks and references to Appendices
COUPELLE- NEUVE	1-11-17		Outpost Scheme with 7th Dragoon Guards	LENS/SLII AMIENS/SLIR Map Topos
	2-11-17		Station training	
	3-11-17		G.O.C. division inspected the Bde in marching order	
	4-11-17			
	5-11-17			
	6-11-17		Section training — Gun drill — firing	
	7-11-17			
	8-11-17			
Mt RENAULT FARM	9-11-17		Bde marched via HESDIN - LABROYE - AUXI-LE-CHATEAU - FROHEN-LE-GRAND - Bde went into hut at Mt RENAULT FARM.	AMIENS/SLII LENS/SLIR
ST GRATIEN	10-11-17		Bde continued to march via BERNAVILLE - FIENVILLERS - CANDAS - TALMAS - VILLIERS - MONCHY-au-BOIS - Sqdn went into billets at ST GRATIEN	
CHUIGNOLLES	11-11-17		Bde continued the march via PONT NOYELLES - CORBIE - VAUX - sur - SOMME - SAILLY - LAURETTE - MERICOURT - Sqdn went into billets at CHUIGNOLLES	
VRAIGNES	12-11-17		Bde continued the march via PROYART - ESTRÉES - BRIE Sqdn went into billets at VRAIGNES	

Army Form C. 2118.

WAR DIARY
or
INTELLIGENCE SUMMARY.
(Erase heading not required.)

13 C.S.A. M.G.C.C. From 13-11-17 To 30-11-17.

Instructions regarding War Diaries and Intelligence Summaries are contained in F. S. Regs., Part II and the Staff Manual respectively. Title pages will be prepared in manuscript.

Place	Date	Hour	Summary of Events and Information	Remarks and references to Appendices
VRAIGNES	13-11-17		Arms Exercise in small parties	AMIENS 56/7 1/100,000
	14-11-17			
	15-11-17			
	16-11-17			
	17-11-17			
	18-11-17		Church Parade	
	19-11-17		Got ready to leave VRAIGNES	
CAMBRAI AREA	20-11-17		Reached BOUZY-LONGAVESNES & FINS. Instantly left DESSART WOOD left at 12-30 to VAUCELLES	
			& moved up towards MARCOING 1 Section (A) attacked & 2 Sgts. missing	MAP 56/12
			3 — wounded 9 horses killed	
			Stayed there all 21st — S.M.	
from MARCOING	21-11-17			
FINS	22-11-17		Reached M MARCOING – RIBECOURT – & FINS killed time	
MARLEY CAMP	23-11-17		Reached via E QUANCOURT – HN NANCOURT – MOISLAINS-CLERY Spent rest — MARLEY CAMP 3	
	26-11-17		MARLEY CAMP — at rest —	
St MARTIN du PRIS	27-11-17		Reached M CHUIGNES & TOUVENCOURT-BRIE – Sgt & Lee Cpl. St MARTIN du PRIS	
	28-11-17 to 30-11-17		Cleaning up —	

13th Sqdn. Machine Gun Corps Cavalry

WAR DIARY or **INTELLIGENCE SUMMARY**

Army Form C. 2118

From 1st Dec 1917 to 31st Dec 1917.

(Erase heading not required.)

Place	Date	Hour	Summary of Events and Information	Remarks and references to Appendices
Sq. W.23.	1-12-17		The Squadron remained all day in the valley till 6.0.p. when it went out to the line near GAUCHE WOOD	Enemy raw Org. amendt. Sy Sk. 2.
	2-12-17		The Squadron still in the line & supported the defence against the German attack. Guns in action. 2.5.p. The left direct fire H.q.rs when it became not intact fire. No casualties in the Sqdn. Sqdn relieved at about 9.0.p. & marched back to the valley in W.23.	
	3-12-17		The Bde. moved back to camp at SAULCOURT	
	4-12-17		The Sqdn took over a part of the Brown Line – 105m in position between W.5 a.7.d. & VAUCELLETTE FARM. Sqdn. H.Q. at GENIN WELL COPSE No 2.	
	5-12-17		The Sqdn still in Brown Line.	
	6-12-17	11.15 am	The Sqdn received orders to march back to SAULCOURT CAMP.	
	7-12-17		Remained all day at SAULCOURT CAMP.	
	8-12-17		Bde. moved back & marched via LONGAVESNES – TINCOURT & CARTIGNY and Sqdn in billets at BRUSLE.	ST. QUENTIN Sh 18.
BRUSLE	9-12-17		At BRUSLE	
	10-12-17			
	11-12-17		Sqdn left BRUSLE & marched via PERONNE – RANCOURT to billets at BEAULENCOURT.	LENS. Sh 11
	12-12-17		Sqdn continued the march via BAPAUME to GOMIECOURT & came under the orders of the 3rd Infantry Division.	

Army Form C. 2118.

WAR DIARY
or
INTELLIGENCE SUMMARY.

(Erase heading not required.)

Instructions regarding War Diaries and Intelligence Summaries are contained in F. S. Regs., Part II. and the Staff Manual respectively. Title pages will be prepared in manuscript.

Place	Date	Hour	Summary of Events and Information	Remarks and references to Appendices
GOMIECOURT	13-12-17		Section Commander went round the runner line.	LENS S.2.11.
	14-12-17		Remained in GOMIECOURT CAMP. In the short notice to move if required.	
	15-12-17			
	16-12-17			
	17-12-17			
	18-12-17			
	19-12-17		Sqd. Left GOMIECOURT at 10.0a + marched via BAPAUME to BEAULECOURT Camp.	
	20-12-17		Left BEAULECOURT at 8.30a + marched via LeTRANSLOY - PERONNE - DOINGT to our old billets at TREFCON. Roads in very bad condition.	
TREFCON	21-12-17		Still at TREFCON. The 28th + 29th on 1 hours notice.	
	22-12-17			
	23-12-17			
	24-12-17			
	25-12-17			
	26-12-17			
	28-12-17			
	29-12-17			

WAR DIARY
or
INTELLIGENCE SUMMARY.

(Erase heading not required.)

Army Form C. 2118.

Instructions regarding War Diaries and Intelligence Summaries are contained in F. S. Regs., Part II. and the Staff Manual respectively. Title pages will be prepared in manuscript.

Place	Date	Hour	Summary of Events and Information	Remarks and references to Appendices
TREFCON	30-12-17 31-12-17		Improving Stables & huts	

Elvaston Payn
O.C. 13th Sqdn. M.G.C.C.

13th Squadron Machine Gun Corps, Cav.

From 1st Jan 1918 to 31st Jan 1918.

WAR DIARY
or
INTELLIGENCE SUMMARY. 31st Jan 1918.

Army Form C. 2118.

Place	Date	Hour	Summary of Events and Information	Remarks and references to Appendices
TREFCON	1-1-18			
	2-1-18		Squadron training. Repairing Huts & Stables.	
	3-1-18			
	4-1-18			
	5-1-18			
	6-1-18		Church Parade.	
	7-8-18		Squadron training. Repairing Huts & Stables.	
	8-1-18			
	9-1-18			
	10-1-18		Preparing to take over the line – Carried out the last mount.	
	11-1-18		Squadron training. Repairing Huts & Stables also roads.	
	12-1-18			
	13-1-18			
	14-1-18		Brought the M.G. limbs to the defences of TREFCON	
	15-1-18		Squadron training.	
	16-1-18			
	17-1-18			
	18-1-18		Grand Model Parade inspected by Corps Cav. Commander.	
	19-1-18		Squadron training.	
	20-1-18			
	21-1-18			
	22-1-18			
	23-1-18		Advance Parties went out to the Trenches.	
	24-1-18		The Squadron went up to the Trenches & took over the M.G. Emplacement at	
	25-1-18		LATE M.G. 47875768 755.00.8916 (b) G & F latr. Forms/C2118/139 in FAGGOT WOOD 49 m in My position.	

Army Form C. 2118.

WAR DIARY
or
INTELLIGENCE SUMMARY.
(Erase heading not required.)

Instructions regarding War Diaries and Intelligence Summaries are contained in F. S. Regs., Part II. and the Staff Manual respectively. Title pages will be prepared in manuscript.

Place	Date	Hour	Summary of Events and Information	Remarks and references to Appendices
LE VERGUIER	26-1-18 27-1-18 28-1-18 29-1-18 30-1-18 31-1-18		Still in the trenches.	

Ellerton Major
O.C. 13th Sqd. M.G.C.C.

Confidential

War Diary.

13th M.G. Sqdn

1st to 28th February 1918.

No. 13 K Squadron Reserve Gun Corps
Seconded Can. Bde.

WAR DIARY From Feb 1st 1918
or to
INTELLIGENCE SUMMARY. Feb 28th 1918.

Army Form C. 2118.

(Erase heading not required.)

Instructions regarding War Diaries and Intelligence Summaries are contained in F. S. Regs., Part II. and the Staff Manual respectively. Title pages will be prepared in manuscript.

Place	Date	Hour	Summary of Events and Information	Remarks and references to Appendices
LEVERQUIER	1-2-18 to 12-2-18		In the Trenches	ST QUINTIN
	13-2-18		Squadron took part in the raid (right flank protection)	
	14-2-18		In the Trenches	
	15-2-18		Canadian Reserve Gun squadron relieved the 13th M.G.C. & proceed to back area at AMIEN	
FLESSELLES	16-2-18 17-2-18 18-2-18 19-2-18 20-2-18 21-2-18 22-2-18 23-2-18 24-2-18 25-2-18 26-2-18 27-2-18		Cleaning up. Weekly horse show to other units	
COEQUEREL	28-2-18		Squadron proceeded by motor lorries to COEQUEREL	

Elliston Mayn
O.C. 13 Sqn Res. Gn Corps

1917
5TH CAVALRY DIVISION
SECUNDERABAD CAV. BDE

MOBILE VETERINARY SECTION

JAN - MAY 1917

SERIAL NO. 249.

Confidential

War Diary

of

MOBILE VETERINARY SECTION, SECUNDERABAD CAVALRY BRIGADE.

FROM 1st January 1917 **To** 31st January 1917.

Army Form C. 2118.

WAR DIARY
or
INTELLIGENCE SUMMARY
(Erase heading not required.)

Instructions regarding War Diaries and Intelligence Summaries are contained in F. S. Regs., Part II. and the Staff Manual respectively. Title pages will be prepared in manuscript.

Hour, Date, Place	Summary of Events and Information	Remarks and references to Appendices
FIEUQUIERES 1/Aug 1917	Routine work. Engaged in weekly admin. and account &c.	
2/Aug	Routine work.	
3/Aug	Routine work. Personnel 7 Squadron 7 Wagon Line for exercise. 2nd Lieut arrived from Reinforce- ment Reinforcements for wagons.	
4/Aug	Received from 7 Squadron R.E. 1 horse. O.C. 75 horses and mules transferred from 3rd Squadron R.E. 1 horse, all for forwarding to these animals to abbeville	
5/Aug	Routine work. From 7 Squadron Spa. 2 horses and horse brigade H.Q. 1 horse.	
6/Aug	Routine work. Paid men.	
7/Aug	Routine work.	
8/Aug	Evacuate sick horses to Abbeville	
9/Aug	Evacuate from horses to abbeville. Proceeded on leave in evening.	
10/Aug	Absent on leave. Routine work carried on as certain. Returns from lines in evening 11	
31/Aug		
22/Aug	Routine work. Also changement hong W.O. Brigade began for filling stores without items. Awarded 5 days C.B.	

Army Form C. 2118.

WAR DIARY
or
INTELLIGENCE SUMMARY

(Erase heading not required.)

Instructions regarding War Diaries and Intelligence Summaries are contained in F. S. Regs., Part II. and the Staff Manual respectively. Title pages will be prepared in manuscript.

Hour, Date, Place	Summary of Events and Information	Remarks and references to Appendices
FEUQUIERES 23/Jany.	Routine work. Mc Kenzie left on leave.	
24/Jany.	Routine work. Received 1 horse from 7 W.9ks and 1 horse from hackies gun funder.	
25/Jany.	Routine work	
26/Jany.	Received 4 horses from 3t Power horse and sent them out there other to Abbeville	
27/Jany.	Routine work. Received in mule (Reservant cadre) from XX Reserve Horse.	
28/Jany.	Routine work. A.D.V.S. visited section.	
29/Jany.	Received from XX Reserve horse 3 horses 2 mules (sick work). Los hand evacuated to Abbeville. Received from new 3t Power horse 7 horses out	
30/Jany.	horse sickguards 2 horses to Abbeville. Evacuated 2 horses to Abbeville	
31/Jany.	Routine work. Received no horse from the Auxiliary Horse transport	

F/S Robert Laffarge
OC Remount 4 at H.Q. Abbn.

Serial No: **249**

Mobile Veterinary Section,

Secunderabad Cavalry Section.

From 1st to 28th February 1917.

Correspondence received

General's Base Office.

oOooo----

                    Date_____

Case on which letter will be found		Initial of Sect Sup.t:
Main Head:	No.	

Army Form C. 2118.

WAR DIARY
or
INTELLIGENCE SUMMARY

(Erase heading not required.)

Instructions regarding War Diaries and Intelligence Summaries are contained in F. S. Regs., Part II. and the Staff Manual respectively. Title pages will be prepared in manuscript.

Hour, Date, Place	Summary of Events and Information	Remarks and references to Appendices
FEUVIERES. 1 February 1917.	Routine work. Rec'd the return howl issued with album outfits.	
2 February.	Routine work. Return of outfits howl issued with albums completed.	
3 February.	No news received from Major Rivers, and one inquiries Army P.O. S.16.	
4 February.		
5/6 February.	Ordinary ambulance work.	
10 February.	Routine work. Gave Infant ambulance to hospital, a child [illegible] to the orderly to the platoon & Lieut. [?]. The ambulance having been by Lieut Holden been hurried and no where was the Lieut have any anything to have but returned to the ambulance with one on arrival then [?] Mr Postmaster Lt Jo[?] Chadwin the [illegible] returned with Capt. Hewers and kept [illegible] himself in two cars for Sergt Harbour and Ambulance and then proceeded in [illegible] to	
11 February.		

Instructions regarding War Diaries and Intelligence Summaries are contained in F. S. Regs., Part II. and the Staff Manual respectively. Title pages will be prepared in manuscript.

WAR DIARY
or
INTELLIGENCE SUMMARY
(Erase heading not required.)

Army Form C. 2118.

Hour, Date, Place	Summary of Events and Information	Remarks and references to Appendices
	the steps taken to recover one of the section mules which had broken loose. He was unsteady on his feet, thick in his speech and slightly incoherent, and also gave out a very strong alcoholic smell. He was placed under arrest for being drunk and Corpl. Kearns was told to take over his (Sergt Baldwin's) duties.	
12 February	In the morning the [illegible] Mobile Vety. Section was inspected by Major General MacAndrew, in marching order. Sergt. Baldwin was brought up and remanded for the following day.	
13 February	Sergt Baldwin was brought up charged with drunkenness and evidence of Corpl. Shifford was taken. Asked if he had anything to say Sergt. Baldwin replied "~~[illegible]~~ Sir, I was not drunk". He was ordered to revert to his permanent grade of private, his rank of sergeant being a paid acting rank. He immediately appealed against this award	

Serial No: 249

Mobile Veterinary Section,
Secunderabad Cavalry Brigade.

From 1st to 31st March, 1917.

WAR DIARY
or
INTELLIGENCE SUMMARY

(Erase heading not required.)

Army Form C. 2118

Instructions regarding War Diaries and Intelligence Summaries are contained in F. S. Regs, Part II. and the Staff Manual respectively. Title pages will be prepared in manuscript.

Hour, Date, Place	Summary of Events and Information	Remarks and references to Appendices
14 February	and asked for beer to [illegible] market. he sent sentry to [illegible] for beer by Court martial. Survey of antenna taken by 2/Lt [illegible] 7 Sharpe. Question of care of Regt. [illegible] in the evening. Wireless [illegible] work carried on.	
15 February	Routine work.	
16 February	Part survey of antenna [illegible] in the afternoon. Routine work. Received wire that Court martial on Sergt. [illegible] would [illegible] place the following day. J. [illegible] in the evening. [illegible] is [illegible] stating that Court martial [illegible] will not be postponed.	
17 February	Routine work.	
18 February	Routine work. A.W.O.L. visited the centre	
19 February / 25 February	Ordinary routine work.	
26 February	Routine work. Comrades has [illegible] by L. 2. 2. Christmas tropics otherwise.	

Army Form C. 2118

WAR DIARY
or
INTELLIGENCE SUMMARY

(Erase heading not required.)

Instructions regarding War Diaries and Intelligence Summaries are contained in F.S. Regs, Part II. and the Staff Manual respectively. Title pages will be prepared in manuscript.

Hour, Date, Place	Summary of Events and Information	Remarks and references to Appendices
27 February	A. & I.R. rifles in the action and in the afternoon proceeded with him out the return to THIEVRE. Then in Companies with the MIDDX, CANADIAN and UMBALLA with the actions the best way of managing the long day and gun pits. Lewis-Hughes Took place at 11 am this morning Capt Dalton, 13 h. Res. Ox Queens Brigade and Capt. Fare, 7 Dragoon Guards with it. Between them numbers. Self electeds and charged with luncheons. In the afternoon evidence to report Capt Clifford E.C. as to the Office his Capt. Ralston and Lunch left however Q.C. used for the picture in subject this Capt. Kaestein and other Rd. Godalm. heartily faced services, the Colonel things we are now called at intervals for the defense and all details that day conducted the usual afterm boxes and drenched Ponp, children and I have & tea & laun's be detail	
28 February		Lt Colonel Jaffer 1000 Lancashire 1.3.7

WAR DIARY or INTELLIGENCE SUMMARY

Army Form C. 2118

Hour, Date, Place	Summary of Events and Information	Remarks and references to Appendices
FEUQUIERES.		
March '17.	Routine work and waiting out orders for month.	
2/3 March		
4 March	Routine work.	
5 March	A.O.C. visits the section.	
	Four horses and two mules received from the	
	Auxiliary Horse Transport (The place where were	
	unable to arrive) i.e. 22 Veterinary Hospital.	
6/8 March	Routine work.	
9 March	Casualty two horses from 7 Dragoon Gds to	
	No. 22 Veterinary Hospital.	
10/11 March	Routine work.	
12 March	Crippled horse cast to 22 Veterinary Hospital.	
13 March	Routine work.	
14 March		
	Two horses of Dragoon Gds. sent broken down	
	lameness and eighteen cast for mules picked	
	evacuated to No. 22 Veterinary Hospital.	
15 March	Six sick horses evacuated by rail to No. 22 Veterinary	
	Hospital.	
16/18 March	Routine work.	

Army Form C. 2118.

WAR DIARY
or
INTELLIGENCE SUMMARY

(Erase heading not required.)

Instructions regarding War Diaries and Intelligence Summaries are contained in F. S. Regs., Part II. and the Staff Manual respectively. Title pages will be prepared in manuscript.

Hour, Date, Place	Summary of Events and Information	Remarks and references to Appendices
19 March 1917 to hand.	Battalion on heavy left by R.H.A. Shared all sick leaves by rail from MONCOURT to 22 Stationary Hospital. Left FEUVIERES and marched through to MLLE BOIRON arriving there 5.30 p.m.	
21 hand. PROUZEL	Marched from MLLE BOIRON straight through to PROUZEL	
22 hand. HAMEL	Marched from PROUZEL to HAMEL	
23 hand. HAMEL	Evacuated the of horse from LA FLAQUE 7 Dragoons Rt. by Broken horse 2 Broken horse 1.	
24 hand. BOIS de MEREAUCOURT.	Marched from HAMEL to BOIS de MEREAUCOURT.	
25 hand. BIACHES.	Find "B" Echelon station near BIACHES Sergt WRIGHT reports to duty from the 2 V.H. HAVRE	
26 hand. BIACHES.	Lt. Indian left the unit in morning as escort for 40 2 V.H. HAVRE. Two horses received from Central Arm.	
27 hand. BIACHES.	Routine work. Received news from the advanced units actions of the division.	
28 hand. BIACHES.	Receiving horses from advance units returning action	
29 hand. CAPPY	Covered horse in the morning from CHUIGNES and	
30/31 hand. CAPPY.	In the afternoon marched through from BIACHES to CAPPY. Routine work.	J.B. [signature] O.C.

Serial No: 249.

Mobile Veterinary Section, Secunderabad Cavalry Brigade.

From 1st to 30th April 1917.

Daily list of
    in Adjutan

Issued to Section_____

From whom.	No. and date of letter received.

WAR DIARY
or
INTELLIGENCE SUMMARY
(Erase heading not required.)

Army Form C. 2118.

Hour, Date, Place	Summary of Events and Information	Remarks and references to Appendices
BAYONVILLERS 1 April '17	Marched from CHOCQUES to BAYONVILLERS arriving 2.3 p.m. The afternoon spent by the units in settling down in billets.	
2/5 April '17 6 April '17	Ordinary routine work. Ordered troops to LA FLAQUE for flooring down in huts of such kind.	
4 April '17.	Remainder troops then hence from LA FLAQUE this morning. In the afternoon firing of two torpedoes by the Coyt. Also 2 L.& O Ordinary routine work Rather sick.	
9/10 April '17 11 April '17	In the afternoon Ample to CAK on instructions of ADVS and was a heart flogging by Royal Engineers. O had to destruction as it not suffering from Mountain Caustic Complaints by stem front. In the evening received orders to be ready to move ordered to a lette hour.	

Army Form C. 2118.

WAR DIARY
or
INTELLIGENCE SUMMARY
(Erase heading not required.)

Instructions regarding War Diaries and Intelligence Summaries are contained in F. S. Regs., Part II. and the Staff Manual respectively. Title pages will be prepared in manuscript.

Hour, Date, Place	Summary of Events and Information	Remarks and references to Appendices
BAYONVILLERS 12 April 917	A.d.V.d. marched Bavton then marching Routine work during the day. Received orders from the Brigade hours in the morning to be ready to move at seven hours notice. Routine work	
13 april		
14 april	Sent the horse in charge of Mr Ireland to LA FLAQUE. These horses was taken over by the AMBALLA MUS. Both the author left BAYONVILLERS at 9.30 am marching through LUHON and CHAULNES, and arriving at TREFCON 2 later	
TREFCON 15 april	Routine work and outlying drives to brunen	
16/17 april	Ordinary routine work	
18 april	Routine work and engaged in making standings. Routine work, making standings.	
19 april	2/s. Andrew changed with Lieutenant to play an place Awarded 7 days Field Punishment No 2	

Army Form C. 2118

WAR DIARY
or
INTELLIGENCE SUMMARY

(Erase heading not required.)

Instructions regarding War Diaries and Intelligence Summaries are contained in F. S. Regs., Part II. and the Staff Manual respectively. Title pages will be prepared in manuscript.

Hour, Date, Place	Summary of Events and Information	Remarks and references to Appendices
TREFCON 20/21 April 17	Routine work	
22 April 17	Ordinary routine work & howitzer teams for athletics	
23/27 April	Ordinary routine work and building stables	
28 April	Evacuate spare horses from NERVE and carry on	
29/30 April	Ordinary routine work	

W.R. Selwyn Major R.A.
O.C. XV Divisional Am. Col.

R.F.A.

Serial No. 249

Mobile Veterinary Section, Secunderabad

Cavalry Brigade.

From 1st May to 31st May 1914.

Daily list o
in Adjuta

Issued to Section

From whom.	No. and date of letter received.

WAR DIARY
or
INTELLIGENCE SUMMARY

(Erase heading not required.)

Army Form C. 2118.

Hour, Date, Place	Summary of Events and Information	Remarks and references to Appendices
TREFCON		
1 hour	Ordinary routine work. Two horsed wounded from NEULE	
2 hour	Routine work	
3 hour	Routine work. No officers or brigade transport left in by the divisional Commander	
4 hour	A short route march on the Boulevard of range and in the section fifteen horses and men were kept amused from Brigade Orders. Remainder at own Regimental Lines. R.H.Q.	
5 hour	Conf. between adjutants to arrange for settling of hay (hay) which was sent round to his during the day	
6 hour	Sergt. Dwight n.c.o. proceeded to 1.3 V.M. HAVRE Ordinary routine work during the day	
7 hour	Routine work	
8 hour	Routine work. Two cables of range received from the Brigade Base Depot	
9 hour	Routine work	
10 hour	Routine work. Two range Cable received from 3rd Dragoon Horse Co. from Royal Canadian Regiment	

Army Form C. 2118.

WAR DIARY
or
INTELLIGENCE SUMMARY

(Erase heading not required.)

Instructions regarding War Diaries and Intelligence Summaries are contained in F. S. Regs., Part II. and the Staff Manual respectively. Title pages will be prepared in manuscript.

Hour, Date, Place	Summary of Events and Information	Remarks and references to Appendices
11/17 May TREFCON	Ordinary trench work. Working and carrying parties and fatigue etc.	
18 " "	Routine work. Firing range.	
19 " "	Carrying party practised bay.	
	Routine work. One wire telephone 2nd Lieut Reid arrived.	
	Received three men draft from N'Rubec. R.M.O.	
20" May "		
/23	Ordinary trench work.	
24 May "	Routine work. Two horses delivered arrived to S.Coy.	
	Also Red Thrush and one horse received from	
	the same unit.	
	Routine work.	
25/26 May "	Routine work. Two lost horses arrived from the Ammunition	
27 " "	horse throughout.	
28 May "	Routine work. Two horses returned arrived to N'Cotty. R.F.A.	
29 " "	Routine work.	[signature]
30 " "	Routine work. Two horses delivered arrived to S.S.Cav. Divn. Fd. O.K. and	Officer Comg 11/D
31 " "	Routine work. One case of mange received from 11 London R.G.A.	

www.ingramcontent.com/pod-product-compliance
Lightning Source LLC
Chambersburg PA
CBHW080824010526
44111CB00015B/2602